THE POWER
of
LETTING GO

transforming fear into love

Nicholas Corrin, L.Ac.

Avisha Publishing

THE POWER *of* LETTING GO - transforming fear into love

First printing, 2013

Avisha Publishing
Friday Harbor, WA 98250
www.fridayharborholistichealth.com

Cover and illustrations by Hank A. Cepeda and Nicholas Corrin

Printed in the U.S.A. on recycled paper

Library of Congress information is available from publisher upon
request

ISBN 978-1-62847-392-6 Perfect Bound
ISBN 978-1-62847-461-9 eBook

THE POWER

of

LETTING GO

transforming fear into love

Nicholas Corrin, L.Ac.

TABLE OF CONTENTS

PART 2
OUR ORIGINS

PART 3
FEAR: DISCONNECTION
FROM THE SOURCE

PART 4

LOVE: CONNECTING TO SACRED POWER

PART 5

HEALING YOURSELF: HEALING THE WORLD

PREFACE

As I look out my window over the slow drizzle and wisps of mist cloaking the fields, the world looks sleepy enough, and perhaps little given to alter its rhythms as fall sets in. Yet I know this is an illusion. I am well aware that the bigger worlds outside, both the human world and the natural world, are in increasingly dire states of turmoil. When I began composing the text for this book in 2006, it was clear to me that many, if not most, people had become trapped in lives that were deeply disconnected from the energies of nature, and therefore from their deeper selves and deeper potential. Life, with all its technological progress, had spawned a culture of excess consumerism, anxiety, and depression. The economic forces that ruled the world had steered us away from the sacred and natural realms, and had increased our sense of isolation whilst dangling ever more artificial attractions and distractions in front of us. Then came the economic crash of 2008, and tidal waves of junk bonds and junk credit debris swept across the world. Eerily, on March 11, 2011, the Japanese tsunami took the whole world by horror, and plumes of radioactive efflux continue to gush out of the crippled facility in Fukushima. In fact, both the financial and environmental situations are catastrophic and fundamentally out of control.

Now, as we near the conclusion of 2012 and ready ourselves for whatever surprises 2013 might have in store for us, we are faced by a much larger version of the economic chaos and decay that occurred just four years ago. It appears that the next ten or twenty years are going to be radically different from what we, as a society, have been used to. Much will likely be swept away or inwardly collapse and need to be replaced by a healthier, less corrupted version. This means that we likely will face enormous challenges, but also great opportunities. The task will be to re-build society at grass-roots levels, and therefore to re-make the world, and the only way we can possibly hope to do this is to re-build who we ourselves are at a core level. We will need to regenerate our relationship with community, and to re-discover powers of compassion, support, creativity and courage that lie dormant within. The post-industrial world, dominated by corrupt banking institutions and greedy corporations, and managed by politicians of feeble mind and even feebler spirit, have led huge swathes of society towards poverty and bankruptcy. But they have also begun to stir an awakening in people that something else is possible: indeed, that it is up to us to de-cide what is possible.

What I saw in 2006 when I started to write this book, was a grip of fear inside people that limited both their per-sonal and collective expression, and that caused them to choose conformism as a coping mechanism. Today, that fear has grown far stronger. Yet fear, at some point, must flip over and become its opposite: love. Love is made of courage, imagination, enthusiasm and a giving spirit. The possibility to re-connect with others, with nature and with the world, and thereby to endow our lives with real meaning and even joy is before us in the gathering chaos of a ruined society. The old archetype of the phoenix, great bird of fire arising from the ashes of the old, has come knocking on our doors and window panes.

Nicholas Corrin
San Juan Island
October 2012

NICHOLAS CORRIN, L.Ac.

INTRODUCTION

What causes us to suffer? Is the source external, or is it within us? In my work with alternative medicine, people come to me with a wide variety of problems and I do my best to help them. Their suffering is usually part physical, part emotional. However, there is something else that can be observed, deeper down. It is a kind of crack in the structure of their identity. Our mind is the real house we live in and, most often, some damage can be found at ground level. It is through this crack that fear enters.

If you ask someone, "Do you feel free?" most people will not give you a straight yes or no answer. Why is this? Because, typically, they will have given up on freedom. They may even perceive it as a threat: the idea of freedom threatens everything they have worked so hard to acquire; it threatens all the beliefs and compromises they have bought into along the way. And if you ask them, "Are you safe?" people often become defensive, because nobody really feels safe. Who does not sense that what they possess (health, looks, job, savings, family, reputation) may be taken from them at any time? And so, in droves, people go in pursuit of security. This pursuit is futile. And should you ask, "Do you know where you are going?" you may well draw from them a blank stare, or a tightening of the jaw-line. This happens because a nerve has been irritated. We all have this nerve.

Deep inside, many of us feel lost, and as a result, we feel powerless. We may appear well put together on the surface, but this is a mask we wear to disguise our fears and uncertainties. We prefer to imagine that we retain control. But in fact, we do not. We can control very little in life, but most of us prefer to ignore this and to pretend otherwise. In fact, the only part of life we can really control is our own reaction to things. This reaction depends upon the way we interpret what is happening to us. It is our core set of beliefs, our fundamental ideas about reality that determine how we experience life, and how we contribute to it.

To reach happiness and freedom, we have to re-evaluate beliefs we hold that have become automatic—that have become controlling programs. This is not something we have been taught about life. We are trained to believe what we have been told. Many of us form beliefs about ourselves and about life that are anchored in the idea of limitation, separateness and inadequacy. We then come to think and react automatically, like emotional robots. Without realizing it, we become controlled by beliefs that shape us from within. We are like cakes with the pan hidden in our unconscious, in our past, in the past of our culture, of our traditions, and of our race. Many voices command us from within, but until we learn to distinguish which of these inner voices are real, which of them speak for us and which against us, we can never be at peace with ourselves nor will the world at large ever be at peace.

When something goes wrong, or our health starts to fail, we may face a crisis that has long been brewing: our sense of having inadequate power to effectively survive in the world, to thrive in it, to feel happy and fulfilled. Many of us are like plants that have failed to put down strong roots. We are disconnected from source energy, and easily fall prey to fear. In order to escape from this fear, we frequently resort to some sort of addictive behavior, whether it be drugs, alcohol, overeating, TV or some spiritual belief system that we wear as armor to protect ourselves from reality. But what is it that we lack?

In fact, it is power, though of a different sort than the

NICHOLAS CORRIN, L.Ac.

power of control. It is the power to abandon control. Now, this might sound very confusing, but the concept of power itself is confusing. Power is not just about acting upon the world and enforcing our will, it is also about being receptive. There is a feminine side to power too. This side makes us receptive to spirit and to a sense of purpose and rightness. This "soft" power is identical with the power inherent in water. It is the power cultivated by the ancient Taoists which gave rise to the internal martial arts. It is the power of receiving, responding and of not doing. The Taoists called this non-action. When we abandon control, we begin to open up to this power of water, the force of non-action. When this force is with us, our "active" power can grow out of it like a beautiful, flexible plant. Usually, when we lose part or all of our power, it is because we have failed to understand the receptive side.

This book is aimed at showing you how the two sides—active and passive—are, in fact, inseparable, and how to go about recuperating your inborn power, but without causing harm to others. Recuperating power does not equate with selfishness or domination. Such types of power as we typically see in the world and in history might be termed raw types of power. Because they always are used to maintain advantage or superiority over others, to force submission or to destroy, we can see there power in its crude state that has not been refined (or "cooked") in the fires of reflection. Conscience exists within us all as an elemental fire or light. This light is also a type of power in the universe, and ultimately is far greater than the crude forms of power which always work to the detriment of something else. The power of light can change this raw power and transform it from destruction into creativity and cooperation. If we observe the great tapestry of Nature, we can see within it countless examples of that raw power as species prey on others weaker than themselves. Yet if we take Nature as a whole, we see a balanced and cooperative display of extraordinary complexity. There is some other kind of power evident in Nature that percolates through all the cruelty and the harshness.

We are of Nature and belong to her. Currently, Nature, in the form of our small planet, is suffering tremendously. We humans have played a large role in the very troubled state of our planet. We cannot seek to heal ourselves without also seeking to heal our planet. There can be no enduring and effective medicine for any of us if our planet remains sick. However, because everything that exists is interconnected at unseen levels, by healing ourselves we can start to help heal others, and the planet too will benefit. In fact, we must. There is no alternative, and already it is late in the day to start. Fortunately, by understanding the different aspects of power resident in the universe and therefore in ourselves, we can assist Nature directly by aligning ourselves with its higher forms of power. When we do this, Nature will assist us in return.

Today, there is much talk about the immune system and how to support it. AIDS has been the global pandemic that has made us focus our attention on the human immune system, but there have, of late, been plenty of other, unexpected menaces to our health, from SARS to, most recently, Swine Flu. The Earth has an immune system too, and the disruption of its eco-systems, the pollution of its waterways, the degradation of the ozone layer, the atmospheric release of carbon dioxide and other greenhouse gases, the use of depleted uranium in warfare plus a daily deluge of chemical toxins have taken their toll on the Earth's fundamental health and its ability to support life. We cannot look at the human immune system without also tending to the planetary immune system.

That is not all: the global phenomena of terrorism and suicide bombings have emphatically demonstrated to us that societies also need immune systems, and when these societ-

NICHOLAS CORRIN, L.Ac.

ies are not functioning and interacting in healthy ways, cellular order will break down. Both terrorism itself, and the heavy handed efforts to kill it, including the recent incarceration and torture of uncharged innocents at Guantanamo, mirror in a strange and interesting way our society's "War on Cancer," where the body is blitzed with chemotherapeutic treatment which does not distinguish between healthy cells and cancer cells. Neither the War on Terror nor the War on Cancer are proceeding very well. It is perhaps early to draw conclusions about terrorism, but our society is showing every sign of losing the War on Cancer and the War on Drugs.

Immunity is part of the natural order. As in Nature, so in the human body. When this order is disrupted or destroyed, disease will enter. Immunity is also a product of the way we think and act, it is not just the body's response at a cellular level. It has been shown, in some cases dramatically, that the way we choose to think and feel can either boost or degrade our immune system. An attitude of fear will bring it down and an attitude of love will enhance it. If we can restore our individual connection to the source energies of nature and the universe, we can enhance our own immune systems and we can even become a kind of immune cell working to the benefit of others and of nature.

As our level of awareness rises, so does our potential to affect the world in a positive way. This means stepping away from fear and into love, the basic theme of this book. Love is a state of real connectedness with others and with all that exists, while fear grows greater depending upon the degree of disconnection felt at the core. Fear will tend to produce more fear, love will tend to produce more love. It is up to each of us to decide which way we want to turn.

NICHOLAS CORRIN, L.Ac.

PART 1

LIVING WITH UNCERTAINTY

NICHOLAS CORRIN, L.Ac.

LOSING OUR WAY

When we are very young we are curious about everything. We want to smell things, touch things, feel things. In adolescence, we start to want to figure out who we really are, even why we are here at all. Since the answers are hard to find, many of us give up, and gradually yield to what society thinks we should do (or be). Yet this submission is bound to create unhappiness in the long run. How many of us have buried dreams that have never seen the light of day? How many of us privately resign ourselves to disappointment as a fact of life? Probably too many to count. Perhaps you are one of them.

There is one lesson we are never taught by our parents, teachers or role models. It is a lesson that life alone can teach us. That lesson is: sooner or later we must deal with who we actually are. There is no escaping this lesson. If we run away from it, it will find us. But if we seek it out, then we can recapture the richness of experience that, deep in our hearts, we yearn for. So who are we, actually? This question has no readymade, off the rack, user-friendly, multiple choice kind of answer. At bottom, all existence, including ours, is shrouded in mystery. It is fluid, cloudlike. One thing is certain, we are not just what we think we are. We are also what we have not yet imagined ourselves to be. We are not just what we have been taught to become. We are also what we dare to become. In a word, we are who we choose to become. As we enter into life, so we become who we are. This means that it is not so much what we are when we set out on our journey that counts, but the way we enter into things that is crucial.

Life can be seen as a vast building, a palace of dreams. This edifice has millions of rooms linked by strange, dimly lit corridors, imposing doorways, stairwells, back entrances, cellars and innumerable windows and skylights. Through which of these spaces shall we pass on our way? Which doorways shall we ignore, fearful perhaps, of what we might find inside? Such choices will determine our lives, both inner and outer. The soul, it has been said, is not inherited but made. Like the silkworm, we must secrete our essence through the workings of our core. As we move, so we become, leaving an iridescent trail behind us. If we freeze, we cease to be. We die prematurely. For life, surely, involves exploration, and exploration involves risk.

In Dante's famous poem, The Inferno, the narrator says, "In the middle of my life, I found myself in a dark wood." This is a place most of us know only too well in our heart of hearts. It is a place of confusion, of lostness, of uncertainty. What previously made sense no longer convinces, what previously satisfied no longer gives pleasure, what previously worked now fails us. Everything has become uncertain. Yet uncertainty is not a bad thing: it is not negative. On the contrary, it is here to release us from the trap we were in, without being aware that we were imprisoned.

EL ACOMODADOR

By what process did we allow ourselves to become "narrowed down," leading us to feelings of dissatisfaction and emptiness? It is as though there were an unwritten law demanding that we stop being open, stop questioning life for its deeper meanings, stop pulsing from the heart outwards, stop searching. Is there such a law, or is it merely human habit, as we grow older, to become duller, more compromising,

NICHOLAS CORRIN, L.Ac.

less fresh, less imaginative, less "all we might be"? Sadly, we usually end up compromising much of our inner freedom without realizing what we have surrendered. And then, perhaps, we despair of ever regaining it.

In the shamanic initiation practices of North Mexico, there is a vital concept known as *el acomodador*. It is a pivot, or turning point in a person's life. Recognizing your particular *acomodador* is the first step towards freeing yourself. For a shaman, in order to access higher powers, it is first necessary to rid him/herself of inner blockages. The same holds true for all of us. Sometimes, we have not just one, but several *acomodadores*, which link up like a chain. If this is the case, then we have become like the prisoner in the medieval dungeon with the ball and chain around our ankle.

So what is the *acomodador*? It is the giving-up point. Somewhere along the lines of our lives, an event has occurred which has stopped us in our tracks. Instead of being a locomotive, moving steadily towards our desired destination, we have stalled. Some traumatic experience has caused us to become immobilized internally. Usually it is a bitter disappointment, humiliation or defeat that has befallen us. Such a disappointment caused us to give up, or to give in: instead of pressing on with being ourselves, we decided to accommodate ourselves to the situation at hand. Because this situation has caused us pain, we opted to minimize this pain by accommodating to it. At this point, our power started to leak out of us, like a punctured balloon.

DO NOT GIVE IN: EMBRACE UNCERTAINTY

Usually, somewhere along the course of our lives, things seem overwhelming or too painful and, without saying so, we lose faith in ourselves. This is when we give in to outside circumstances and influences. It is when the innocence of self-belief gets damaged. This is the meaning of the *aco-modador*. Though we continue to function externally, some parts of us have become frozen inside. When we trade in our actual self for an acceptable self, we lose the keys to a richly meaningful life. Such a life is only accessible to us when we are in touch with our true natures. In effect, with the *acomo-dador*, we have traded in the actual contents for the shiny wrapping paper.

Why is there so much depression around? If you think about it, depression comes from viewing one's future with a kind of dread certainty: *Oh, things will always be this way. They'll never get better. This is just the way it's going to be.* When we speak to ourselves in these terms, we are, effec-tively, fixing our future ahead of us. We are dictating what it is supposed to be. It is a security of sorts, but a negative one that we are generating, locking out the possibilities of change and improvement. *Rest assured*, we say to ourselves in the silent language of the unconscious mind, *this is how it is going to play out.* Such a depressed state of being is another way of giving in, and giving up our power to draw positive changes towards us.

Life, in essence, is uncertainty. Were it not for uncer-tainty, there could be no possibility, no freedom. Life shifts, and it can shift for better or for worse, but shift it will, unless we tell it not to, by pinning it down. But even then, eventu-ally, it will shift, for life cannot be pinned down. So the very first step to escaping the *acomodador* and re-entering the life flow, is to embrace uncertainty.

LIGHT IN THE DARK

All of us, beneath the surface of our personalities, seek love: to love, and to be loved. This is not always obvious at first—many things may seem more attractive and more im-

NICHOLAS CORRIN, L.Ac.

portant, but ultimately, they prove to be illusions. Only love can give meaning to our lives. So to live from the heart is the only way to live, for, in the end, only living in this way will have felt real.

But what is love? Surely, love exceeds and eludes any of the various concepts we may have formed about it. On the other hand, love is something very simple to apprehend, a light in the dark. If love lights up the darkness, it is everything. There is light, and there is nothingness. If we think about the light in the universe, much of it is traveling from extinct stars. As physical bodies, the stars themselves are long gone, yet their light continues to stream forth, illuminating the black vastness of night. What power there is in this image: the light endures even though its fuel (the star) is gone.

This also gives us an image of hope: light is also hope, and hope comes from love, which is light.

Hope carries us forward through the pitch darkness of night. For life is full of unknowns and uncertainties. And despite the sunlight which returns each morning, and despite all our electrical lamps and fixtures, there is a tide of darkness around us that will not go away. So we need hope to navigate through this vast space we call life, ringed as it is with shadows. Hope requires trust, some source of trust deep within us that things will work out well. That we will be somehow recognized and loved, just as the light pouring forth from distant stars is caught and wondered at in the remoteness of our eyes.

Yet love has to be earned, and both hope and trust depend, in fact, on risk. Risk is inevitable, for life is an adventure into uncertainty.

LIVING WITH UNCERTAINTY

Knowledge waits on certainty, but certainty is never quite certain.—Chuang Tzu

I suppose we might all agree on one thing—that life is nothing if not challenging. On the day of our birth, our tiny, water-bound bodies must navigate their way out the birth canal, still bound by their umbilical cords. Once the cord has been cut, however, we are, in a sense, on our own. There is no longer an uninterrupted connection to the mother. For us, whilst in the womb, the mother had been the entire universe, and we lived in the protection of her waters. No longer is this the case. When the waters broke, our security broke with them. This is a theme that shall repeat itself in various guises throughout human life: the shock of the unexpected comes to break down what previously felt secure.

Birth is actually the first trauma of separation. And the very word nature actually derives from the Latin word for birth, *natura*. All of nature must pass through the doors of separation. Seeds and insects are swept off by high winds, sometimes traversing an entire ocean and landing on another continent. Fish emerge from spawn and must take on all the dangers and unpredictability of the sea. Each one will be viewed as food by unseen predators. But with animals and plants, some type of instinct keeps them always connected to the totality of nature. With humans, this is not so, and to be an individual and therefore a separate being can lead us into feelings of loss and disconnection. Civilization, for all its benefits, has removed us further and further from our natural, instinctual connection to nature and has thereby delivered us into the hands of anxiety and fear. Such anxiety

NICHOLAS CORRIN, L.Ac.

that comes from disconnection from nature will generate its own artificial types of uncertainty that stream out of anxiety itself.

It has often seemed to me that our most fundamental problems originate in the experience of disconnection. If we are fearful, anxious, depressed, imposing, judgmental, hateful, delusional or excessively willful, such states of mind stem from feeling disconnected from others, from society or from the entire universe. Ultimately, however, this disconnection is from our deepest self, our soul.

It does not matter what belief system you may have, or whether you are religious or atheist. The innermost part of you connects with nature no matter what you believe. In fact, there is a law of connection that transcends belief. It is like a river of energy: when we are carried by strong, positive motives and feelings deep within ourselves, we become empowered to accomplish remarkable things. It is as though the universe were supporting us like the magic circle of an inflatable tire as we navigate our way through rushing white waters. There is a hidden current that we have tapped into, regardless of what our minds might be telling us up there on the surface. When this happens, we have connected with something beyond words. It is a state of awareness rather than a state of mind. In such a state of awareness, we become harmonized with currents of universal energy and are no longer in our disempowered state of separation.

THE OLD MAN
AND THE ROPE

Here is a true tale I heard from the musician Prem Joshua at one of his concerts. Prem was in his early twenties and had traveled to India and Nepal for the first time. He wanted to get close to the source of the Ganges, high in the Himalayas, and to experience its vital energies for himself. He had trekked up to a small village that nestled in those cold uplands, with the fast river rushing close by it. Prem crouched down on the stony ground to observe the swift movements of the currents.

There was a rickety footbridge overhanging the river with a rope hanging down from it about half the way across. Over to his left, Prem could see the frothing waters cascading over huge rocks into a precipitous waterfall. The waters swept by with astonishing force and speed. They also looked really cold. Prem took off his shoes and socks and gingerly dipped in his big toe to test the river temperature. He quickly withdrew it: the water felt glacial! At that moment he heard a pattering of feet behind him, growing louder and louder. Turning around, he noticed a small, wizened old man dressed only in a loincloth, sprinting full tilt towards the river's edge, and exclaiming, *Om Namah Shiviyah*! (God is Great!) The old man leapt into the river and promptly disappeared beneath the raging currents. Every so often, his head would bob up like a cork and then go under again.

Prem watched in consternation as the man was swept along towards the rapids, where he would surely be smashed to pieces on the rocks. For a second, his head was visible beneath the overhanging footbridge. Suddenly, Prem saw the man reach out a thin arm and grab the rope dangling into midstream from the bridge above. Now, he took it with two hands, hauled himself up, clambered on to the swaying bridge and made his way calmly over to the other side.

SAFETY VERSUS SECURITY

Yes, life itself can be compared to a dangerous river. But as the story of "The Old Man and the Rope" shows us, we can only find true safety when we let go of security. This is the paradox: the more we cling to security, the less safe

NICHOLAS CORRIN, L.Ac.

we become, because we have become ever more invested in what we possess, and therefore have more to lose. Conversely, the more we abandon security, the closer we get to safety. How to make sense of this riddle?

If you really think about it, you realize that true safety is impossible for a finite creature. We humans are very much finite beings (though some of us might pretend otherwise!) Our finite little lives are surrounded by the vastness of infinity. How can we possibly feel safe? It is like being thrown into the middle of the Atlantic Ocean and then told to swim to the shore. Or being projected into outer space, abandoned on some dusty outpost of a distant nebula, and then told to find your way back home, alone. If space can seem hostile, time is not on our side either: tick-tock, tick-tock goes the grandfather clock. We busy ourselves with all sorts of activities, but underneath this, in our silent moments, we must face the inevitability of aging and death. How to feel safe under such conditions?

Then again, how did the little old man make it? His safety, and ours, can only be drawn from what is not finite. Our bodies and our individual existences are bounded and limited, but what put us here is not. We emerged, each of us, from the boundless universe, to find ourselves enclosed in a particular body and personality, living at a particular geographical location at a particular period in history. The energy that produced us, however, transcends time as it transcends space.

Are we to think of this universal energy as hostile or indifferent to us? If it brought us into being in the first place, did it do so without any sense of purpose, or without valuing our existence? If our unconscious programming is convinced of this reasoning, we will only try to protect ourselves from life itself, which we really believe, deep down, is dominated by death. But if we can trust the universe as a loving and supremely intelligent source, we can surrender to its embrace and to its guidance, like a child does to its parent. Which will it be for you?

You might answer, "So what about the thousands of people crushed in earthquakes, or those recently killed by the tsunami? Or what about the innumerable people who, through no fault of their own, have been ravaged by war? Or the perennial victims of torture, of rape, of genocide? Or what about all the thousands of animal species going extinct in our very own lifetimes? Surely, if the universe were as you say—loving and supremely intelligent—it would not allow these things to happen?" This dark side of life is an indisputable part of reality. Without question, there is a seam of terrible destruction that runs through creation, from galaxies to atoms. But there is also an unfathomable beauty and order. The universe, perhaps, has two faces, like most of us do: one creative, the other destructive. Do we feel, deep inside, that the universe is actually neutral, or does it somehow value creation and kindness over destruction? Does it value life over death—or is this just a sentimental human dream?

A LOVING UNIVERSE

How can we possibly see this vast, incomprehensible universe as filled with love? It dwarfs us into insignificance, on our lonely little planet, surrounded by an infinity of blackness. We live the lives of mayflies, here for a few brief moments, then gone forever. We may venture out bravely on rockets and space probes, but what echoes back at us is our own smallness and vulnerability.

This tenuous sense of our place in the universe has been the price we have had to pay for our scientific and technological progress. The more deeply our telescopes penetrate into distant galaxies, the greater the emptiness can seem. Yet when the American astronauts made their historic voyage to the moon in April, 1971, they came back profoundly affect-

NICHOLAS CORRIN, L.Ac.

ed. Ed Mitchell could only describe his experiences out there in a mystical way.[1] What was he exposed to that acted upon him so deeply? It had to be very powerful frequencies of consciousness that exist in what we call "outer space": the astronauts were exposed to these frequencies without the normal filters that the earth's ionosphere and stratosphere generate. The earth has atmospheric filters to protect us from harmful ultraviolet radiation, such as the much damaged ozone layer. In a similar way, the atmospheric density around the earth also absorbs much of the high frequency energy that streams through outer space, energy that is capable of radically affecting our consciousness.

In the novel, *Solaris,* by science fiction writer Stanislaw Lem, Chris Kelvin, a psychologist, is sent up to help with a space station manned by scientists monitoring an outer planet called Solaris. A number of uncanny sightings and occurrences have recently been reported from around the planet's ocean, apparently destabilizing the sanity of the resident scientists at the station. (Two movie versions have been made of this book, one by the Russian director, Andrei Tarkovsky, and another, more recently, by Stephen Soderbergh, starring George Clooney). The planet's ocean appears to be intelligent, sentient and aware, yet nothing in its biochemical makeup matches with human biochemistry. Some of the scientists at the station are going mad, and the ocean appears to be able to read their minds, as the past erupts into the present as a series of apparitions or "hallucinations." Exposure to the presence of this ocean dismantles any thoughts which allow human beings to lie to themselves, as though the effects of the ocean were to generate an extraordinary field of "conscience", merging the individual self into it like granules of sugar in warm water.

The idea of consciousness—and conscience—existing outside the human being, and specifically outside the brain, is a difficult concept for many modern people to swallow.

But our present view is simply a consensus view of reality that has been produced by historical forces. These forces have been a blend of the social, the intellectual and the political. Originally, the power of the Catholic Church solidified itself by identifying nature worship with heathenism, with witchcraft and with the devil. The Church would not tolerate any "views" other than the laws and interpretations it promulgated, and it soon came to burn alive those persons it considered heretical. (Heresy was, in effect, the crime of offering an alternative interpretation of reality and the word heretic actually derives from a Greek word, *haeresis,* which means "to choose." Freedom of choice was not acceptable in the eyes of the Ecclesiastical authorities and was punishable by death). Later on, once science had wrested intellectual control from the Catholic Church, it continued the latter's repressive attitudes.

Science as an institution became thoroughly entwined with technology and therefore with new forms of social and political power. The dogma that science issued was that of Rational Materialism, which effectively reduced all other beings, nature and the cosmos itself to the status of raw materials. Rational Materialism became the prevailing religion, in effect, though one that had dispensed with the need for God, and it continues to hold sway in the world today, but its grip is weakening steadily. With the advent of twentieth century developments in physics, specifically with the emergence of quantum mechanics, the edifice of certainty we are calling Rational Materialism began to crumble. The quantum world presents us with a deep reality which neither materialism nor rationality can completely account for.

Heisenberg's Principle of Uncertainty is a foundational concept of quantum physics. It explains why events cannot be understood entirely via logical sequences of cause and effect, as quantum interactions are simultaneously multiple, and their outcomes can only be gauged in terms of probabil-

NICHOLAS CORRIN, L.Ac.

ity, thus making the future intrinsically unpredictable and unknowable. The Uncertainty Principle describes a world at the subatomic level which appears to be in constant flux and indeterminism.

Objectivity disappears with the so-called Observer Effect whereby the experimental results obtained are not independent of the thought process of the persons conducting the experiments.[2] The observations made by the observer cause the observed item to take a particular form, such that the act of viewing is effectively altering the configuration of what is being viewed.

The Principle of Complementarity precludes the possibility of knowing two attributes of a particle simultaneously, so the location at a particular point in space and the pathway of the moving particle can only be determined separately, not together. This gives rise to the wave-particle duality of matter, which is, effectively, a function of the observing human consciousness which is inextricably engaged in the results of its inquiries. Consciousness, then, no longer fits neatly inside the human brain. Instead, it begins to appear to be some kind of interactive field which, far from being inert, participates in all that we think and do. Physicist David Bohm called this, "The Implicate Order," and posited the idea of a continuous field of inexhaustible energy which has come to be known as the Zero Point Field.[3]

As I have said, for most of our time on Earth, humans have not seen themselves as radically separate from the rest of life, and solely possessed of consciousness. Possibly the oldest cosmogony we have today derives from the Vedas and from the Samkhya philosophy of Yoga. Far from being a mere physical exercise, Yoga is part of a complex spiritual and intellectual discipline extending back some ten thousand years to the dawn of human history. Central to its teachings is the idea that the entire universe is in essence a conscious being, the *Purusha*, which means "Person" in Sanskrit.[4] According to Yoga, the Purusha is an ineffable field of consciousness that pervades everything in the physical world, from galaxies to ants, but also transcends them as what is beyond all form or name.[5] Such an awareness may be recovered by any individual eventually if sought for with deep sincerity over many lifetimes, but only by dissolving the illusory separateness between the observing self (the ego) and that which it observes (the rest of existence).

In fact, all pre-scientific cultures have tended to view the world animistically, as pervaded by spirit and cosmic intelligence. This meant that all its contents were to some degree alive, conscious and sentient. When this perspective was undermined by scientific materialism, the floodgates for the destruction of the planet were opened. Today, that destruction is already well under way and most of it has occurred in very recent times. There is only one way to halt this and to restore health and balance to the planet, and that is to see nature as imbued with spirit, the breath of life. Science studies life from a cognitive point of view, but this is not the only way for us to "know" things. Awareness can also arise from deep within and can be better expressed through symbol, image, music and poetry. Nature then becomes an articulate system, a living language of the unknown through which we discover the meaning of our own presence here, and which expresses ourselves back to us.

The mystical lunar experiences of Ed Mitchell are not directly replicable by most of us. However, if we climb a mountain where oxygen is sparse, or travel into desert terrain, we will nonetheless experience a comparable exposure to high frequency energies, providing us with a sense of the extremely high frequencies of conscious power that stream through outer space. In Yoga, high mountain energies are associated with *Shiva*, the god of pure contemplative consciousness whose name means "The Auspicious One." Many spiritual traditions have seen the mountain or other

NICHOLAS CORRIN, L.Ac.

high point as the residence of sacred forms of awareness. Other natural places have been deserts, caves, cliffs and volcanic craters. Nature has a vocabulary of forms which serve to promote heightened awareness in us. And wherever space and emptiness exist, we can begin to experience a kind of fullness at our core, which is also a kind of purification.

In the yogic tradition, there is a direct correlation between space and life force, and thus between space and potentiality. Space is the original element out of which all the other elements, air, fire, water and earth have emerged, just as Being has emerged out of Non-Being and Form out of Non-Form. Wherever space exists, life-force (*prana*) is generated. We have only to look up into the deep blue sky to experience this and to understand it. To look out into airy space is to give wings to the spirit, and when we observe a bird circling high above us in the sky, our consciousness binds with its movements and we begin to draw into ourselves the very vastness in which it gyrates so effortlessly. One easy way to meditate and to increase one's life force is simply to spend time walking alone under the vault of the sky, or to sit down inside and visualize it internally: close your eyes and allow your boundaries to expand in all directions, as if a blue wind were blowing through the walls of your skin, and carrying you into infinity.

Sooner or later, we all have to deal with infinity. Why not start now? For a solitary human being, this place we call the universe can appear to be a terrifying absence. Certainly, it challenges us, and requires that we probe deeply into things. But space is not simply something that exists out there. It is also right here, in our living rooms and bedrooms. Whenever we reach out a hand to pick up a cup of coffee, or to touch a friend's arm, we are reaching across a small piece of infinity. If we can establish a different relationship with this space we dwell in, we can be in the universe in a different way. Our hearts can open and we can become more loving and peaceful. It is then that the true nature of the universe might begin to reveal itself to us as existing as much in our own hearts as in anything we perceive "out there."

Who has not experienced that strange phenomenon of being seen, or watched, by some invisible presence in nature? Whether in the midst of a forest or under the gathering dusk on a lonely path, a sense can descend that you are not the only one doing the seeing; you are also being seen by some invisible eyes. The habitual conviction that we are the subject uniquely possessed of consciousness is then turned on its head. Many people, simply by being removed from their normal environment become nervous and fearful. The experience of being watched by an unknown presence is usually scary and even terrifying to people, the more so the more in denial they are of their own inner darkness.

Yet such experiences do not have to be the basis for horror movies and all the usual clichés about fear. Rather, experiencing oneself as being seen can lead to heightened awareness and also to true compassion. With this experience we can begin to sense the reality of consciousness existing not only within us, but around us, and beyond us. That strangeness at the core of things—what the philosopher Heidegger referred to as "the uncanny"—disturbs us from our complacent assumptions and restores to us a reverence for the unknown forces that brought us here. In the words of the English scientist J.B.S.Haldane, "The universe is not only queerer than we imagine, it is queerer than we can imagine."

Strangeness breaks down the doors of familiarity and allows us to sense mystery. This sense of mystery is as important for our inner wellbeing as food or water. The ancient Anglo-Saxons saw life as a mystery filled with strange connections, and they referred to this interconnected realm with reverence as the *wyrd*. Their sacred term *wyrd* is the root of our modern word, "weird."[6] Strangeness is the basis for sensing presence beyond the human, and therefore for

NICHOLAS CORRIN, L.Ac.

holiness, which really means wholeness. In Loren Eiseley's words, "One does not meet oneself until one catches the reflection from an eye other than human." Perhaps the greatest mistake human beings have made as a species has been our attempt to eradicate strangeness from life and to reduce it to what we can explain. That could only produce illusions which would lead to separation from the source, and to states of unhappiness and decay. We can understand this idea more clearly through the two contrasting images of a security box and the wind.

THE SAFE DEPOSIT BOX AND THE WIND

The wind created all the islands of the sea
—Pablo Neruda

A safe deposit box at the bank is rather like a coffin: its structure symbolically demarcates a boundary line with the outside world. *Do not enter here*, its shape cries out. By contrast, the wind, which owns nothing and clings to nothing, moves freely about the planet. Our inner state of mind can either be like the deposit box, or like the wind. The box, though sturdy, must be entirely focused on guarding its contents. The wind has nothing whatever to lose and is free to experience without any fear. Have you ever watched birds surfing on the wind?

I used to live in West Seattle and it was only a short walk from my house to the waters of the Puget Sound. On fine days, you can see over the bay to the high crags of the Olympic mountains. Elegantly silhouetted against the sky, their mostly grey flanks glisten in luminous patches where deep snow has fastened to the upper rock face. On low pressure days, the mountains are shrouded in cloud or mist. Occasionally, a strong wind will blow up and stir the normally placid sound into a lively sea covered with whitecaps. When such a wind blows, a very interesting phenomenon can be observed amongst the bird population. Seagulls and pigeons, which normally seem the most ordinary and unremarkable creatures, become transformed into aerial acrobats. The pigeons start to glide and dart through the air with a wild, ecstatic sort of energy, as though they had just woken up from a long dream and discovered their true nature. The gulls stop fighting and bickering and they allow themselves to be carried by up-draughts of wind, as though in moving meditation. And if you follow with your eye the line of the beachfront into the distance, you will start to see a gyrating procession of birds, twirling effortlessly in the air exactly above the line where the sea turns to land. It is as though the birds have become one with the wind, the water and the earth. They seem to allow the wind to express itself through them and, at the same time, they mysteriously echo by their aerial positioning the boundaries of sea and land.

Phenomena such as this give you an overpowering sensation of the oneness that exists under the surface of things. And if you pause to consider the message of the birds, it might be that nothing is more delightful than surrendering to the free movement of the wind, a movement that is part of a deeper order of which it is only one expression. There are many examples of these types of movement in nature. But not security in the shape of a box. Nature does not produce such things because in nature, everything must flow.

And so it is for us: our lives must flow, and must participate in the flows and rhythms of nature. If we choose to turn away from nature and focus on our own security, we might lock ourselves in, and even suffocate in there. Too much security can be like a prison. Our social self has devised prisons, and not only for those we have judged guilty of crimes: too frequently we inwardly imprison ourselves on

NICHOLAS CORRIN, L.Ac.

an unconscious level. Our unconscious programming that there is something unacceptable about us means that we effectively convict ourselves, refusing to allow ourselves full expression. Instead, we aim for the straight and narrow. In deep reality, however, freedom and uncertainty co-exist in a beautiful partnership, like wind and water. In nature there are no prisons, because in nature there is no guilt.

RISK AND TRUST

It is part of being human to crave safety. We all like to feel safe. But it is also human to seek risk and danger in some form or other. Life and risk come together, it would seem. There is something life enhancing about risk itself, while too much security can be suffocating, even deadly. As long as we are alive, it is obvious that we can never be completely safe, for we never know quite what tomorrow may bring. At the same time, we know that all of us live, essentially, on borrowed time. From whom, or from what, is "our" time borrowed? If "our" time does not really belong to us, then who is the rightful owner?

We generally do not think of risk and trust as compatible, let alone similar. To risk something seems to imply that there is danger involved, whereas trust suggests that everything is going to be okay, and that we are being protected. But what if risk and trust are the same thing, illogical as this may seem? Was this not the case with the Old Man and the Rope? If we risk everything by surrendering ourselves willingly to a greater power; if we align ourselves utterly with that power, and if that power is benign, how can we fail? But if we risk something and rely only on our own resources, of course we face the greatest potential dangers, and possibly even death.

But how are we to conceive of such a "power" if it indeed exists? As we know, generally speaking, no "saviour" will come to our rescue when we find ourselves in deep trouble;

fate is harsh, life cruel in its sudden twists and turns. Time, apparently benign, turns out to be savage; death, old age and sickness inevitable. Is self-reliance the only cure for the troubles and indifference we must face or is there another way? Perhaps meaningingfulness and purpose can also be found by accessing an ancient, buried set of instincts binding us to the natural world, signals that give rise within us to a sense of personal responsibility sustained by freedom of choice.

Many years ago, I was hiking in the high altitude back country of the Dominican Republic. A small group of guys, mostly composed of local youths plus myself and my close friend Hank, a native Dominican, set out on a four day 75 mile hike across rugged mountainous terrain, intending to climb up and over the mist-laden Pico Duarte. The first night, we pitched tent by a stream and it pretty much pelted down till dawn. My tent was not up to the task of keeping out the tropical downpour, and everything that could get wet got not just wet, but drenched. By sunrise, however, the skies had cleared. Carefully, I removed my valuables—passport, wallet and airline tickets—from the rest of my sodden gear, and attached them to the low lying branches of a nearby tree by means of some string I had brought along with me. I wanted to give these things a chance to dry out a little as we prepared a quick breakfast and gathered our stuff together before setting out on the next stage of our hike. I remember watching the steam rising out of my wallet and passport as they dangled from the tree in the early morning sun.

It was not until midday that I realized something was wrong. We had stopped by a cool river to take refreshment and eat some lunch. The sun was high in the sky and it was hot. We lit a small fire and began brewing coffee in an open pot. It was at that moment, smelling the intense, black aroma of the coffee whilst watching the sinuous river water rushing by that it suddenly dawned on me that I had left my valuables behind on that tree.

NICHOLAS CORRIN, L.Ac.

There were two problems I now faced. The first was that we had been hiking already for almost four hours across unmarked terrain, along rough, meandering paths that frequently bifurcated or even petered out in dense undergrowth. How to trace my way back through that? The second problem was that the members of the group were unaccustomed to being in the mountains. They were young and inexperienced and they were easily afraid. Far from being close-knit, the group members had more of an every-man-for-himself kind of attitude, and were not to be relied upon for help. My friend cautioned me that the others were likely to abandon the two of us if I got lost, or took too long finding my way back. I only had one small water bottle with me, and unless you knew where the mountain streams flowed, you could easily get dehydrated in that back country.

I made a split second decision to return to that tree and recover my things. My friend would wait for my return: neither of us knew what the others would decide to do. My reasoning mind might have persuaded me that I was insane, but I decided to silence it. I put all my trust in risk—or I risked all of myself in trust, I cannot say which exactly. But I knew I was going back to that tree. I started running, and fast. It would be a marathon of sorts, that I knew, but I would not admit the possibility of failure. I banished all doubt from my mind and held one image firmly in the center of my consciousness. That image was of my passport and wallet hanging from the branch of that selfsame tree, bathed in strong, golden sunlight.

And I ran, without once stopping. Whenever I encountered a fork in the path, I did not pause to think, I allowed my feet to make the decision, trusting them implicitly. I cannot say how much time passed because, in a way, I felt outside of time. And suddenly, there I was, in front of the tree, and there before me, exactly as I had pictured them in my mind's eye, were my belongings. My heart leapt briefly in exultation.

But I had no time to rest or to celebrate. I took my things off the tree, silently thanking it for holding them there for me. I made a swift about turn and broke into as fast and steady a run as I could muster.

Again, whenever I met with a fork in the pathways, I let my feet decide. I carried in my mind the absolute conviction that I would trace my way back to that river where the others were waiting, and that they would still be there. Which turned out to be exactly the case. And even though I had been running at high speed over many mountain miles of rough, rock-strewn terrain, I felt almost no fatigue—even my thirst was under control. And once again, upon my arrival back, it seemed as though time had somehow been slowed down to give me the chance to do what I had to do. Everyone appeared relaxed. It was almost as though the entire episode had happened in another time zone.

THE EMERGENCY HANDLE: PANIC OR FAITH?

Those of us who have ever traveled on a railway train or ridden a subway car will be aware of a special handle set into the wall of the car and accompanied by a sign which reads, "In the event of an emergency, pull handle down to stop the train." Painted fire engine red and shaped like an upturned and slightly curved T, the handle's presence on the wall silently reminds everybody that, "You never know, an unanticipated problem may arise; something could go badly wrong…"

And it is this very "uncertainty principle" that we individuals must face on a daily basis which provides the seed for anxiety within us, just as for the physical disease anxiety can give rise to. Conversely, this very same uncertainty and unpredictability of life can liberate us from the grip of habit and from fear—they can set us free. How is this so?

NICHOLAS CORRIN, L.Ac.

The truth is that although most of us prefer not to think about the red handle, and avoid looking at it, inside our hearts and minds we wish we had a personal emergency brake that could be applied to life, a handle that would slow things down or stop them when we feel out of control. But there is no such handle in actuality, no magic red brake that will stop the train of life when something goes wrong: the train hurtles on regardless of our pain or predicament.

Anxiety in essence is a feeling of lack of control over the future. The future is experienced like a river that unwinds in front of us, like the swift Ganges into whose frothing waters the old man plunges in the tale of the Old Man and the Rope. The river of time pulls us forward with its unstoppable current, but the phenomenological experience we have is also of our future rushing towards us, as though pursuing us from the front. This is the common shared condition of many in today's unstable world of rapid and deregulated change where even the forms and rhythms of nature appear to be collapsing around us.

Anxiety is another word for stress, which is the main contributor to disease. Anxiety, even at low levels, will place constant stress on the homeostatic systems of our bodies, unleashing streams of free radicals which are unstable particles with an unpaired electron. It is a well known fact that free radicals produce breakdown of regulatory systems and matrices and direct degradation of cells, thus leading to premature aging. Free radicals are the most active part of the interface between mental anxiety and stress as they affect our physical and physiological systems. There is no red handle inside us by means of which we can switch off the barrage of free radicals at will; however, this does not mean there are no effective ways to cancel out their deleterious effects, and rejuvenate our bodies and minds. We will explore this subject later in the section entitled, "Love: Connecting to Sacred Power."

When anxiety reaches a certain point of intensity it turns into panic. Some people have a constant low grade condition of anxiety of which they are really quite unaware. Most commonly, it is masked by antidepressant or anti-anxiety medications which have been prescribed for vast numbers of people, (including many doctors and therapists themselves!) At times this anxiety will rise up and cross a certain threshold and these people will experience what is known as a panic attack. But it is not an attack from outside, it is an attack from within.

In a state of panic, the entire outside world suddenly appears threatening or devastatingly unstable. Yet panic is purely an individual's response to exterior stimuli—to things as they are—it has no independent reality. A panic attack is simply an attack from within one's own psyche. We must then ask, who is this doing the attacking, and who, exactly, is being attacked? It is interesting to note, as an aside, that in the commonly used term "heart attack", it is not clear what

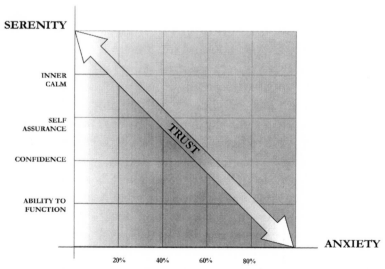

Anxiety can be represented mathematically as existing in inverse proportion to trust [Fig.1].

NICHOLAS CORRIN, L.Ac.

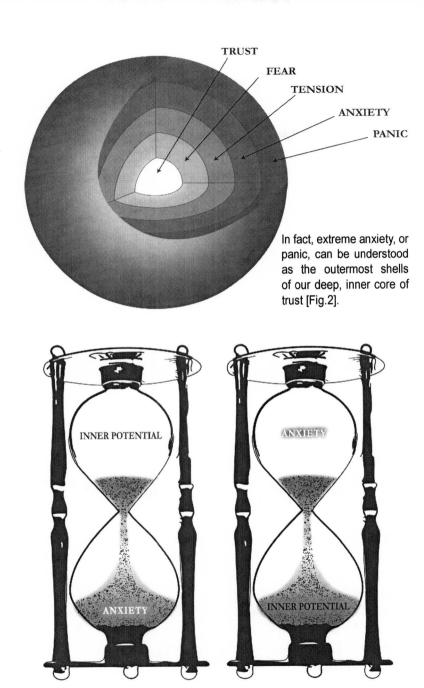

TRUST
FEAR
TENSION
ANXIETY
PANIC

In fact, extreme anxiety, or panic, can be understood as the outermost shells of our deep, inner core of trust [Fig.2].

INNER POTENTIAL

ANXIETY

ANXIETY

INNER POTENTIAL

Anxiety also has an inverse relationship with the release of our inner potential [Fig.3].

PART 1. LIVING WITH UNCERTAINTY   43

is signified. Is our heart under attack, or is our own heart attacking us? Even in our use of language we can see here the "principle of uncertainty" at work, like a seam of ambiguity running through the ground rock of life itself. This is because life was never made to human specifications; and despite that famous phrase of the ancient Greek philosopher Protagoras, man is not "the measure of all things."

THE FULL MOON

There has been considerable research into the correlation between urban crime rates and the full moon, and considerable evidence documenting the unbalancing effects of the full moon on human behavior. It is worth noting that our English word lunatic also derives from the Latin word for the moon, *luna.* The original meaning of lunatic seems to be associated with great variability and change rather than with madness. The moon represents for all of us the cyclic nature of change in contradistinction to the sun, which represents the unchanging aspect of reality, the transcendent or divine truth.

The moon, therefore, has also been closely connected with moodswings and with the irrational side of human behavior, whereas the sun has usually been associated with reason and clarity. In the ancient Mediterranean cultures, the Greek God *Apollo* was associated with the sun and came to represent the objective and dispassionate part of human beings. This side was historically claimed by males while irrationality, associated with the moon, was associated with females. However, in the East, this has not been the case at all. While the moon is typically associated with the feminine side of our nature, the full moon can represent a type of transcendent, enlightened clarity. The modern Korean Zen master Seung Sahn speaks of clear mind as being like the full moon: "Clear mind is like the full moon in the sky." If

NICHOLAS CORRIN, L.Ac.

The battle within us can be represented as proportions of light and dark, a volatile state subject to fluctuations [Fig.4].

we imagine a cloudless, moonlit night, with the contours of hills and trees etched clearly against the velvety black sky, the entire scene shimmering with soft light under the scattering of stars, we immediately sense in our imagination the

The source in us of this transcendent lunar water is the crown chakra, our highest energetic center [Fig. 5].

transcendent calm of the full moon. It is like deep, unruffled water, a state of quiet, joyous serenity. In the spiritual origins of India, perhaps the oldest spiritual tradition in the world, water and the moon are also associated with the highest form of consciousness. *Shiva,* the god represented as dancing in a circle of fire, is also identified with the water principle which exists in the universe as a principle of consciousness, not simply as a principle of matter.

NICHOLAS CORRIN, L.Ac.

Yet it is also true that the werewolf awakens howling at the full moon. Unclear mind also emerges when the full moon is in the sky. We might therefore question why the moonlight should affect us negatively. In fact it does not. It merely amplifies what is already there within us, pulling it up like a magnet. (Drugs and alcohol also do this: they bring up what lies buried within). If our mind is muddy, the effects of the moon will intensify this muddiness. If our mind is clear, the full moon will intensify that clarity.

This is one reason why fasting and detoxification are usually most effective when the moon is full. One physiological explanation for this is that inorganic minerals toxic to our bodies such as lead, cadmium and copper, and other toxic wastes are leeched out of their storage sites in the liver under the magnetic influence of the full moon. From here, they enter the bloodstream and travel up to the brain where they unbalance brain chemistry, thus disturbing the psyche and possibly contributing to violent and criminal behavior, especially in those people who are pre-disposed to act in this way.

However, if we probe still more deeply into the problems of anxiety and panic attack, we will realize that there is not so much an opposition between faith and panic as there is a split, a cut-off. As I have already suggested, all the problems of human beings appear to originate from a state of disconnection from ultimate reality, from what has variously been called God, Tao, Brahman or All-That-Is. In Ayurvedic medicine, this disconnection is considered to be the root of all disease, mental or physical. By contrast, aligning oneself to the sacred, natural order is to re-align with wisdom and thereby heal or protect oneself from accident or disease. This perspective predates even Ayurveda, which is at least 5,000 years old, and has its roots in shamanism, mankind's oldest spiritual and medical system. In shamanic culture, humans attempt, via the journeys of their tribal shamans into the spirit realm, to restore good relationships with those spirit beings who speak for the transcendent order, an order which operates throughout the natural world, not just through human society.

For us today, panic means a nasty, frightening state of mind, an extreme accentuation of anxiety. The geo-political and environmental disasters affecting the world generate a kind of dormant or latent panic in people, beneath the threshold of their normal daily consciousness. On the surface, people may go about their normal daily lives as though there were not too much to worry about, but somewhere inside they have to be aware that the forests are being felled, the wildernesses ripped to shreds and covered with asphalt, the ice-fields of Antarctica melting, the sea-levels rising, the flora and fauna dying, militants plotting their next terrorist attack; in many parts of the world, innocent people are being incarcerated and tortured without trial or judicial representation, and the global stockpile of nuclear weapons is still being added to, moreover by those countries and regimes that may not have sufficient self-control or wisdom to refrain from launching them.

There is a strong hunger in mainstream American society for disaster movies where horrible states of panic occur and violent chaos engulfs masses of people. Why is there this hunger, if not to satiate the unconscious recognition that the flip-side of "normal" life, the dark underbelly, is resident in the world and very much alive? But reducing reality to mass entertainment, though it is good for the box office, is completely counterproductive in terms of political progress or healing of the consciousness, two processes which have to go together if either are to succeed.

The word "panic" derives its name from the ancient Greek god *Pan* who was—and to this day, still is—revered in many parts of the Mediterranean. *Pan* was a nature deity, and he represented the irrational delights of blending with nature and its vital, exuberant, ecstatic energies. Wandering

NICHOLAS CORRIN, L.Ac.

through the olive groves or the open countryside, *Pan* would play on his pipes. The music that was produced by *Pan's* breath as it blew through the pipes was so entrancing that it would overcome the minds of all who heard it, transporting them into a kind of uninhibited communion with nature. Later, with the advent of Christianity which became the state religion in most Western countries, *Pan* became associated with dark forces and with the devil. Hence our modern term panic for a state of the soul in complete disarray.

But *Pan* was not the agent of evil forces. As an archetype we carry within our psyche, *Pan* represents communion with nature without moral or intellectual self-control mechanisms. Today, we have almost lost touch with this part of ourselves and nature is something we look at rather than participate in; even then, it is usually through photographs or TV. Part of the reason we, as a society, have so much anxiety is that we have been "unplugged" from the source of our being in the natural realm.

The panic we hold under the surface, the unacknowledged strata in our psyches of isolation and disconnection, stem from our deep divide from the natural realm. The natural realm can supply us with calm and with ecstasy, two apparent opposites. The wild aspect of nature is as vital to our inner health as anything else. The more we lose touch with the wildness in nature and allow it to disappear, the more prone we become to a different, shadowy kind of violence that ferments in our own psyche. Nature provides vital nutrition for the human soul. Without this nutrition, the human psyche grows imbalanced, as a body does that lacks essential vitamins and other nutrients. In this sense, Faith (connection to the sacred dimension) and Ecstasy (communion with nature) are not warring opposites, they are complementaries. They are like fire and water, yin and yang, heaven and earth.

THE SAFETY HANDLE

The red emergency brake on the train represents, meta-phorically speaking, "panic stations". But another kind of handle exists which does not operate a braking mechanism. Rather, this other handle adjoins us to the bracing flow of universal energy and offers us the protection of a greater power. Such a handle is an archetype that we carry in our own psyche. It is also an energetic structure that forms part of the subtle, non-physical architecture of the cosmos. Let's examine all this in greater detail.

In his book, *The Power of Intention*, author Wayne Dyer relates a very interesting experience. He tells how, as a small child living in Detroit, he would travel with his mother by streetcar to Waterworks Park.[7] He remembers looking up at the leather straps hanging down from the ceiling of the trolley car. The adults were tall enough to reach up to these straps but as a small child all he could do was gaze up at them, high above his head. Dyer explains that he would have loved to have been tall enough to reach the straps, so he pretended to himself that he could simply float up to them, like a balloon moving against gravity. There, in his imagination, he held on tight, with the easy confidence of an adult, and the swaying, accelerating or decelerating trolley car no longer disturbed him. Instead, he felt totally safe, one with the car and its motion, its speed and its destination. He further explains that now, as a grown man, whenever he feels stressed, anxious or worried, he imagines a trolley strap dangling above his head but out of reach. Then he imagines himself floating up to grasp the strap. As soon as he takes hold of it, he experiences tremendous "relief and comfort."[8]

Dyer explains this as letting go of ego thoughts and entrusting himself to the ever present field of intention, which he considers to be a benign energetic intelligence at the heart of the universe. He recommends this visualization to anyone

NICHOLAS CORRIN, L.Ac.

to use at any time they feel anxiety or disturbance. In essence, it is a technique to establish re-connection.

Safety and connection, literally, go hand in hand. This is the core essence we return to again and again. In the womb, we are connected to the mother via the umbilical cord. The universe, for us, is the mother, and we are bound to her and fed by her, safely enclosed in an inland sea. This dim recollection that we have of life in the womb stays with us all through life and underpins our search for security which we can never find again in quite the same way. But the memory we carry inside is important because it expresses an archetypal relationship we seek with the universe itself, not just with the mother who bore us. We seek to be held and intimately connected to the actual universe that we now see as stretching vast and impersonal around us, all the way to infinity. Because this is very difficult to achieve, we do not feel safe. We feel afraid. And because we feel afraid, we opt for security, which is not the same thing as safety. Security is a reinforced box, a castle, a bullet-proof tank, a shell, whereas safety requires no walls, no locks, no buffer zones and no armor.

WHEN SAFETY APPEARS IMPOSSIBLE

If we look at the state of the world today, we must wonder how safety can be anything but an illusion for human beings. Vast numbers of the world's population continue to live at subsistence level, deprived of basic medical care and exposed to virulent infections and parasites. The global economy, ravaged by greed and speculation, has destroyed the savings as well as basic employment opportunities for millions of hard working people left without a viable future in a crumbling economy. Corruption and greed at governmental and corporate executive levels have lain waste social safeguards such as medicare and pension schemes, and have also spawned a spike in violent crime plus the erosion of human rights and privacies. For all the many freedoms it has brought us, the internet is no less a jungle filled with dangers of identity theft, snooping and scam merchandising. In the U.S., infrastructure maintenance has been profoundly under funded and mismanaged during a period of spiraling debts and junk credit culture. Add to this the unpredicatable behavior of the weather now characterized by frequent storms, flooding and earthquakes. In the so-called developed countries, global transmission of disease has been occurring at accelerated speeds due to the frequency of air travel and the development of tourism. The human immune system is being challenged by a sharp decrease in the effectiveness of antibiotics against new strains of bacterial disease such as MRSA while older diseases such as TB are again on the ascendant, especially in Asia.

Both the former Soviet Union and the United States have littered the globe with land mines in their attempts to hold control over territory, and children as well as adults the world over are stepping every day on these mines and having limbs blown off. Weapons grade plutonium has been pilfered from decaying military installations in Russia, transported across Europe on urban transit and sold (to whom we do not know) on the black market. Meanwhile, nuclear proliferation into states with extremely militant, fanatical regimes such as Iran is proving very difficult to control. The United States, on the other hand, has used depleted uranium shells in both Gulf Wars and in Bosnia, leaving a trail of sickness amongst local populations and even amongst its own soldiers.

In the environment and the biosphere, mineral depletion of the soils has gone hand in hand with chemical pollution from effluents and industrial waste. Dumpsites are more than just heaps of undesirable toxic debris. The chemicals in these dumps interact and recombine in unforeseen ways,

NICHOLAS CORRIN, L.Ac.

generating new forms of toxin which slowly leech out into the groundwater and make their way across the entire world, as the planet has a system of water connections similar to our bloodstream with its arteries, veins and capillaries. Our attention was first drawn to the urgency of taking action against pollution by Rachel Carson's classic book, *Silent Spring*. Since then, writers such as William Thomas have shown that the United States military is the nation's biggest and most noxious polluter.[9]

On political, economic, military, medical and environmental levels, is safety then nothing more than a pipe dream? Is the best we can do to hunker down and duck when the shadows deepen? Is security the best we can hope for, and safety a ridiculous myth? This is the belief we are being pressurized to have by all the media forces constantly re-iterating their message of fear and corporate paternalism. We are being bombarded with "information" whose basic purpose is to instill fear and at the same time make us trust the status quo as the best, the most desirable option.

The media's trick is to work people into a state of fear and complacency at the same time. This extraordinary feat is well illustrated by ads that are now commonplace on television during prime time. The ads are for over the counter or prescription medications for common ailments such as migraine, lumbago, arthritis, sinusitis and so on. Such ads, while confidently extolling the efficacy of a drug, casually list its possible accompanying side effects. The list typically runs something like this: dizziness, fatigue, fainting, increased blood pressure, cardiac arrest, renal (kidney) failure, liver toxicity, and stroke. Yet the ads obviously work and, strangely enough, people feel sufficiently lulled into a trusting state of security that they will purchase and consume medications with all of these known possible side effects!

It is obvious that security goes hand in hand with high levels of irrationality. The explanation for this is that the unconscious mechanisms of the population have been infiltrated by the pharmaceutical giants and their colleagues in the advertising industry. It is sufficient to show a cozy image with a happy looking couple, smiling on a beach or gazing into the sunset, and all the threatening information of the listed side effects will be canceled out by the warm, fuzzy visuals. It will be the visuals and the confident, reassuring voiceover that penetrate people's psyche, not the information itself.

Yet all is not lost. In fact, there are always alternatives and every problem has a solution. Although this might seem self-evident, the majority of us act as though this were not true. Or we feel utterly engulfed and overpowered by a world run by interests hostile to us and to the general wellbeing of the planet. That makes it all the more vital for individuals not to sink into a state of despair and defeatism. Rather, it is necessary to draw strength from the knowledge the universe itself is filled with healing powers which can be tapped into if we so choose. All human knowledge, for good or ill, all human discoveries and so-called inventions have been drawn out of the latent field of intelligence and potentiality that constitutes the universe. Humans never operate in a vacuum. We are ourselves a product of the universe, and all our applied thought and technology has been mined out of the creative field of intelligence that we are calling the universe.

Let's take just one example: bacteria. We typically think of bacteria as our nemesis, and it is very hard for us to feel kindly towards them. Yet we have "friendly" bacteria in our gut which are vital to the functioning of our immune system. *Acidopholus* is the best know of these strains. Others are *Lactobacillus Longus, L.Casei* and *L.Bifidus*. These microorganisms live in us and support our health, a little like low paid workers on a farm. Or take the mitochondria, which is the powerhouse of the individual cell, responsible for the production of ATP, which is the actual fuel that runs the cell.

According to the esteemed biologist, Lewis Thomas, the mitochondria may well have been originally a bacterium, which penetrated us at a much earlier evolutionary stage, and eventually fused with the cell, becoming an integral part of it. We should remind ourselves that nothing in this world of ours, not Michelangelo, not Einstein, not Buddha, not Mother Teresa, no corporation, government, army, football team or rock group would have been possible without the existence of this lowly bacterium, which decided to make a home in us millions of years ago. If we always maintain our attention on potentiality, the miraculous becomes the possible.

Recent scientific application of bacteria to clean up toxic waste has been a case in point: some strains of bacteria actually thrive on effluent that is deadly to humans, converting it into harmless residues. This causes no harm to the bacteria themselves. The success of this application is profound, for it proves that there exist solutions to some of our worst problems already available within nature itself. It is astonishing to think that nature would have created micro-organisms that are able and willing to clean up the terrible pollutants that we have generated. It brings new meaning to the phrase of the Roman philosopher Lucretius, "One man's meat is another man's poison." Man's poisons can be five star cuisine for bacteria. This fact alone symbolizes the field of potentiality within nature and the universe. If we can re-connect more effectively with this potentiality, we can also start to re-grow the thread of trust, and therefore have more of a feeling of safety within the universe itself, the only means for us to grow from a state of fear into a state of love.

THE UNCERTAINTY OF
THE COLLECTIVE SHADOW

*As far as the laws of mathematics refer to reality, they
are not certain; and as far as they are certain, they do
not refer to reality.*—Albert Einstein

In the natural world, life without danger is unthinkable.
Only death is free of danger, and only because nothing can
happen anymore. When we cast an eye over the beauty of
nature we realize the whole panorama is made up of destruction and menace as much as peacefulness and calm. Over
here, placid water buffalo graze on wild prairie grasses. Over
there, the lionesses are stalking. Or, closer to home, it is July
and the skies over the mid-Western states show patches of
brilliant blue and a few scudding summer clouds. Yet, somewhere not too far off, a tornado is brewing that will decimate
one small town in a matter of minutes. Danger and destruction are that part of natural reality humans fear and reject.
We want security, but the truth is nothing is ever secure.

In Hinduism, the god Shiva is associated with the cosmic aspect of destruction. There is an acknowledgment that
creation and destruction are complementary poles of one
transcendent reality. We have a vivid sense of this when observing the brilliance of stars in the night sky: many of these
stars disappeared eons ago, and it is only their ghostly light
that still streams towards us, entrancing us with the illusion
of their long vanished presence. The stars may be gone, yet
their light endures. And if we choose to reflect on this fact,
the ensuing paradox may instill in us a sense of hope and
trust in this unfathomable cosmos.

But Shiva represents the powers of the cosmos, not the
powers of man. Because human beings have free choice and

NICHOLAS CORRIN, L.Ac.

access to power, we can use that power for destructive ends that have nothing in common with the destructive forces of nature and the cosmos. When the tiger or the tornado kills, it is not the same as when man kills. For us, killing and destruction can never be innocent. Human beings, especially in recent times, have exhibited a grisly capacity for cruelty beyond compare. The atrocities of ethnic cleansing in Rwanda and the former Yugoslavia are the human version of the tornado, and it is impossible to compare the two without concluding that the human variety is infinitely more sinister.

Some fifty years earlier, during World War II, some seven hundred thousand men, women and children of Serb, Bosnian or Jewish extraction were killed at Jasenovac camp by Croatian militiamen using "saws and sabers, axes and hammers, and leather cuff-bands with fixed blades that were fastened on the lower arm and made especially in Solingen for the purpose of cutting throats."[10] These items were the militiamen's "preferred instruments of execution."[11] This one example can stand as a symbol and testament to the depth of darkness dwelling in the human heart. Author and poet Robert Bly speaks of this shadow aspect in us as something very ancient, inherited from our ancestral and animal past and also "ineradicable".[12] He suggests that it is a dormant part of us that a change in circumstances can awaken, and that when such a change occurs, human beings may then become capable of the greatest inhumanity.

If we are even subliminally aware of this aspect of ourselves, how can we feel safe in the world? The answer to that question is clear enough: the more we turn our heads away from the shadow side of life, the more likely it is to rear up and surprise us. That is the basis for shadow work in Jungian psychology: only by looking within, retrieving and then assimilating rejected aspects of our self can we hope to avoid feeding the shadow. On the other hand, if we honestly explore and engage with all aspects of our psyche, we can bring light on to these same dark parts. When we do this, the dark parts turn into light. In that respect, shadow work can be called auspicious. For through self-examination, there proceeds a "bringing to light" of the darkness within. This is perhaps comparable to Shiva, the Auspicious One, who destroys ignorance through the light of awareness. There is a Native American story that addresses the issue of our shadow side and our personal responsibility quite succinctly. A tribal elder is narrating to a group of young men about a battle going on within his own soul. The fight is between two dogs, one white the other black. It is an intense fight to the death. One of the men listening is too eager to know the outcome of this fight and interrupts the elder saying, "Which of the dogs will win?" To which the answer comes, "The one that I choose to feed."

THE POWER OF LIGHT

But if we have inherited a dark side from our collective past, we have also inherited a light side. All the kindness, compassion and generosity that humans have expressed in the past somehow exists as a deep pool in our collective consciousness. We can call this light side our supra-conscious and the dark side our sub-conscious. The light is more potent than the dark, but the dark may be more attractive to us. We can think of light and dark as magnets of a psycho-spiritual nature exerting their influence on us (Fig. 6).

For most of us, the subconscious is a more powerful magnet than the supra-conscious. Anything self-serving would pertain to the sub-conscious magnet, and anything giving would pertain to the supra-conscious magnet. Yet each of these magnets has an influence on us, and what I am describing metaphorically as magnets has a presence in the energetic structures of the universe itself.

I have suggested that the light force is more potent than

NICHOLAS CORRIN, L.Ac.

the dark force. If we examine human history with all its barbarism and cruelty, or if we look at the current state of the world, we might form a different conclusion: we might say that it is the dark force that is the more powerful, and the dark force that is winning. But this would be wrong. If we shine a light into a dark space, that space will become illuminated. But we cannot "shine" darkness into a bright space. It is physically impossible.

The only way to darken a space is to cut off the source of light. Light is energy vibrating at different frequencies. Some of this light falls within the visible spectrum and some is beyond it and thus outside our normal range of vision. But the light force within us—what I am calling the supra-conscious—is more than just physical light, and it vibrates at extremely high frequencies. When such a light force interacts with darkness, it will imbue that darkness with some of its own energy and

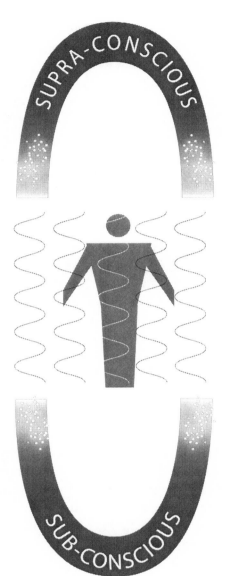

The Magnetic Pull of the Sub and Supra Conscious [Fig.6].

transform it. This we can perhaps say is an unacknowledged law of the universe: that light overpowers dark. It is the basis for all spiritual teachings of whatever type, and for the effect those teachings have had upon humanity.

Men and women who have embraced the light principle without fear such as Martin Luther King, Rosa Parks, Nelson Mandela and Gandhi, have been able to affect the world in dramatic ways, and disarm what appeared to be intractable prejudice and hostility. Another collective example of light triumphing over dark was the country of Denmark during World War II. Although the country was under German occupation and overrun by the Gestapo, the Danish people refused to go along with the Nazi anti-Semitism, and the King and Queen actually wore the yellow star on their clothes in solidarity with the Jews who were being deported and massacred. Interestingly, this had a softening effect even on the Gestapo who refrained from their typical actions and behaviors under the magnetic influence of the Danish people.[13]

This phenomenon of light holding sway over dark, infusing it with its higher frequency of vibratory energies is also known as "entrainment". The higher frequencies will affect the lower in such a way as to speed these up and attune them to the higher ones. The phenomenon of entrainment can easily be experienced whenever we are in the company of a person who is calm, generous, non-judgmental and compassionate: it is as though some of this rubs off on us, and we feel altered in a positive way.

Part of the uncertainty that we must deal with living in human society is due to the interplay of supra-conscious and sub-conscious forces, or light and dark. This is a very complex matter since they interact in very many ways, both individual and collective, in families, in the workplace, in cities, nations and above all perhaps, globally. But to hold to the light is the only way to find safety as opposed to security for ourselves and for others.

NICHOLAS CORRIN, L.Ac.

THE FULLNESS OF SPACE

As children we have all marveled when, in late afternoon, the sun sends slanting beams of light into our bedroom or living room, and suddenly, as if from nowhere, millions of dust particles appear, gathered into some slow dance in the midst of these diagonal shafts of light. Where did all these dust motes come from? Our childish minds are struck by the contrast between what had appeared to be empty (the air) now being shown to be full of... dust. Now dust, we have been taught, is not generally considered a good thing. Yet here is this otherworldly phenomenon, a ray of light, dancing with worthless dust right in the middle of our living space.

Much of the dust in our homes is actually made from human skin that has flaked off or been brushed away, and gradually disintegrated. When the sun illuminates this dust it is allowing us to enter a strange museum we did not realize was there: the air. The air contains more than just oxygen and other gases; it contains traces of ourselves. One cubic foot of air in fact contains minute components of thousands of different kinds of insects, invisible to the naked eye. But it also holds far more than this. It has been estimated that one cubic foot of air will contain molecular residues of matter that once formed part of almost every being that has yet lived. This means that when we inhale, we bring into our lungs molecules of what once were Jesus and Buddha, and, for that matter, Genghis Khan and Tyrannosaurus Rex. In a very material sense, we inhale human and planetary history with every in-breath we take.

But it is not just smithereens of particulate matter that co-exist in this cubic foot of air. There are also waves of every type and variety: radio waves, microwaves, gamma rays and all sorts of other cosmic pulsations beyond the threshold of our perception. This cubic foot of air, apparently so neutral and placid, is vibrating with millions of different wave-lengths of energy and information. Some of this information is man-made, streaming out of broadcasting stations, satellites and radio towers. But many of these waves are of cosmic origin, emanations from distant parts of outer space. They are what might be called the silent speech of the universe, vibrations which swim through our immediate environment just as smoothly as neutrinos swim through solid matter. So much for consensual reality. Based on what we refer to as common sense, consensual reality is perhaps common nonsense. To see the air as empty—and "space" as even emptier—is not sense; it is the product of limited perception and limited understanding bound together into something called habit. By habit alone we accept the space around us as empty, not full.

BEYOND EMPTINESS AND THE ZERO

It is not at all innate or "natural" for human beings to see the space surrounding us as empty. Nor is it scientifically valid. The new physics has taught us that matter and energy are different manifestations of the same unitary field, and thus they are interchangeable. The universe is not a vast empty chamber with bits of stuff floating about in it. It is an unfathomably complex web of interlocking and intercommunicating systems. What appears empty is really a dynamic field alive with vibrations and gravitational nodal points which cause warps in the field and generate substantial bodies we refer to as matter. Really, they are densifications of ever present energy which swirls around under the sway of cosmic laws that science is trying to understand.

Everything is connected, and we are connected to each other, to our planet and to this cosmos in multiple ways,

NICHOLAS CORRIN, L.Ac.

from the food we consume, which is actually a concentrated form of solar processes, to the circadian rhythms and lunar influences which act upon our endocrine system and regulate our internal secretions. The universe is in a sense, a great body: in a way, a lot like our bodies, where we can find great complexity, but no emptiness. The old saying, "As above, so below," applies still as we are beginning to comprehend, or learn anew, how the human being mirrors the state of the greater universe.

The old way of seeing still dominates however. It holds sway in our politics, technology, industry and medicine, even though science has shown us a very different basis for reality. We continue to act in the world as though it were really a case of solid objects surrounded by empty space.

The old way of seeing originated in our intellectual history, which was then applied to commerce, technology and industry. The principal basis for this way of seeing was based in part upon the theory of atomism. This philosophical assumption that there were basic indivisible building blocks of matter called atoms was part of the equation of our materialism. The other part was the idea of zero.

The zero, which we are accustomed to seeing everywhere from bank accounts to sports results, probably originated in early Indian mathematics.[14] From there, it was adopted by the Arabs, whose period of high culture formed a bridge between the older classical systems of knowledge and the modern, emerging scientific world of the West. The zero, which previously had not been used in the quantifications of Western mathematics, began to take hold in secular society as it allowed traders and merchants to calculate quantities and exchanges much more swiftly than before, where large numbers of integral numbers had to be used and this involved tedious amounts of notation.

From here, the zero soon moved on to become the single most important numerical device for the application of mathematics to science and technology.[15] And at the same time, it infiltrated our basic world view, changing our relationship with the universe from one of reverence to one of exploitation.

Zero exists nowhere in nature. It is a figment of the human mind, and as such cannot be the basis of reality. Nature, as the saying goes, abhors a vacuum. The older mathematics of Egypt, India, and Greece was based on the number one, which signified a unitary Oneness in the universe. This Oneness was sacred and indivisible. It was the foundation for the multiplicity of experience, but it encompassed and transcended such multiplicity. Oneness is the spiritual basis for all great religions as for our reverence for nature which we experience as the physical manifestation of spirit.

When the number one was replaced by the zero as the basic numeral for mathematical calculus, everything changed. The zero became the mathematical foundation for a rationalism which rapidly replaced the idea of a living nature with machines, and even with the idea of the universe as a machine. It suggested the existence of a void, or nullity surrounding objects. In this way it provided the implicit moral justification for exploitation of the Earth's natural resources, projecting nullity or worthlessness on to the "ground" and value or quantitative worth upon the extractable resource. It was at the root of imperialism and corporate colonialism. It was the hidden intellectual agenda which provided the driving force for slavery, the Industrial Revolution and the depredation of Africa as described in Conrad's famous novel, *The Heart of Darkness*. In our day it is also the driving force behind contemporary attempts to justify drilling for oil in the Alaskan wilderness.

However, the implicit philosophical, scientific and spiritual connotations of the zero have been proven by theoretical physics to be obsolete. Moreover, our forefathers and pre-scientific peoples never saw the natural world or the heavens

NICHOLAS CORRIN, L.Ac.

as a field of empty space in which certain "things", either natural (such as trees) or man-made (such as buildings) existed, like pieces of furniture on a stage. For them, the entire surrounding universe was alive, and imbued with spirit.

Centuries of scientific rationalism have worn away our internal connections with this living universe so that we no longer can draw its energies into us in a direct way. Supposedly, this scientific rationalism was the empirical basis for our society's materialistic approach to life, which has led to over consumption of resources, wastefulness and planetary depletion. But as we have seen, this empiricism and rationalism is really based on the twin myths of the atom and the zero: the atom and the zero are really mental constructs rather than natural phenomena. As such, they cannot form the basis for our relationship with the universe. Theoretical physics, by contrast, shows us a universe made of flowing inverse relationships between wave and particle, matter and energy, a universe of constant interconnections and interactions between myriad levels of one cosmic field.

However, as a collectivity, we continue to "see" and experience our total environment, including our bodies and ourselves as objects (atoms) surrounded by space (zero). We do so because historical and economic forces have conditioned us and programmed us to "think" in this way, and since perception follows conception, we see only what we believe to be real. We see according to the formulas that have been embedded in our brains. And without most of us being in the slightest aware of it, we have inherited the Newtonian idea of classical space as an empty container with a certain number of solid objects inside it. Such is the world as we have been conditioned to conceive and perceive it. And this then became the basis for our technology, our architecture, our medicine and our entire lifestyle.

Unfortunately, this world view based on the zero and the atom has inevitably led us to plunder the natural environment, in thoughtless disregard for such intangibles as ecology and natural harmony. Our greed-driven societies have sought to enrich themselves with "solid" gains from "empty" and worthless surrounding space. As a result, our cities have become largely a mirror image of these tendencies. Power and extraction have gone together in an unholy alliance of global economics based, ultimately, on this conception of space as emptiness (worthless background) with bits of valuable stuff (natural resources, fossil fuels, energy supply etc.) there to be extracted from it.

From an evolutionary and ecological point of view, this alliance of power and extraction is the alliance of Dumb and Dumber. It has also led, on psychological levels, to isolation, pessimism and anxiety. The craving for consumption and hence, the overly rapid and unsustainable depletion of the Earth's resources has gone hand in hand with an inner emptiness at the heart of the consumer. The consumer seeks to fill the inner void of disconnection with the acquisition of objects drawn from the material realm. It is a vicious circle. This vicious circle is like a distorted version of the sacred circle that represents the unity of all life in the cosmos and that is the geometric equivalent of the number one. It is like the primordial interconnectedness reflected in a distorting mirror: the warped, and cracked mirror of collective human consciousness.

But let us remind ourselves again that we have not always seen the world this formulaic way, nor is it at all inevitable that humans should continue to do so. Post-Einsteinian physics has given us the scientific foundation for reviewing our past erroneous assumptions about the nature of reality. The new physics is remarkably in accord with the spiritual philosophies of the ancient world. It is, therefore, the harbinger of global healing. For it can offer us the theoretical basis for radically altering the way we do business with each other, and with the rest of nature.

NICHOLAS CORRIN, L.Ac.

On a personal basis, personal healing can start by refusing to approach one's life on an atom-and-zero basis any longer, and by taking personal responsibility for cultivating an alternative vision. We need to stop conceiving of ourselves as separate atoms of humanity and view ourselves as interconnected with each other and with nature at fundamental levels. The universe did not produce us as an extraneous element. It made us out of its own raw materials, and it carefully built us in the womb over nine months, slowly feeding us with nutrients through the umbilical cord that we might walk fearless, free, joyful and respectful through the theater of life.

EMPTINESS
CAN BE FULLNESS

In point of fact, emptiness and fullness are just constructions of the mind: in reality, they do not exist in any objective or absolute way. We can experience something as full or empty, depending upon our point of view. The classic example here is the glass half-filled with wine, or other beverage of your choice. Is the glass half full or half empty? It is entirely a matter of our individual attitude. This old proverb reminds us that our reality is not really independent of us at all. It requires our active participation. The way we look at things will re-condition what they are. If we see things differently, the very things we are looking at will change. If we apply this notion to our lives, we can create dramatic shifts in our circumstances. An apparently hopeless situation can become hopeful, a loss can lead to a gain.

Another way of approaching this theme is to think of an empty space as full of possibilities. Imagine yourself on a crowded subway car, crammed to the hilt with passengers. Now imagine yourself on a deserted, windswept beach, with no-one around. In which place are you freer to make any movement you please? The empty beach is actually full of potential. And so it is with many circumstances in life: the less we bind ourselves to possessions, the less attached we are, the less clutter we have around us, the more possibilities are open to us. What is empty in one sense, is full in another; what is full in one sense is empty in another. This even holds true in evolutionary terms: animals which have developed highly specialized bodies have historically been the ones to have succumbed to extinction, whereas those that have remained somewhat unspecialized, with something in reserve, have been able to adapt to changing environments and avoid extinction. Exactly the same is true in the economic and employment sphere. Those who retain some inner space of adaptability will survive, those who have become too "filled-up" with one specific specialization, likely will not.

Often our minds and emotions can be "filled" with an assumption about the way things are. The assumption may be idealistic or pessimistic, but we are in the grip of the assumption and lack the "space" to see clearly. Many years ago, I believed I was doomed to die a young man. In the course of my work, I had accidentally been cut and exposed to blood I later learned was contaminated with HIV. When I realized what had happened, I went for a series of tests, convinced that I myself must have been infected, and that I faced an inevitable descent into AIDS. I clearly recall going into the clinic and the nurse looking at me with compassion and concern, asking me if I was likely to attempt suicide. (This was even before my blood sample had been tested, such was the prevailing conviction back then that any exposure to the HIV virus was tantamount to a death warrant).

I called up a good friend of mine, an older man in his seventies who had earlier in life been a theologian and a professor of philosophy at Yale University, before giving this up to work in theater and teach in art school. I invited Richard out to dinner, and announced to him in a somewhat shaky

NICHOLAS CORRIN, L.Ac.

voice that I was probably HIV positive. I was shocked by his response. I was fully expecting him to look downcast and upset, but he didn't. Instead he mumbled a word in Latin, *potentia,* which he attributed to Aristotle, his favorite philosopher. I just sat there with my forkful of food half raised in the air, frozen like a statue. I looked into his wrinkled, absent minded expression as I saw his eyes gaze off pleasantly into space. What on earth was he getting at?

Instead of pressing him on the matter, I just let it drop, feeling even lonelier than I had before. Here am I telling my friend I don't have long to live and here he is spouting in Latin about potentiality. What kind of solace is that? Not long after, my blood test came back negative, as did all the subsequent tests which are necessary to determine whether one's system has produced antibodies to the virus. (HIV itself has never been isolated, and infection is deduced from the presence of antibodies in the patient's blood). I soon began to re-assess all my previous assumptions about health, disease and the immune system. I read all I could find about the supposed die-hard causal relationship between HIV and AIDS and discovered that it was not so self-evident at all.

My entire view shifted and I began to recognize that this entire causal theory was full of cracks and gaps. Indeed, there were many long-term survivors of HIV infection who had eschewed conventional medicine. I then began to devote a great deal of my time to researching alternative, drug-free protocols for treating HIV infection. A great space had opened up in my understanding, and the potentiality to use this understanding to help others. Richard had been right.

In the spiritual traditions of the East, emptiness or formlessness is the basic ingredient, and the one that seems strangest and most alien to Westerners. But what is meant by this emptiness? In Buddhism, the idea of a Supreme Creator or Godhead is rejected from the teaching. The highest aspect of our self is considered to be *Anatman,* which means non-self or non-soul. To attain enlightenment is to transcend the limited awareness of the ego, which always experiences things in terms of likes and dislikes, and personal judgments which create the illusion of dualism in the world. But dualism is not truth, it is the product of the ego and its fantasies and judgments. Hinduism, with its ancient roots in the Vedas, does speak of an absolute Godhead, which it refers to in different ways as *Brahman* or *Atman.*

However, despite this basic difference, both spiritual traditions view truth as something which cannot be encompassed by the mind, or by language. In the earliest Upanishad, the Brihadaranyaka, truth or the Absolute is described in terms of what it is not: *"neti-neti"*, which means "not this, not that."[16] Such a "negative"way of describing God, or the ineffable source of everything that is, was also common in Jewish literature and commentary, where the transcendent deity is often evoked by listing what it is not. So emptiness and formlessness imply a supreme reality that transcends things, names, ideas, dichotomies, language and mind itself. They do not imply emptiness as a barren or dry state. They imply a supreme consciousness that the ordinary mind cannot hope to access unless it empties itself.

In Judaism, God cannot be seen. In the Book of Exodus, Moses only "sees" God on Sinai as God turns His face away. There is, for Moses, a holy encounter with emptiness mysteriously filled with presence. And the name of God itself is ineffable: God cannot be named, but His presence may be summoned up through the vibratory effects of prayer. In Hinduism there is a similar idea: God is beyond names, but can be invoked through mantra. In prayer and mantra the mind must empty itself first if the calling out to the divine is to be heard.

Zen Buddhism also speaks about an "original face" that we had "before our parents were born." In fact, a classic zen meditation is based on this: sit in *zazen* (or just sit quiet-

NICHOLAS CORRIN, L.Ac.

ly without distractions) close your eyes and visualize your Original Face before your parents were born. If we stream backwards in time, passing through evolution in reverse, we can see ourselves becoming pre-hominids, then invertebrates, then just elements of water and fire encoiling in the pristine beginnings of the primal universe. Our Original Face is shrouded in steam and mist, like the summit of a mountain. Such is our Original Face: the journey from and back to the unfathomable source. Zen speaks about Beginner's Mind, a mind without assumptions, conditions or presuppositions. It also talks about "Don't-Know-Mind". Seung Sahn, the Korean Zen master writes, "Always keep this don't-know-mind. When this don't-know-mind becomes clear, then you will understand."[17] Don't-know-mind is the same as clear mind. "Clear mind is like the full moon in the sky. Sometimes clouds come and cover it, but the moon is always behind them. Don't worry about this clear mind; it is always there."[18]

THE ART OF
NOT KNOWING

Don't-know-mind is the mind that accepts uncertainty. That is why it is clear. And that is also why it is spacious. Relaxing into a state of unknowing creates an openness in our hearts. We become gentler and more humorous. When we rest in the "sense" of the unknown, we gain the same freedom that the wind has to blow across continents and oceans. Emptiness, as we have seen, is never quite empty, just as certainty is never quite certain. The emptiness of not knowing is like the emptiness of the lungs that can now take in a deliciously deep inhale of fresh air. When we develop the art of don't-know-mind, we sense a kind of fullness in the emptiness, a kind of fertile presence there.

Confusion always erupts from ideas and interpretations, not from uncertainty. When we accept uncertainty, we are not confused. But when we proclaim absolute certainties, whether these are religious or scientific, we are in a thick fog, a fog so thick that we do not even realize we are in it. Even at the quantum level, this state of uncertainty expresses itself: things are never quite what they seem to be, or the way we interpret them. So the key to living well is to embrace uncertainty. If you can let go of the grip of your interpretations and assumptions about the way things work, you can relax into a more receptive state. This relaxed state will allow you to absorb and assimilate information in a deeper and more integrated way.

The ancient Taoists cultivated the art of uncertainty. They understood that any hard and fast ideas about spirituality or religion reflected only immaturity. It is childlike to want simple answers. This fluid skepticism that they practiced enabled them to be in tune with the energies of nature, and to cultivate them directly. And living with uncertainty does not mean that we need to switch off our minds. Quite the contrary. Our minds need to be agile and alert. It is not a matter of denying thought or ridiculing the mind. It is a matter of enriching it and developing it by placing it in a "cloud of unknowing."

Every day, morning and night, we wash and brush our teeth. We consider this normal behavior. Strangely enough, we do not extend this to our minds. Think how much plaque can build up in there, day after day, month after month, year after year… The point is not for the mind to be empty or absent. The mind must be present. The mind is supposed to be active and purposeful. However, when the mind is not properly centered in a "cloud of unknowing", it becomes dangerous to ourselves and to others. How many times have your best laid plans blown up in your face? How many times have your absolute, sure-held convictions proved illusory?

NICHOLAS CORRIN, L.Ac.

Ironically, it is when we are unconsciously trying to control things that they go awry. If, on the other hand, we accept our place in uncertainty, we acknowledge implicitly that there is more to any situation than we had assumed: so we pay closer attention, we look, we listen, we respond. Also, we have become relaxed, and instead of forcibly controlling something, we are much more likely to find the most advantageous result in any given situation.

COMPASSION

A person without compassion is like a tree that can give no shade. Compassion is what makes us human, and without it, we descend very quickly towards brutality. Those acting without compassion for others are always in thrall to what I have called "raw" power. This is the type of brute, active power that has not been refined by the light of the imagination. The imagination is what permits us to enter into the experience of others, and therefore to acknowledge the validity of their existence. So the imagination is the real basis for compassion, and without it, compassion is not real; it is only a soft, sentimental state that does not connect one being to another. To connect, one of these two beings must attempt, with understanding, to enter into the life experience of the other.

The imagination is our amazing faculty to see and feel things from another's point of view. Without this faculty, human beings have little to boast about. When the heart and head are not united, a human being is little more than an uncalibrated machine. The head is as necessary for compassion as the heart is, for there needs to be a conscious attempt to penetrate and to understand what is unfamiliar. Inevitably, uncertainty will give rise to compassion: all of us share, temporarily, a flickering existence beneath the stars, as we shuffle around on our habitual pathways under that dark overhang of infinity. Are we not all on the same raft, all trying to navigate down the unpredictable river of experience? There is only our capacity to love and to be loved that can bring meaning to any of this, to our lives and equally, to our deaths.

EXERCISES
AND MEDITATIONS

The following exercises and meditations have been designed to help you absorb the ideas in this section, and apply them to your own life.

SET YOUR DAY

Set your day. When you awaken in the morning, before you do anything at all, take a few moments to prepare yourself inwardly. Your day will change accordingly, because the way you approach it will shift the way you experience it and even what occurs. Don't expect good things or bad things to happen to you, but tell yourself that you can affect the day's events and that it will turn out well because of the way you are approaching it. After all, it is your day. Think of the day as a river into which you are about to plunge. Plunge in with confidence, like the little Old Man, knowing that if you do so, the water will support you and take you to the safety of the bridge. Approach each day this way and note the differences from previous days.

PRACTICE NOT KNOWING

Practice not knowing. Whenever you are in a meeting or any situation where people have conflicting opinions, hold back a little. Don't express your views as quickly as you normally might. Pause and hold back a little. Suggest rather than dic-

tate. Cultivate the sense that the best ideas and solutions are not always obvious at first. They may be hiding some place! Tap into not knowing and see how this will make people listen to you with greater attention and with more respect.

WALKING MEDITATION

Walking is a great way both to be present in the body, and to reconnect to the elements, earth, water, air, fire (light) and space. For walking to be meditative, it must not be mechanical. Think of your body as lithe and supple, like an animal. Think of it as an expression of nature, like a stream or a bird. Move in a relaxed way, enjoying the lilt of your hips, the swing of your arms, the gentle rotation of your spine. Go as fast or as slow as you need to preserve an inward state of mind.

1) Use your peripheral vision, taking in what you see with the "sides" of your eyes, not just what is directly in front of you.

2) If you are on a path, move in a sinuous, curving way (for this is how energy always moves, spiraling forward). Instead of keeping to a straight line, see what it feels like to veer rhythmically from right to left.

3) As you walk, observe without judgment the multiple things going on around you, which might otherwise pass unnoticed. This could be people's gestures, small pebbles on the path, the shape of a gateway, the color of someone's shoes. Absorb these details like a sponge, then let them go. Keep, however, whatever details really strike a chord with you and make you feel more intensely alive. Perhaps it is a heron, poised for hunting, or the shape of a cloudbank by the horizon. Perhaps you want to maintain a diary of your walks: just note down the beautiful details that came to you on each occasion.

NICHOLAS CORRIN, L.Ac.

WATER MEDITATION

Being near water is always healing, especially flowing water. Here are some options. If you listen to water sounds, this will start to wash away the internal "fixities" that are causing you stress and blockage. The sounds will open you up to the freshness of new possibilities.

1) Sit near a natural source of water—at the beach, by a waterfall, a stream or a fountain—and let yourself be thoroughly absorbed into the sounds. Let yourself become the water sounds.

2) You may also choose to follow the movements of the water with your eyes, so that your sight and attention flow in complete harmony with the water itself. Notice how the water that forms waves on the sea appears to move but really does not, whereas the waves and ripples on a river appear to be static but are really composed of moving water. Perhaps, if you grow meditative enough, you will feel yourself carried off by the water.

RAIN SHOWER MEDITATION

1) Stand in a quiet place, indoors or outdoors. Close your eyes and breathe slowly and deeply into your abdomen.

2) Make sure your shoulders are soft and relaxed, your chest concave, and your arms freely hanging (make a little space at your armpits).

3) Now, very slightly bend your knees just an inch or two, and sink downward with your mind, feeling your energy sinking down into the earth.

4) Place your hands in front of your navel, palms up, as though you were holding a beach ball.

5) *Now gently raise the ball up to your chest, keeping eyes closed.*

6) *Now, let go of the ball, and turn your palms first outward, then upward.*

7) *Press your upturned palms up above your head, and imagine your hands were reaching into the sky, a sky full of soft rain clouds.*

8) *Now turn the palms face down over your head, and imagine your two hands have become clouds: a beautiful, silvery rain starts to descend from your hands, washing down over your entire body.*

9) *This electrically charged, silvery rain is showering down about you, and even through you, and you are being cleansed of all the debris, stale energy and blockages that have built up. When you feel clean, let your hands fall by your sides, straighten your legs, and slowly open your eyes.*

EMPTINESS MEDITATION

1) *Sit or stand in a quiet place. Close your eyes and slow down your breathing. Consciously relax all your muscles.*

2) *See yourself seated or standing in empty space. Form a clear mental image of yourself in this position.*

3) *Now watch your left leg disappear into nothingness, leaving only a faint contour.*

4) *Then watch your right leg disappear in the same way.*

5) *Now watch the same thing happen, first to your left arm, then to your right arm.*

6) *Then make your torso disappear. Only your head and neck*

NICHOLAS CORRIN, L.Ac.

are left. Now erase these. What now remains is just a faint trace of your outline in empty space.

7) You now have no name, no face, no substance.

8) Imagine clouds of chaos beginning to swirl around what little remains of you.

9) Then, look deep inside your belly, which is just a dark, empty space. See stars and galaxies start emerging like spiraling buds of light within your core. Watch as your outline brightens with their light, becoming ever brighter and more distinct. Watch as your face and body re-emerge in full detail, but different from before, filled with light. Your body now has a new found freshness and power. Beam that outward to the world, to whomever might need to receive your brightness. Emanate compassion to others.

SITTING LIKE A MOUNTAIN

1) Sit on the floor (or outside in good weather) in a cross-legged or lotus position. If this position is at all uncomfortable for you, sit on a meditation cushion or other support.

2) Make sure your spine is erect and your pelvis sits evenly on the ground. Let your energy sink down into the earth.

3) Extend your arms in front of you and rest each hand, palm down on your knees.

4) Half close your eyes, or fully close them. Breathe slowly and deeply down into your belly.

5) Become aware of your seated body as a part of the landscape. See it as a kind of pyramid, rising out of the ground, like a mountain. It has the strength, stillness and calm of a great mountain. Clouds play around the summit, where the air is thin and bright, and the sunlight intense. Become this mountain.

6) Breathe slowly, with the kind of breath rocks take, as though each inhale and exhale took a thousand years. Feel yourself deeply grounded into the body of the earth. You have become a mountain, massive and serene. Nothing can disturb or deflect you.

STANDING LIKE A TREE

1) Stand upright, but relaxed. Let your arms hang by your sides, but retain a little space at your armpits so that the energy can circulate. Drop your shoulders and allow your chest to become slightly concave.

2) Now bend your knees slightly, about two inches, keeping your spine erect and tilting your pelvis forward slightly (by tilting the tailbone forwards, without forcing it).

3) Imagine roots growing from the soles of your feet down into the earth.

4) Feel steady, grounded and rooted.

5) Breathe slowly and fully down into your lower abdomen.

6) Now gradually lift both arms in front of you as though you were holding a large beach ball. The fingers should be extended, and the fingertips of the left hand should point towards the fingertips of the right hand, about six inches apart.

7) Make sure your arms are not higher than your shoulders and that your elbows and wrists are relaxed, not tense.

8) Stay in this position for several minutes if possible. Eventually, you will be able to work up to twenty minutes or longer.

NICHOLAS CORRIN, L.Ac.

9) Visualize yourself as a tree in a landscape: still, patient and grounded into the earth. This simple exercise will strongly stimulate an energy flow up and down your legs and spine, increasing your stamina, willpower and overall health.

SEARCHING FOR YOUR ACOMODADOR

1) Sit in a quiet, protected place where you will not be disturbed. Perhaps it is best to take a long walk first.

2) Sit on the edge of a stool so that your spine is erect (and the energy can flow smoothly up and down).

3) Now imagine yourself sitting in a sphere of light: this light will protect you from all harm, and from all negative criticism.

4) Now imagine you are the sole person sitting in a movie theater, and it is your life that you are watching on the screen.

5) See which periods of life flash by, which ones return or linger. Watch to see which faces come up, which expressions occur on which people who have affected you. Notice if there are periods of your life where the movie is black and white rather than color.

6) Eventually, some scenes will be repeated or will seem more dramatic and crucial than others.

7) When you are done, slowly come out of your meditation and note down in your special notebook the details you have observed, as though you were noting down a dream. Repeat this meditation regularly until you have begun to form a clear understanding of when, where and to whom you gave up your power—and gave up the possibility of really being yourself. This process might take some time. Don't worry. Be patient, the images are there inside you, waiting to be summoned up.

NICHOLAS CORRIN, L.Ac.

PART 2

OUR ORIGINS

NICHOLAS CORRIN, L.Ac.

A SENSE OF MYSTERY

Who are we, where are we from, why are we here, and where are we going? These are the eternal questions that come with being human. Though we may not give voice to them directly in our daily lives, they are ever ready to well up in our private moments.

Strangely, these almost unanswerable questions are as much a part of what we are as our bodies, our bones and our blood, let alone our faces, names and identities. The human being, said the French philosopher Sartre, is that creature that questions the reasons for its own existence. Or could it be that the universe, acting through us, requires these questions in order to learn more about itself? Does perhaps our own self-questioning mirror a more intangible self-questioning that proceeds at unseen levels? And might it not be that the strange spread of biological evolution stems from the same source of experimentation and exploration that occurs within our own minds?

One way or another, both individually and collectively, we put together a story about ourselves that we call our biography. It sews together past and present, and it anticipates the future. But behind this outer story there exists a more wordless sense of who we are. It is in this strange, wordless part of ourselves that we chance upon the realm of the deeply felt, and perhaps it is here that our "real" lives are lived. These are unspoken parts, unexplored parts, dismissed parts, parts that are like open ground leading to unknown places. There are also those deep strata in us that feel strongly connected to other people, and indeed to the whole of life: animal, vegetable and mineral. These parts give us that thread of connection to the source.

The source is nameless, shapeless, fluid, mysterious. It is the opposite of something fixed and distinct, such as an apple. It is the spiritual ocean in which we swim, beneath the surface of our consciousness.

Without doubt, it is important to have a good sense of personal identity. But this is really no more than a fine set of clothing. It is not what we are inside. Inside, we have another type of body: airy, fluid, spatial, luminous. This has been called the spirit or the soul. Our soul comes close by us when we are in a contemplative state, when we grow quiet and still. Then the dense, physical body seems to be less what we are, for we have entered a feeling state that is more cloud-like, or more like dusk, when the light mixes with the darkness, and shapes of things become delicately blurred as they melt into oneness.

The soul is more of a vapor than a solid. That is why we say we feel "expanded" at moments when life is experienced as elusive, yet rich in hidden meaning and also in delight. When life seems to lack these attributes, we tend to feel contracted, hardened or shrunk. In a depressed state, the vaporous nature of the soul solidifies, like steam condensing then freezing into ice. In such a state, we become literally frozen into matter. (There is an equivalent of this process at the quantum level: please see chapter entitled "Science, Fire and the Human Light Body" in Part 4).

If it is our wish to live in a more expanded state, it is vital that we cultivate the art of not knowing. This way, we remain receptive to the sense of mystery, not locked down by explanations and interpretations. It is not that there is anything wrong with explanations and interpretations. It is just that they are partial. They pin things down, and they do so in an incomplete way; they fail to get to the bottom of things, where the true source is located, and where lies our capacity

NICHOLAS CORRIN, L.Ac.

to be one with all of life. Intuition guides us better towards this source than do explanations, but to activate intuition, we need to be in a relaxed state.

WHERE ARE WE FROM?

We have already seen how, by embracing uncertainty, we can start to free ourselves. Out of this very uncertainty, our intuition starts to grow. When our intuition and spirit are strong, we draw to us that which, deep in our hearts, we yearn for. That is, the real essentials for us to feel good about being alive—things that we frequently forget or undervalue in the bustle and confusion of normal life. So-called normal life, which is goal-oriented in the extreme, can take us very far from what we really require in our hearts. We are greatly strengthened by this sense of inner knowing, and instead of feeling adrift, we start to believe our dreams will not fail us.

The entire universe is a dream of sorts. We are dreamers who have been dreamed into existence by the mysterious powers of creation. If we aligned ourselves inwardly with such creative powers, would we not be better able to realize what the universe has in mind for us? If there is some sort of creative design behind appearances, and if our lives, as they unfold, are part of that design, it follows that when we live from the inner heart, in touch with our true natures, then our lives will unfold with the creative force of the cosmos behind them. They will be part of an unblocked current, a river of energy. And our own powers of intuition will tune in to whatever brought us into existence. By intelligent design I am not referring here to some naïve fantasy of a religious nature, but to an elusive over arching reality that cannot be contained by human words, concepts or rational logic.

Don't-know-mind helps us stay in touch with this mystery, and it encourages us to trust our ability to navigate the current. However, at school, in the media and in the world at large, another kind of mind is dominant, one we might call know-it-all-mind. This phenomenon of know-it-all-mind keeps us restricted. It does so by the filters imposed by society and history. It makes sense of things for us, but it simultaneously depletes us of our vital connections with the unknown by joining up the dots so that everything has been already mapped out for us. Now, maps are very useful things, but as we all know, maps are not the same thing as the places they represent. And stories are another kind of map.

There are two mainstream, competing stories explaining how we got to be here. One is religious, the other is scientific. One says creation, the other says evolution. The religious story says that Spirit put us here. It is common to all traditions and cultures, with the possible exception of Buddhism which denies the existence of a Creator. The scientific story says that we evolved out of primates. These primates evolved out of more primitive mammals which evolved out of amphibians which evolved out of fish, all the way back to mono-cellular beginnings in the prehistoric oceans. And all this "evolved" out of the Big Bang. But creation and evolution are by no means as mutually exclusive as these rival stories make out.

The universe dates back approximately 15 billion years, and the Earth, approximately 4.5 billion. The human species can trace its evolution back to primitive, single-celled organisms floating in the warm waters of prehistoric oceans. Later, we would pass through various gateways of form— amphibian, small mammal and pre-hominid—before assuming the shape we now possess, which itself is changing under the impress of technology, chemical pollution and sedentary lifestyles. We are no more than a costume for the life principle itself, which may cast us off in disgust if we do not treat it with greater reverence. There is no warranty for the permanence of the human species, and we may turn out to be

NICHOLAS CORRIN, L.Ac.

no more than a failed experiment by nature. Those species that have become extinct in the past have generally been the ones that have backed themselves into a corner, becoming so over-specialized that they have been unable to adapt to shifts in climate or the environment. We may have become such a species, despite all our inventiveness and technological prostheses.

Biological evolution is eminently mysterious in that it appears to have developed in sudden spurts, not in some slow, gradual, generic sort of way. This series of "pulsations" which caused shape-shifting amongst species is not reducible to the dogma of genetic mutation espoused by neo-Darwinists. Pulsation is basically a phenomenon of rhythmic, variable energy output, which can be represented by means of a simple wave. Cellular growth in plants has been shown to occur in such a rhythmic, pulsed mode, "each pulse exhibiting a rapid uplift and then a slower, partial recoil of about one quarter the distance gained."[19] In other words, the way a plant grows is in spurts followed by periods of rest. Each spurt is immediately followed by a brief recoil. Thus, the sequence of growth in plants is: four steps forward, one step back.

The pulsating mode of biological evolution is in fact consistent with the idea of a higher consciousness "dreaming" forms into being. Such a view is intrinsic to the Dream Time of the Australian aborigines, which is a time both within and outside of historical time. The Dream Time is both the original creative impulse which gave rise to the land and its creatures, and the maintenance of creation through a consistent dreaming by sacred forces, the Ancestors.[20] In the Vedic tradition there is an analogous idea: natural forms are the result of divine thoughts or images which "imprint" themselves on the world of space and time at different intervals. There is a creative hand at work which "sculpts" new and emerging forms through subtle energy fields. We can invoke a cosmic artist or dreamer whose ideas reverberate down into the material plane, where they engage with the flow of time, influencing evolution accordingly. Thus we can see how biological evolution, developing by strange shifts and leaps that do not occur at uniform speeds, could be the result of divine dreams (or templates) affecting the biological world and contributing to its evolution.

Two striking examples can illustrate this idea. First, the miraculous presence of flowering plants, with their inexpressible array of colors and aromas. Flowering plants appeared suddenly on this planet in what has been called "a sudden, violent explosion".[21] The angiosperms—plants which produce flowers—first made their appearance around 100 million years ago during the Cretaceous era, towards the end of the Age of the Great Reptiles. Up until that time, the world had been cloaked in monochrome; heavy and somnolent with thick, green vegetation beneath which slow moving reptiles grew to improbable bulks. The earliest plants were mosses and primitive ferns which reproduced, not by air-borne seeds, but by water-borne plant sperm swimming through the surrounding wetlands to fertilize the female cells. Later, vast trees loomed upwards, dropping their simple, woody cones directly to the ground beneath them, close by their roots.

When the flowering plants erupted on to the scene in just the blink of an eye of geological time—a few million years of the Cretaceous—the planet clothed itself in a multi-colored coat every bit as remarkable as the coat of Joseph, the famed dream reader of the Old Testament. The planet began to glow with intense saturation, rather like a black and white picture suddenly taking on color, except that the prior world had been, in effect, green-and-white. The new plants also produced encased seeds as their reproductive mechanism. This husked type of seed with its dense, nutritious core provided an oily concentrate of energy that would allow warm

NICHOLAS CORRIN, L.Ac.

blooded birds and mammals to thrive at their high metabolic rates.

The human species itself would be unthinkable without the prior, explosive emergence of the angiosperms and their beautiful relationship with movement and exploration. Human mobility and exploration has a definite precursor—one might say, an Ancestor—in the flowering, seed bearing plant. For these seed casings developed adaptive mechanisms whereby they could venture into new territory: burrs by means of which they might hitch a ride on the coats of animals, tiny helicopter-like blades, or sprigs of down, which enabled them to be carried by the wind and thus spread their color and scent beyond the limited compass of their forbears.

Darwin himself called the phenomenon of flowering plants "an abominable mystery", so illogical and incomprehensible did it seem to the rational mind.[22] Just as astonishing is the sudden, rapid growth of the human brain, which developed its large frontal lobes only within the last 50,000 years. Surely, the idea of "biological" evolution is not at odds with the idea of a spiritual universe. The principal problem with the mainstream scientific story is that it rests upon the assumption that consciousness is merely an epiphenomenon produced by molecules. According to this view, our human capacity to think and feel is little more than a side-effect of genetics which produced complex neurological systems capable of generating consciousness. In other words, consciousness results from neurons, which result from bio-chemical structures, which result from molecular configurations, which result from genetic "adaptations" over long periods of time. Such a belief system is like the snake eating its own tail. How can particles of matter have the capacity to organize themselves in such a way as to study the origins of the universe that gave birth to them?

Such absurd beliefs are in part generated by our innate tendency to look at things dualistically, splitting reality into opposites. This gives us spirit and matter, faith and science, body and mind, human and animal, good and bad, right and wrong, and so on. This tendency of the human mind has been hardened through centuries of education and conditioning. Part of the conditioning is dogma repeated over and over so that it becomes inviolable and unquestionable. This produces a kind of false faith that most religious people cling to. In the past, it was used to obstruct new knowledge and to attack scientific discoveries.

The other part of the conditioning is logic, which overlays our dualistic disposition and appears to validate it. Such logic probably goes back to Aristotle: if A and B are dissimilar, and if A = C, then B cannot also equal C. This logic produces a kind of false truth which most "scientific-minded" people cling to. It is false not because it has no truth as, quite obviously, this logic does apply to much of ordinary reality as we experience it. But it does not apply to reality at deeper levels.

The Complementarity Principle recognizes this as it acknowledges the entanglement of subject and object.[23] How we choose to observe something will have a bearing on how, and what, that something will show itself to be. So we will encounter either a particle or a wave depending on how we bring our attention to observe a phenomenon. Yet both particle and wave are aspects of the same elusive phenomenon. Only our way of looking at this phenomenon varies, and in so doing, this very act of observation will "shape" the outcome. To us, the phenomenon can only appear either as a wave or as a particle. Yet at some deeper level beyond the questioning mind, the phenomenon exists as both. In such a case, A and B are dissimilar, yet both equal C.

In one of his movies, the great Russian film director, Andrei Tarkovsky, projects his formula on to the screen:

$$1 + 1 = 1$$

NICHOLAS CORRIN, L.Ac.

He means to show by this that all things—and all of us—originate in and belong to the realm of spirit, which is oneness. It is a spiritual equation. Another, more humorous way of saying the same thing was expressed by the Catalan painter, Joan Miro, when he wrote:

2 + 2 does not equal 4. Only accountants believe that.

If we consider the origin of life as spiritual, this is in no way incompatible with science. What could be more suggestive of spirit than evolution itself? There we see Life seeking ever more refined and complex structures, Life abandoning the security of the known in order constantly to venture into unknown territory and don unknown forms: does this not amount to search, courage, quest, aspiration, and even love? What could be more indicative of a spiritual foundation than this? Creation, even according to the Bible, did not happen overnight. It is a work in progress, an unfolding, and evolution is its dynamic template.

Evolution is not simply a biological phenomenon. It is a function of consciousness itself. We can sense such a calling within ourselves if we choose to look inside. There is a kind of thirst at our core—a thirst for greater and higher understanding—a thirst for deeper connection with all that surrounds us. And a thirst for more evolved ways of being, feeling and living. In fact this impulse is itself due to the presence of Light in the universe. Light is not simply a physical phenomenon, but the presence of spirit itself seeking to light its own journey through the unknown. We are part of that journey, each in our individual way. And we can choose to follow the light or to extinguish it. But following the light must take us deep into the night where we must confront our darkest fears.

THE SEARCH FOR MEANING

One does not meet oneself until one catches the reflection from an eye other than human.
—Loren Eiseley

There is a sort of hunger in the soul that requires the food of a meaningful life. Jesus expressed this idea when he said that man does not live by bread alone. We might even suggest that this phenomenon has been hard-wired into human consciousness. Hard-wired by whom, or by what? Perhaps by the mysterious process of biological evolution itself. When the frontal lobe of the human brain grew in size due to rapid evolutionary changes during the interglacial era, human consciousness also shifted dramatically in its potential. Meaning, and a link to the sacred dimension, became another kind of food sought by early mankind.

Long before the time of Christ, Paleolithic societies had developed contemplative rituals honoring the sacred dimension, from which all meaning flows like a river. The cave paintings at Lascaux in France show how early humans revered Life in all its mystery. On the walls of caves situated deep within the living rock, far removed from the daylight at the entrance way, they painted the images of the animals they hunted. Through these images they invoked the spirit of these creatures: mammoth, bison, deer and antelope. Early man knew that even though hunting was necessary for survival, and hunting was itself a skill, to kill anything was to take away something that belonged to Spirit. And Spirit was also the Guardian of meaning. Man knew that the gods lived in the animals he hunted.

Animals, along with plants and herbs, were early man's way of finding meaning and purpose in the world. Animals, with their powerful, swift bodies and graceful movements,

NICHOLAS CORRIN, L.Ac.

embodied spirit itself. There was a mysterious beauty to their form and to their presence which early man revered deeply.

Flowering plants, on the other hand, reflected the cyclic processes of time. Besides this, they held the magic of delicacy and transience, qualities, we might also say, of the soul. Man, early on in his development, felt the stirrings of his own soul through the presence of animals and flowering plants. We know that even Neanderthal man would lay wreaths of flowers on the grave sites of the deceased. Flowers were an expression of this creature's connection to the divine, a kind of common language capable of expressing the sacred. Laying flowers on a grave enabled him to express both grief at the passing of a tribe member and his reverence for the mysterious powers that ruled the universe. The flowering plants allowed this doomed, transient creature, soon to be annihilated by emergent homo sapiens, to express its own pre-hominid soul.

As for herbs with their healing powers, traditional peoples learned by following and observing animals. Humans discovered which plants heal by observing how animals sought out and ate medicinal herbs. This process of observation must have begun a very long time ago, perhaps in early pre-history. Animals, in a sense, were the first teacher-doctors, as they led man to the identification of medicinal herbs, and thus taught him to practice herbal medicine. By observing sick animals forage unerringly for the most helpful herbal plant, humans learned further information about the inner powers of both animals and plants. Beyond this, they learned about the profound interconnection between the animal and plant kingdoms. Humans witnessed a kind of spiritual ecology at work between animals and plants. Here was a realm of intelligence beyond human intelligence linking animals to plants. It was the realm of Nature, the House of Spirit. And it was into this realm that the shamans, mankind's earliest doctors, would make their healing journeys.

How many of us living in this twenty-first century can say that we feel our lives to be deeply meaningful? Not too many, I'd guess. Have we then lost something our primitive forebears apparently had, and that perhaps animals, plants and even rocks share, in forms of consciousness outside language? When we pause to observe these aspects of nature, we tend to feel a sense of peace that carries with it overtones of deep meaning. We human beings experience this in an almost primal way. Nature, for sure, is an elaborate field of interlocking ecosystems, weather patterns and other biosystems. But when we walk beneath the sky and gaze up at the swirl of cloud formations, or when we bend down and look at the spreading fronds of kelp on the beach at low tide, or clusters of barnacles stuck to the rocks beneath old jetties, we do not feel dizzy with too much information.

On the contrary, it calms us. Nature appears to organize its information differently than we do. We can consider the natural realm and the cosmic realms to be extraordinarily complex series of interrelating informational fields. Together, they produce in us profound feelings of wonder and awe, so clearly there must be a difference between the way the universe organizes its information and the way we humans organize ours. Perhaps here is the key to the lost kingdom of deep connection, a kingdom we have mythologized as Eden or Paradise.

Our era has been called the Information Age. For all the wonders that information provides, we are almost glutted with it. It is as though human beings can only assimilate so much information. Most people in the so-called developed world are caught up in overloads of information and in busy work routines which leave them little time for reflection. It is as though the mirror has been placed in some back drawer and almost forgotten. In the impoverished societies of the third world, or in the debt-stricken, collapsing economies of once affluent first world societies, people have little luxury

NICHOLAS CORRIN, L.Ac.

for contemplation as brute survival is often the main concern. People must face up to malnutrition, infectious diseases, war or natural disaster before they can reflect on the meaning of life. In huge, developing economies such as China or India, the allure of material affluence following centuries of subsistence living is understandably greater for most people than the quiet space of inner reflection. And yet, the fact remains: the human being is a microcosm of the macrocosmic universe.

This universe is spiritual at its core. The universe is ever enigmatic and beyond our comprehension. What Jesus said about bread being not enough for life still applies and always will. Man has a spiritual hunger, not just a physical hunger or a sexual hunger. Man exists on many different planes, reflecting the multidimensional nature of reality and of the universe. There is no way that human beings can ignore their spiritual dimension without self-destructing. We have seen, for example, in the late twentieth century how the anti-spiritual political behemoth of Soviet communism was brought down by the weight of its own dullness and inertia.

We have already discussed the famous zen meditation: Meditate on what your original face looked like before your parents were born. Our true origins are in the universe itself, above and beyond family, nationality, ethnicity, beyond even our human species. There is something outside us that demands recognition from the depths within ourselves. It is the call of the other, the strange gaze from the face of otherness, for this is our Original Face, the face that might be glimpsed only in an uncracked mirror.

LOOKING IN THE MIRROR

Does Life in general have a purpose? We know that science and religion have differing views on this subject. Most religions suggest that man was placed here by God as part of

God's design. Nature is simply interpreted as the backdrop against which human beings engage with their own spiritual destinies. Science, on the other hand, views man as a by product of biological evolution. Life is basically a struggle for survival and genetic mutations have allowed man to rise up to the top of the food chain where he now sits (somewhat overweight and bloated, for that matter). But if you ask yourself, privately, "Does my own life feel purposeful? Does my own life feel meaningful? Do I own what I am doing, do I know why and to what end I am doing it?"—what will your answer be? Plants and animals do not have to pose these types of questions, nor, for that matter, do machines. But we humans do. We are driven to look in an internal mirror and examine ourselves, and always the question returns, what am I doing here?

Looking in the mirror, whether internal or external is not an easy thing to do. We find it very difficult to look at our own image with any objectivity. After all, it's ourselves looking back at us! Either we dislike what we see, or else we are somehow in love with our own image. Or, more likely, both at the same time. To look into the mirror and actually see yourself is very difficult as you will tend to see only the way you think about yourself reflected back at you. This may well change from day to day, depending on your mood. So we cannot expect to go to the mirror, gaze into it and try to find out the core of who we are.

In the Greek myth, Narcissus died as a result of falling in love with his own image reflected back at him from the surface of a pool. Attempting to embrace it, he fell in and drowned. This can be seen as a metaphor for self-absorption. The more absorbed we are in our idea of ourselves, the less connected we become to others and to the greater world around us.

Buddhism gave us the concept of the cracked mirror. The idea is similar. The cracks in the mirror represent fault lines

NICHOLAS CORRIN, L.Ac.

in our vision, that is to say, in our capacity to perceive reality. This has been damaged. What has caused this damage? What has cracked the mirror? For each of us, it is a different story, but the further we get stuck into our self-absorption, the more cracks will appear.

Cracks appear on the mirror because our heads have got all stuffed up with unreal ideas: ideas about others and about ourselves, and ideas about the way things work. We project these ideas on to the space of reality so that we are no longer capable of seeing anything but our own ideas. Perception follows conception; what we believe to be there, we end up seeing, and what we do not believe to be there, we fail to perceive. Our feelings get entangled with these thoughts so that we are always comparing ourselves to others, passing judgments on other people, on the world, and on life in general. Some of these judgments are similar to sound bytes that keep on repeating and repeating inside us, and causing us to act in repetitive ways.

We could also say that all this inner noise creates a sort of screeching vibration, and that these dissonant vibrations coming from our hearts and minds cause the glass face of the mirror to crack. A cracked mirror cannot reflect our true image back to us. According to spiritual traditions, our true image, the image we can see in an uncracked mirror, is the image of our soul. The soul is really the state of consciousness in which we experience the interconnectedness of all things. The soul is hidden in our core but it exists simultaneously in everything that surrounds us. In a sense, the soul is the mirror itself. When we feel ourselves at one with the rest of life, we find our soul-image reflected back to us. This is the inner peace that is spoken of in spiritual traditions. But the soul will appear to us only when it is not cracked by the pressures of the "I".

There are easy ways of looking into the mirror. One is to immerse ourselves in nature. When I hike over windswept hills and cliffs, I sense the sky and the clouds reflecting "me" back to myself.

As a child growing up in the north of England, winter was typically a long drawn out affair, and spring arrived, shall we say, tentatively. But each year I would be mesmerized by the presence of living buds on the bare branches of trees and bushes. Each day brought a slight change in the shape and color of these buds: some were deep brown, others lime green, yet others a sort of maroon shade, with a touch of pink. As they opened, slowly but with an extraordinary, unstoppable power and sense of inevitability, I felt so absorbed in all this that it was as though a part of myself was participating in it.

Now, as I look back to those simple experiences of childhood, I can say that the annual festival of spring buds was as much a part of me as anything that occurred at that time within my family or at school. I can now see myself mirrored back in this display of tightly bound bundles as, slowly, hour by hour, day by day, they unleash their inner potential until the fullness of leaves and blossoms, in all their tremendous variety, hangs from the trees and bushes around me.

SPIRIT AND MATTER

In deep reality, there is no dualism, there is only oneness. We, however, break things up into fragments and thereby create the illusion that there are real and distinct boundaries between things. We see things as separate because we think of things as separate. For us, a table is a separate "thing." So, for example, if we look at a table, we "see" the edge of the table as the place where table stops and air begins. Same thing with a person: we see the skin as the place where the person "stops", their ultimate boundary. We see the horizon as the line where the sea "stops" and sky "starts". Yet all this is just true in terms of our level of perception.

NICHOLAS CORRIN, L.Ac.

A housefly will see this all differently: if we are seated at the dinner table with our plate of food in front of us, the fly will see a continuum. Plate-food-table-person will not appear separate and distinct at all. They will form one continuous zone, a zone of considerable interest to the pesky housefly. Probably this is one reason we hate flies so much: they do not respect us, they do not even distinguish us from other forms of matter!

But flies have something to teach us here. Like them, we do not see what is actually there in some absolute way; we see what we conceive of as being there. Perception follows conception. We conceive, mentally, of table, plate and person as distinct and different. And we extend this way of conceiving to just about everything so that we end up seeing "things" separated by "space." We also think the same way. We have abstract ideas about things separated by a kind of mental space. For example, we have an idea about spirit and an idea about matter, and we assume there to be a kind of mental "space" separating these ideas.

None of this has any reality; it is just the product of the way we happen to think. But the consequences can be very damaging to our psychological and also physical health. Because we have assumed, at a deep level, that there is a separateness surrounding all things and all ideas, we tend to feel ourselves threatened by that very separateness. Deep inside, we feel exposed and isolated. We feel like islands in a sea of emptiness and we strive to protect ourselves from this emptiness, which terrifies us. Out of this fear of emptiness, we generate anxiety, phobias and depression. And we cultivate all sorts of habits, tricks and illusions to pretend that it is not actually there.

But flies do not experience such anxiety, nor, apparently, does any other species of animal or plant, and certainly not rocks and elements. Only we humans do. Is this because we are more intelligent or less intelligent than the rest of life?

Perhaps both. Humans are capable of thinking themselves into a corner, or into outer space for that matter. We might say that it comes with the territory of evolution.

Most of our problems can be linked to a mind-body split, and the split between mind and body can be extended to a perceived split between spirit and matter. In the West, we have a long history of regarding spirit and matter as distinct from one another as table and air are. But, as we have seen, this is not the way the fly experiences things, and perhaps flies are better attuned than we are. What we call "matter" is really a densification of vital energy whose point of origin is in unknowability, or "spirit." There is a slowing down of vibrations until they "coagulate" into the form of solid objects. This can be understood schematically as an inverted cone of downward spiraling and inwardly contracting energies that "materialize" as they slow down and become perceptible to our ordinary senses.

The word "matter" actually originates in the Latin word for "mother" (mater) from which the word "matrix" also derives. The root meanings of the word matter show an ancient understanding that what is material has something alive and even spiritual to it: Mother Earth is generative and creative. This is because matter is not separate from spirit; rather, it is simply the form taken by spirit, it is spirit taking form as matter. Spirit inhabits matter, or devolves into matter without ever ceasing to be spirit.

THE SPIRITUALITY OF MATTER

Your existence and your body originate in infinity. Imagine an invisible thread, or root, extending from your head into limitless space. Through this root, you draw the strength to live. This strength can be amplified manifold.

NICHOLAS CORRIN, L.Ac.

Everything knowable to our senses pours out of infinity through the inverted cone into the realm of matter. This happens continuously, second by second. What is knowable is sustained by what is unknowable, what is finite is fed and nourished by what is infinite. Matter is still spirit, however. Matter is simply spirit slowed down so much it becomes visible, tactile and audible.

It also has taste and smell. Ordinarily, matter is experienced by us through the senses and spirit is experienced by us through the soul, or through what we can call "the eye of the heart" (Fig. 7). But matter can equally reveal its spiritual nature whenever we look at it with imagination or with love. Children do this automatically. For them, inanimate objects are alive and are given names and identities just like people. Artists and poets also have the capacity to see everything as alive and imbued with spirit.

In order to commence the path of healing, it is very im-

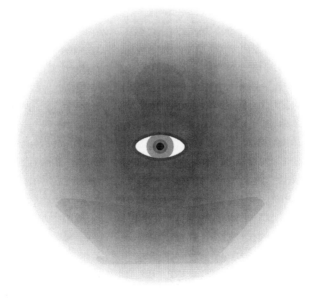

The Eye of the Heart [Fig.7].

portant to re-evaluate your relationship with infinity. Another word for infinity is universe or God. It is not important what word you choose. What counts is to begin to form a relationship with what is beyond all limitations. This is the source of your being and, consequently, it is the source of your power to heal. Illness and unhappiness are intrinsically limiting to us and they are the result of limited or impeded energy flow within body and mind. If this energy flow is increased and expanded, it will overcome such limitations as illness and depression. Remember that your root is in what is infinite. If you tap into that root you can draw in energy to make you stronger and clearer, and thereby to heal both physically and mentally.

All true healing, whether it is induced by a shaman or by a white-coated doctor in a Western hospital, is mysterious. Healing occurs from the inside not from the outside. Even with surgery this is the case. Surgery can assist the healing of the body from disease or from serious injury. But surgery by itself does not heal. Rather, it facilitates the process of healing by creating more favorable conditions within the body. The body can then tap into its own resources, which are the resources of life itself. This is what is called the life-force. This same life-force runs through all of nature: rivers, trees, flowers, clouds, fish, animals and insects. It runs through us, through our bodies and our minds.

The basis for this life-force is spirit, which really means breath, the breath of the universe, or the breath of God. In a very real sense, the universe is breathing life into us with every breath we take. As is quite obvious, we do not really take breath in, our lungs do it for us. When we are sleeping or unconscious, the breathing does not stop. Something beyond our personal will is doing the breathing for us, just as something else is making our hearts beat, pumping our blood and running our digestion. Would Life arrange all this for us for no reason? Would the universe breathe each of us

NICHOLAS CORRIN, L.Ac.

into existence and continue to breathe life into us, second by second, all for no reason at all? Is mere absurdity what lies at the very bottom of things?

We all like to feel special and everyone likes to feel unique. We like to feel not just important, but irreplaceable. It is an instinctive part of being human. Yet deep inside we are very much afraid that none of this is true at all. For we have been taught that we are basically the product of genetic mutations that gave rise to our shape, color and personality. This means that we are really the product of chance more than anything else. Beneath our desire to feel truly validated in our particular existence is the gnawing fear that we are just the playthings of chance, as though the universe were a roulette table, and we were just the number that happened to come up—and, worst of all, it may not be a winning number! Deep inside, underneath the facade, we suspect that we are not very important at all in the scheme of things. In fact, we may be just an accident. Silently, and often unconsciously, we question our reason for being here, for living, especially when things are not going our way.

This disempowering set of feelings occurs because we are disconnected from the source. That source is infinity, infinite potential and infinite power to create and to flourish. Our culture has provided many material comforts, but it has certainly not provided us with the comfort of feeling connected with the rest of nature and with the source. We appear to have largely lost the skills of earlier peoples to tap into that source.

Regarding health, although we have made some real progress in eliminating many fearful infectious diseases, conditions which decimated earlier generations, other diseases are also showing up to take their places. Also, we in the so-called developed world are plagued by stress, chronic ill-health, reduced vitality, obesity, anxiety, a toxic environment and a profound and growing disconnect from wilderness and from the subtle forces of nature and the universe. It does not have to be this way. What keeps us stuck in these conditions is the culture of fear.

THE UNIVERSE AT OUR CORE

Just as slime-mold organisms thrive in damp conditions wherever there is a paucity of fresh air and where, due to neglect or indifference, human hands fail to wipe things clean, fear thrives in conditions of emptiness, isolation and disconnection. If human history is filled with blood and terror, it is perhaps because the human heart has been unable to wipe itself clean of its own film of darkness. Yet even though ancient cultures had many barbaric practices that would appall our modern sensibilities, they generally cultivated something we have let wither on the vine: a profound sense of connection with the mysterious forces of the cosmos.

It is generally well-known that ancient civilizations spent a good deal of time observing the movements of the planets in the night sky. In this way, both astronomy and astrology were born. The Mayans, Persian Zoroastrians, ancient Egyptians, Chinese and Indians were inducted into these sciences through the unpolluted darkness that fell about them. It was this rich ambiance of true darkness that allowed the stars to be observed in all their glistening presence. The deep, brilliant blackness of night enabled those early students of the heavens to see, map out and track the movements of the pristine heavenly bodies.

It is quite ironic that in today's advanced world, where we have so much ambient light pollution, it is very difficult to get any unadulterated view of the night sky, and thereby to feel strongly re-connected with our source the way early peoples could. Simply gazing into the night sky has always

NICHOLAS CORRIN, L.Ac.

been a way of restoring our energetic lines of connection with the greater universe.

THE SACRED NAVEL IN THE SKY

The ancient Chinese went farther than this. Noticing that there was one light that remained fixed and unmoving in the night sky, they named it "Master of Heaven".[24] Today, this is what we call the pole star, which in our period of history is Polaris. The pole star appears to us as static because it is in alignment with the Earth's axis. As the Earth rotates, all the stars and planets appear to move, except for stars in direct axial relationship with the Earth. This phenomenon proved invaluable for navigational purposes.

But the Chinese saw the pole star not just as a fixed point for navigation, they saw it as the wellspring of cosmic energies. From it, divine energy came streaming down to Earth. They identified it with the *Tai Ji*, or "Great Ultimate".[25] This fixed lamp in the sky was the point from where yin and yang, or the play of opposites, rained down to Earth. It was the most powerful point in the universe, the source of all light and power.

The Chinese conception was comparable to the *ain sof* of the Kabbalah, which is an original point of light containing cosmic energy. It can also be compared to the *bindu* of Tantra, which is a cosmic seed: from this seed, divine creative energies stream from the formless into these realms of form which we inhabit.[26]

Both the Chinese and the Indians saw correspondences between these heavenly points and points on the human body. The Vedic Indians placed this correspondence close by the center of our chests and named it the *hridaya*, which means spiritual heart. Such a point is not to be confused with the physical heart, nor merely with the heart center or heart chakra. It is deeper than these.[27]

The Chinese placed the correspondence between the pole star and our bodies on our abdomens, close by the navel. In this way, the abdomen itself became a sort of mirror plate for cosmic forces. In the center of the abdomen is the navel, just as in the center of the heavens is the polestar. They discerned a vital reservoir in the abdomen itself, just below and behind the navel. They called this the *Lower Dan Tian*. In this energy center, cosmic energy can be gathered and stored, for health, for longevity or for the development of our individual consciousness.

The Taoists understood this place to be that special region in the human body which is a portal into the original formless void of the universe. If we cultivate it, they held, we can tap into the primal energies that gave birth to the universe itself. We could think of this as a kind of "stem cell" of vital energy. And to this reservoir they also gave the attribute of empty power; for when we stop imposing ourselves, when we abandon the need to control through ego, we may then re-enter the swirling force fields that sustain the physical presence of all that exists. This is what we have referred to several times as the feminine side of power, the power of water, the power of non-action and of inner stillness.

The ancient Chinese even named two acupuncture points on either side of the navel *Tian Shu*, which means "Master of Heaven". This was the same name they gave to the pole star. So they understood the human being as a microcosm of the greater universe. We are built in the image of the universe, and we have power points of access distributed on our torso just as the universe has them in the sky. The Chinese knew that vital energies stream into us from the cosmos via these entry portals around the navel. The navel itself is much more than a scar indicating where the umbilical cord was once attached. It is at the center of a zone where we continue to

NICHOLAS CORRIN, L.Ac.

receive an influx of vital energies throughout our adult lives.

This influx of positive energy can be enhanced with certain practices which you can find at the end of this section. These exercises allow us to "plug-in" to the universe in a non-rational, non-mental way, and to draw energy up as from a well. This can be only be felt internally at our deepest point. And depth as experience is equivalent to expansion of consciousness: in point of fact, our English word God derives from an earlier Germanic root which means "depth."[28]

OUR SUBTLE ANATOMY

In the most basic sense then, we come from the stars. We are made of light, and we originate in a cosmic source of energy which the ancient Chinese, as we have seen, identified with the polestar. This energy still streams into us all the time. However, we can amplify it or we can block it off. At the end of this section are some preliminary exercises to tune into this cosmic energy. The more aware we become of this cosmic source of energy, the stronger and more expanded we can become.

What we call our physical body is just the densest part of us. It is the most slowly vibrating layer, and we are so used to seeing this layer as "reality" that we have become blind to the luminous ocean of energy swirling around us. This energy ocean consists of light that is not visible to the physical eye. However, if we develop our so-called Third Eye, we gain the possibility to see some of this "hidden" light.

Our physical bodies are actually maintained by organizing fields of energy that overlap the physical structures. We can think of these fields as our energy body, or energy envelope. It weaves through us and distributes energy to the cells via a subtle distribution network. The Chinese perceived this network to consist of the acupuncture meridians, while the ancient Indians saw the network as made up of the nadis.

Both meridians and nadis are systems of distribution for the subtle life force to enter our physical bodies. If this subtle life force is diminished or blocked, we grow sick. If it is cut off completely, we die.

The abdomen plays a major role in energy distribution. It is like an inner sun, sending out rays in all directions. Two of the seven major chakras are received into the abdomen: the Solar Plexus chakra in the upper abdomen, and the Sacral Chakra in the lower abdomen. These chakras channel into us the energies of fire and water respectively. The navel is the centerpoint of the abdomen, and from it energy can travel into that vital storage tank in the body, the Lower Dan Tian. We will utilize this important energy zone in some of the exercises described on the following pages. This zone is an energetic womb, and it can serve both our creative impulses and the re-growth and re-vitalization of our bodies and mind.

It is important to know that many negative feelings we carry around unconsciously and self-limiting beliefs such as "I am not worthy of being loved", "I am inadequate", "I will never have what I want…" and so on, are coded into our abdomens. When we begin to send vital energy down there with our mind's eye, we can begin to unravel these negative programs that are working against us, and we can start to flush them out of our systems.

The following exercises and meditations have been de-signed to help you absorb the ideas in this section, and apply them to your own life.

NICHOLAS CORRIN, L.Ac.

EXERCISES
AND MEDITATIONS

LOOKING IN THE MIRROR

Stand or sit in front of a large mirror. Stay at least five feet away from the mirror if possible. Now become aware of what you see from the sides of your eyes, using your peripheral vision. Now look at yourself in the mirror, but making use of your peripheral vision. Don't look at your face at the center so much as around it. As you perform this exercise, you will see the shape of your face start to shift, as though the inner structure was changing. Watch how your face starts to melt and suggest other faces. Some people believe that this exercise allows us to glimpse our faces from past lives. However this may be, it will bring you closer to a sense of your Original Face, and to the quest for your true self.

PRACTICE SEEING LIKE A FLY

Practice seeing the way a fly does. Look around you, but don't allow yourself to see things as separate objects with separate names: door, floor, desk, person, window etc. Practice looking at things and keeping the words out of your brain, so that everything starts to merge into one field. If you do this exercise regularly, you will begin to experience a renewed sense of possibility and freedom.

ACTIVATING THE ABDOMINAL CENTER

1) Sit comfortably on the floor or on a stool with spine erect. Stay away from noise, and from electrical devices such as computers.

2) Close your eyes and slow down your breath.

3) Use your inner sight to look back at your brain. Imagine your eyes turned backwards, and use them as searchlights to scan your brain from top to bottom.

4) Observe all the activity buzzing around in your brain.

5) Now gather all this distracting, busy energy into a beautiful spiral and send it down through your neck and chest into your abdomen.

6) Now place your attention in your heart. Send a spiral of loving energy from your heart down into your abdomen. Feel great tenderness and care for yourself.

7) Observe a deep, hollow place within your abdomen, behind your navel.

8) Watch the spirals of energy from your head and heart enter into this space.

9) Sink pleasantly into this space in the abdomen, and feel it fill with calm energy.

10) Smiling and relaxed, dwell inside this deep, dark part of your body, trusting that it will support you and provide you with the answers you are seeking.

NICHOLAS CORRIN, L.Ac.

11) Stay in this meditation as long as you feel comfortable. With practice, you will be able to enter it more quickly and easily, and to stay in it longer.

BREATHING INTO THE NAVEL

1) Sit on the edge of a stool in a quiet place. Stay away from computers, phones, TV sets or other electrical devices. Make sure the air is clean and fresh.

2) Close your eyes and relax. Breathe deeply. Slow down inside. Keep your spine straight and erect.

3) Now focus on your navel. See it become your center-point.

4) With eyes closed, curl your lips into a gentle smile. Smile inwardly down to this point.

5) Place your hands, one on top of the other, over your navel.

6) Start breathing quickly and forcefully expelling breath out of your nostrils with a slight snorting sound. Use your abdominal muscles to push the air out of your nostrils. Feel your abdomen being woken up and becoming warm. Do this for one full minute.

7) Relax. Place your hands in your lap, one cradling the other, with tips of the thumbs touching. Now focus on the Third Eye, which is located at a point between your eyebrows. With eyes closed, visualize through the Third Eye the deep night sky with trillions of stars and galaxies spreading before you.

8) Breathe the light from these stars down through that point and into your navel. Concentrate it there. Using your mind's eye, begin to see a point of light that is growing in intensity just behind your navel, inside your abdomen. Smile down to this point of light as it grows and your abdomen grows warm around it.

9) As you exhale, expel stale, stagnant energy from your abdomen down your legs and out through your feet into the earth.

10) Continue this for several minutes.

11) When you are ready to finish, place both hands back on your navel and hold them there gently. Feel the warmth, calm and energy that has collected behind your navel.

12) When you are ready, slowly open your eyes.

CONNECTING WITH THE POLESTAR

1) Sit with erect spine, preferably on the edge of a hard stool with your feet on the floor. You may also sit cross-legged on the floor. But it is very important to feel yourself grounded.

2) Close your eyes and touch the top of your palate with the tip of your tongue.

3) Visualize the night sky above and around you, with the stars and constellations slowly rotating.

4) Now find the fixed point of light in this great wheel of stars: the Polestar.

5) Connect with it mentally, and notice a violet tinge of color to it.

NICHOLAS CORRIN, L.Ac.

6) Smile inwardly as you relax deeply and secure yourself to this still point in the sky so that you feel completely calm and safe.

7) Now start to breathe in the light from the polestar through a point at the top of your head. As you inhale, draw this stream of light down through your inner body until it reaches a point in between your navel and your spine.

8) Now exhale this light back up through a thin, light conducting tube inside your body, out the top of your head and all the way back up to the polestar.

9) Now inhale again in the same way. You should start to feel a kind of flap or valve opening and closing on the top of your head as you breathe in and out.

10) Continue this breathing for as many minutes as you can, maintaining half your focus on the polestar, and half your focus on the point within your abdomen behind the navel.

11) When you are ready to come out of the meditation, place both palms, one on top of the other, over your navel, take several, slow, relaxed breaths and gradually open your eyes.

It is best to do this meditation after dark when the stars are out in the sky.

FLOWERING
PLANT MEDITATION

1) Sit in a quiet place, preferably close by trees, plants or flowers.

2) Make sure your spine is erect and your pelvis is evenly balanced.

3) Breathe slowly, inhaling down into the lower abdomen.

4) Close your eyes and visualize the void of space, with the Earth as a small sphere in the distance.

5) See the Earth as a gleaming, green and blue gem in the surrounding blackness.

6) Now zoom in on the planet and see hillsides, valleys and fields covered with flowers. Observe the many different colors and shapes of the petals, and smell their scents.

7) Now focus on the point between your eyebrows, and breathe in these colors down to your lower abdomen, slowly forming a multicolored ball inside you, just below and behind your navel.

8) Feel it glowing and warming you from inside.

9) Once you feel lit up and warmed by this color energy in your core, slowly open your eyes, look over at whatever plants or flowers are near you and reflect on how their ancestors (the first flowering plants) emerged suddenly, millions of years ago, in a mysterious explosion of color and seeds, making life possible for human beings.

NICHOLAS CORRIN, L.Ac.

PART 3

FEAR: DISCONNECTION FROM THE SOURCE

NICHOLAS CORRIN, L.Ac.

FEAR AND LOVE

This book is about the power of letting go, the power to abandon control. Part of letting go involves the power to let things in. Letting in is also a power, because it can improve our lives by embracing change. This power is blocked when we are too stuck on the way things are right now, when we are fearful of change, fearful of the fruits of uncertainty. Whatever is too full is also empty of opportunity. Can you cram any new clothes into a suitcase that is already packed tight with old ones?

Many people live what they feel are unfortunate lives, never breaking free of the carapace of limitations. They live in a cocoon, a cocoon of fearfulness. Gazing out from their cocoon at the threatening world outside, they conclude they must protect themselves at all costs. They refuse to venture outside the cocoon, and they refuse to let anything extraneous come in. They just want to live in the world of the known and the world of the secure, even though such a world may be suffocating them. In this way they will have suffocated the power of letting in. They will have closed out opportunities that might have blown their way, opportunities that could free them from a blocked or otherwise unsatisfactory existence.

But for these possibilities to come to us, we need to be ready to receive them, and to act on them: strike while the iron is hot! Opportunities will sometimes whirl around us, but if we fail to see them and to act on them decisively, they will pass us by, and it may be that they will not return.

When we align ourselves with the adventurous energy of love, we remain open and receptive. When we align ourselves with fear, we hunker down and frequently fail to see good opportunities even when these might be staring us in the face. Our own negativity will have blinded us.

Fear and love are not normally thought of as opposites. And this, in fact, is true, they are not literal opposites. But if you search deep inside yourself and ask what emotions are driving you at your core, what will you find there? I suggest that fear and love are the two primary emotions that color our hearts, like red and blue. Fear could be also be called the absence of love, and love also could be called the absence of fear. Fear is a seed which can sprout into hatred, resentment, pessimism, blame and violence. Love is another seed which can sprout into generosity, tenderness, tolerance, creativity and peace.

If we turn our eyes to the world about us today, we can see that we are in real trouble. Ever since the attacks on the World Trade Center in September 2001, the world has become increasingly polarized. Fanaticism and fundamentalism have sprung up like poisonous mushrooms; innocent victims have been beheaded and videotaped for global viewing; human rights have come under attack both at home and abroad; corporate greed has been extended through junk credit bonds and banking fraud plus a barbaric doctrine of pre-emptive war aimed at securing control of cheap oil resources. War itself has been publicly declared as a necessary (and endless) state of affairs. All this should be set in stark contrast to the behavior and achievements of a man such as Gandhi. Gandhi preached non-violence, equality, tolerance, respect for all human rights, and co-operation. How has the world come to sink into such a dangerous trough of fear and hatred?

It is true that the power of letting in also has a dark side. Those who choose to live inside a cocoon are not completely wrong: the world is a dangerous place, and life itself is threaded through with darkness, as much as with light. To let in successfully we must do so from a position of self-awareness, from self-confidence and intuition. Otherwise we might be swept away by what we let in, for our personal lives are lived under the influence of powerful collective forces. And influence means, literally, a flowing in. Whether we realize it or not, our thoughts and feelings are being strongly affected, even shaped, by these collective forces. What are these forces I am speaking of? There are two of them, and they fit together like a hand and a glove.

One is external, the media. The mainstream media forces a constant stream of distorted pictures into our psyches, pictures as filled with violence, moralizing and jingoism as they are with trivia. Much of what passes as news today is controlled propaganda. In many instances, news clips have even been staged, with actors posing as broadcasters.

A second force is internal: our sub-conscious minds. Most people have some idea of the existence of their personal subconscious, but far fewer understand the workings of the collective subconscious. We are actually rather like fish, swimming daily in the great pond of our collective, societal and cultural subconscious. Our collective unconscious mind will absorb much of the fear-driven "information" from the media and start to program us from within.

How can we protect ourselves from this barrage and affect the world in a positive way? We must start by taking better care of ourselves. This might sound strange to some, but it is only by loving ourselves more that we can generate a more loving world. Love is more than an emotion, it is the strongest form of energy that exists. We can say that love is the energy that brings life into being out of nothingness, and that sustains it second by second. From a mystical point of view, love is the glue that holds all the pieces of life together so that all may thrive.

The more we tap into this energy of love, the more we will be sustained by it. Conversely, the more we succumb to fear, the more it will rule our lives. The world itself is only made up of individuals. For it to be transformed, we individuals must somehow change ourselves. Human beings are strangely different from the rest of nature in that we are endowed with freedom of choice. This freedom allows us to rise very high or to sink very low. With freedom also comes responsibility: a free being is a responsible being and is willing to take the initiative rather than to let others decide what should be done. If you are willing to reconsider your relationship with life itself, you can rediscover the sacred nature of freedom that you embody. Living this freedom more fully is also a way of loving. Abandoning this freedom is sinking into fear and allowing negative forces to control both you and the world.

The power of letting go demands that we release any need to depend upon outside sources of ready made information, much of which is warped, trashy or toxic—or just plain old misinformation. Letting go of this stuff allows one's intuition to come up for air. Careful reflection from within creates freedom in the individual. And only free individuals can contribute to a free society. Yet freedom is a fragile plant, and when fear grows past a certain threshold, freedom will perish altogether.

Fear is a potential energy that constantly eats away at us, like dark waves lashing against the shore. So we need now to examine what fear is all about.

THE MORPHOLOGY OF FEAR

Man is always marveling at what he has blown apart, never at what the universe has put together, and this is his limitation.—Loren Eiseley

NICHOLAS CORRIN, L.Ac.

If we look at nature without any sentimentality, we might see it mainly as the story of the eaters and the eaten. Every millisecond there are innumerable endings: tiny creatures of one species get devoured by slightly larger creatures of another species which, in turn, are consumed by creatures of yet another species and so on, all the way up the so-called food chain. This can be a fearsome spectacle to contemplate. If nature produces such a rich variety of life-forms, it does so by insisting that its children feed off each other. The abundance is profligate: fish typically produce vast numbers of spawn (according to some natural historians, herring produce as many as seventy thousand) but, if they hatch, the overwhelming majority of these will perish in the jaws of predators. In the natural world there is almost no safety, and there is ever present danger.

If we consider the physical attributes and coloring of many animals we might speak of a morphology of fear. Take for example, the armadillo, whose body recalls some of the armor-plated dinosaurs of the Jurassic period. Or the rhinoceros, with its exceptionally thick hide and intimidating horn. Another type of morphology of fear would be camouflage, where the potential prey has grown to look almost identical to the branch or leaf it is resting on. The trouble for prey is that the predator also has access to this option. Both zebra and tiger stripe their bodies with lines that mimic the shafts of long grasses. The chameleon is perhaps the master of this device, or morphological attribute, being able to change color many times to synchronize with different surroundings. Fleetness of foot also falls under the morphology of fear: the antelope and the hare, amongst many others, have opted for speed to outpace the predator.

These adaptations indicate a sort of fore-knowing on the part of species of the dangers lurking out there, and genetic modification is steered, as it were, by an intrinsic caution, or what might be called a fear based intelligence.

Predation can occur even before birth. Sandtiger shark embryos develop a full set of teeth whilst still in the mother's womb (female sandtiger sharks actually have two wombs). The hungry embryos devour any unhatched eggs before attacking each other. Of these, only one shall prevail and enter the ocean waters already well schooled in the art of killing and swallowing down prey. Fingernail clams and sea slugs display similar cannibalistic proclivities in this most violent form of sibling rivalry. In the nests of Spanish bearded vultures, it is a similar story. There, the mother will lay two eggs some days apart. The first-born, and therefore larger chick, will peck the smaller one to death with blows to the head, before devouring it as food. Perhaps what strikes us as one of the harshest characteristics of nature is this callous indifference to the defenseless newborn. We shudder at what we inwardly recoil from: the sight of the child preyed upon by its siblings, or even by its own parents.

In the insect kingdom, the male, typically smaller than the female, is frequently devoured during or immediately after sex, and has no protective instinct to cover him. It is as though the possibility of fear has been overcome by erotic urgency, a scenario we can observe equally well, at times, amongst humans. The male Serromiya biting midge, commonly known as no-see-ums, is penetrated by the female during coitus and injected with acid which quickly dissolves his innards into a liquid. The female imbibes this like a protein shake, then makes off, leaving the husk of the male behind minus his genitals, which typically remain stuck fast to the female's, like some romantic souvenir.[29]

I lived for about a year in New Hampshire, where no-see-ums proliferate in the warm summer months. There the winters are bitterly cold, the type of cold that can penetrate through many layers of protective gear and that hurts the very bones beneath your flesh. And the winters are long. When you live with such unforgiving cold, you long for any

NICHOLAS CORRIN, L.Ac.

kind of respite during the summer months. Yet that is when the no-see-ums arrive. They will torment you like an invisible enemy whenever you expose your skin to the sun. In Alaska and in Siberia, at the height of summer, mosquitoes descend like a deluge in the air. It appears to be a characteristic of northern climates that the short idyll of long, balmy days is corrupted by the presence of bloodsucking insects. In itself, this is an interesting example of the natural interplay of light and dark forces.

If we look at nature scientifically, and without sentiment, we will find a theater of horror, mitigated only by the need to survive. In such a theater, fear and violence prevail. There is neither true harmony nor kindness. Rather, there is a kind of consensus that anything goes as long as it ensures your survival. What kind of God would have approved of such a scheme? Human beings have probably rejected nature, or sought to tame it or alter it because of their primal fear of the violence and lawlessness of nature. Yet to see nature this way is not to see it as it actually is, but only as we experience it to be. And we can, and do, also experience nature in a contrasting and opposite way.

Admittedly, this next example is from a zoo, but nature itself does not care about artificial boundaries. At the very unusual Sriracha Tiger Zoo in Thailand there are some remarkable things to be seen.[30] Not least among these is the sight of a mother pig suckling baby tigers, and a mother tiger suckling baby pigs. In the former case, the zoo staff has found that if they feed unweaned tiger cubs pig milk, they grow up stronger—and gentler—than with tiger milk.

Sai Sai is a female tiger who was born in captivity and, as a cub, was nursed for four months by a pig who treated the little tiger as one of her own, loving her and caring for her just like her own piglets. In adulthood, Sai Sai has not forgotten any of this or "reverted" to what we might project as her true, savage nature. On the contrary, there are pictures of her playing gently with a large litter of piglets, cuddling up to her or just spreadeagled over her wide flanks as though she were a cozy fireside rug. Visitors to the zoo can see tigers, pigs and dogs peacefully sharing the same spaces.

What does all this mean? Surely it brings into question our habitual assumptions about animal nature, and about the "fixed" personality of predators and prey. It suggests that, below the surface, something far more fluid than our preconceptions is at work in nature. Given the right circumstances, there is an innate love, caring and playfulness that transcends not just species, but the hostilities and survival mechanisms of creatures that occupy opposite poles on the food chain. If the harsh conditions that nature imposes are taken away (and this is what the staff at Sriracha appear to be doing), an innate gentleness and commingling of species comes forth that would have been deemed impossible. But what is impossible is only what we have decided in our own minds to be so.

This idea will continue to be a recurrent theme throughout this book. Never fix an artificial boundary line between what is possible and what is impossible. With don't-know-mind, this attitude is not hard to maintain. It is not that we become credulous, it is that we are not rigid and fixed in our opinions which are, after all, merely scripts we have inherited from others. With don't-know-mind rather than know-it-all mind, reality can always teach us something unexpected and profoundly revealing, as at Sriracha Zoo, fifty miles or so outside of Bangkok.

We have to wonder about what amazing qualities there may be in pig's milk that are able to bring out the latent gentleness in a tiger. Could it be that the tiger's aggression is refined by certain ingredients in the pig's milk, ingredients that affect the consciousness of the tiger as much as its body which, strangely enough, responds better to pig milk than to the milk of its own kind? Yet we ourselves treat pigs, such

NICHOLAS CORRIN, L.Ac.

extraordinarily intelligent animals, with the most appalling disdain. We raise them in industrial misery in gigantic hog farms, processing them into luncheon meats preserved with nitrates. We do this to animals whose very milk seems to contain some intelligent coding that none of our human books or computer chips contains. Surely, this is yet another example of the strangeness that lies behind surface appearances. Reality is both more fluid and, perhaps, more deeply loving than we realize. Our own religious myths point to this very idea. Before Adam sinned, all animals, it is said, lived in harmony with each other and there was no killing of one species by another. The bloodshed only started as a consequence of human sin. Perhaps this pre-Christian myth underlies the findings at Sriracha Zoo. Perhaps, at some deeper level than we realize, there is a latent tenderness across species that we cannot begin to fathom because we cannot find it in ourselves.

Have you ever listened to a concert of frogs? If, on a summer's eve, you happen to walk down a lane off the beaten track and pass by some pond or marshy terrain, you are liable to hear a mesmerizing concert put out by frogs. Sounds which have no particular melody or tune have the capacity to enthrall our minds, and the "chorus" of frogs is one such sound. Except that scientists have informed us that these musical and meditative effects are really the result of competitive male frogs, shouting out for all that they are worth, in hopes of attracting a female mate. It is all about the sexual marketplace, science informs us, and the driving force is the gene seeking replication, and acting as servant of that great principle, "The survival of the fittest."

Which is true then, the "scientific" view or your experience of meditative harmony as you walk by the rural pond on a midsummer's eve? Actually, it is not a matter of either-or; it is really a matter of intellect and imagination. The intellect works by catabolism (breaking things down). The imagination works by re-combining everything into a profound one-ness. It is not a matter here of right or wrong. It is a matter of different levels of perception. They are not mutually exclusive. But imagination is greater than intellect and can absorb it, just as an anaconda can swallow a whole cow, or just as the night's enveloping blackness can absorb the landscape below. Often, kicking and screaming, the intellect will refuse to yield, asserting its supremacy as The Knower. Yet knowledge based on breaking things down and then re-assembling them into artificial syntheses—in brief, into mental constructs—can never capture the true essence of things. Only via the right portion of the brain, with its cavernous vaults of intuition and imaginative insight, can we hope to refine intellectual conceits into cosmic awareness.

THE TWO-SIDED BRAIN

The human brain has a left side and a right side. Although this is strictly true only in a very general sense, the left side of the brain appears to organize our rational, analytical thinking, while the right side organizes our intuitive, creative thinking. The left side is more verbal, computational and logical; the right side is more visual, poetic and artistic.

Can fear be assigned a particular location in the human brain? It may be more a matter of how the brain is communicating within itself than with any particular place. If the right and left sides of the brain are not talking to each other, the person will be in a disconnected state of awareness—and remember that the state of disconnection from the source seems to lie at the origin of all our problems. In between the right and left lobes of the brain lies a central area known as the corpus callosum. This fibrous section of the brain's interior functions as a kind of switchboard between right and left. If it is left unattended, guess what is going to happen?

NICHOLAS CORRIN, L.Ac.

We can easily see how states of anxiety and imbalance, even paranoia and delusion, might occur when the two sides of the brain are not talking to each other effectively.

To reach a condition of well-being at both mental and physical levels, it is necessary to be in a state of balance. Without a daily return to balance, we are bound to experience stress at some level of our being. And to gain a deeper relationship with the cosmos, it is important that our various aspects come into balance, for the universe is extremely varied and filled with complementary energies and paradoxes.

In ancient Greece, Plato distinguishes two ways of knowing, which correlate with the two sides of the brain. *Mythos*, the silent, intuitive way of knowing, is bound up with the right brain. *Logos,* the word-based, discursive way of knowing, is bound up with the left side of the brain. Both ways of knowing are equally necessary, but must be in relationship with one another. Intuition and silence can take us far deeper than mere thinking, but thinking is a vital part of being able to act in the world and to relate to others. Logical thinking is basically a way of "sharpening the arrow"whereas intuition and silence can take us much deeper into reality, beyond what can be spoken of.[31] The word myth shares close roots with mystery and comes from a Greek word, *mutus*, which means "to close the mouth."

This aspect of us is the receptive, meditative aspect. It correlates with what I have called the feminine side of power. Letting go involves becoming quiet enough to balance both parts of the brain and to "ground" the active, thinking responses of the left brain in the silent knowing of the right brain.

(*Please refer to the exercises at the end of this section for techniques to balance the right and left sides of the brain*).

HQ OF FEAR:
THE AMYGDALA

Yet there does exist one specific area of the brain which articulates fear and anxiety and it is called the amygdala. The amygdala is formed by two knobs at the very front of the limbic system, which is the central portion of the brain that processes our emotional life. If we take a look at the structure of the limbic system, we can see that it looks a bit like the Starship Enterprise. At the very front of the limbic system, forming a double prow, the amygdala points forward into the neo-cortex and towards the forehead directly beyond it. In between these two "horns", right in the middle of them, hangs the hypothalamus. The hypothalamus is that crucial part of the brain that receives and coordinates all incoming information. It processes this and relays it to the body via commands it sends on to the ANS (autonomic nervous system) and the endocrine system. So keep in mind a triangular spatial relationship between the double-pronged amygdala, and the hypothalamus, below and between the prongs.

Because it is such an important player in the mind-body system, the hypothalamus has often been seen as the CEO of the brain.[32] It listens to incoming information from the corporeal senses, and also to information streaming from the psyche within the neurons of the brain and, on the basis of this input, sends messages down to the autonomic nervous and endocrine systems so as to maintain homeostasis, or internal balance. Now consider the proximity of the amygdala to the highly influential hypothalamus, and imagine how a current of fear and anxiety might affect the capabilities of the hypothalamus to keep everything running smoothly.

NICHOLAS CORRIN, L.Ac.

The CEO may get highly stressed and may want to check himself out!

The amygdala is very interesting structurally: it is composed of two knob like horns, that "discharge" to the body, via the hypothalamus, information it produces.

This information is mostly made up of fear and aggression, emotions that the amygdala specializes in. Now, if we imagine us extending the amygdala forward and outward, through the frontal bone of the forehead, we would have, in

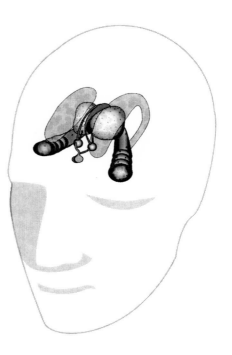

The Amygdala [Fig. 8].

effect, two protruding horns. This imaginary exercise gives us a very striking image of the relationship between fear and aggression: all violence and aggression originate in fear, the primal state of disconnection from the oneness of the source.

Most of the time, our bodies and minds are not in a state of optimal balance, and when this is the case, we cannot be as successful or as healthy as we would like to be. We can never navigate as skillfully or as long through the river of life if a part of our inner resources has to be constantly spent on trying to bring things back into balance. Imagine trying to start up a new enterprise when you are still obligated to finance old debts: that is what it is like when the system is out of balance in some way. Ancient Chinese and Ayurvedic medicine understood that although there are external causes for our health problems, the real causes tend to lie within and correlate with disruptive emotions or states of consciousness. In yogic theory, these are known as *vrittis*, which mean waves, or vibrations. These *vrittis* can become aggravated into *kleishas*. *Kleishas* can be understood as disturbed choppy wave forms, like turbulence at sea. They are emitted whenever fear and anxiety get the upperhand.

Since the hypothalamus, as it attempts to maintain balance, will be forced to relay much of this inner turbulence down to the body, all the various organs such as the heart, stomach and kidneys can be affected, and indeed every cell of the body, as it is the hypothalamus that tells the pituitary gland (the master gland of the endocrine system) which hormones it should release or withhold, and when. Hormones are chemical messengers traveling throughout the body and instructing other glands or individual cells to instigate their own secretions or metabolic responses. So when fear or anxiety are being emitted for long periods from the amygdala, the hypothalamus is going to be directing much of this influence down into the body.

(Please refer to the exercises at the end of this section for meditations to calm the amygdala and benefit the hypothalamus).

THE PHYSIOLOGY OF FEAR

If fear is a primal emotion for human beings, what is it based upon? Fear is indissociable from pain, and it is related to the sense of the future. Fear is an anticipation of pain or loss projected on to the future. Fear might also be called a state of the body-mind when survival is threatened. Fear in humans is connected to the so-called *flight-or-fight* syndrome that correlates with adrenal hormone activation. From

NICHOLAS CORRIN, L.Ac.

a biological perspective, fear is a necessary emotion. It is necessary because it is allied to the survival instinct. The survival instinct has, in its simplest form, the nature of a reflex. It is a primal reaction of the nervous system. First, an outside threat is perceived by the creature's sensory system; second, a bio-chemical signal is sent via neural channels to the organism's control center (ie. its primitive brain) warning of this threat and the signal is cross-linked with an innate roster of dangerous forms; third, the organism reacts in a defensive mode by up-regulating its response to the perceived danger. For example, an electric eel will become "hot-wired" in the presence of a predator.

However, the human experience of fear as we are describing it is far more complex than with primitive organisms, since it is also an emotion as opposed to a mere reflex, and thus entails a more evolved reaction. There is an identifiable subjective experience involved, not simply a neural signal transmitted to the organism warning of an outside threat. At least, this is what we humans tend to assume. It explains why we find it much easier (more ethically acceptable) to kill flies and mosquitoes than mammals such as cows, cats or dogs. In mammals, we tend to see our own evolved nervous systems reflected back at us. We more easily recognize ourselves in furry, warm blooded mammals, and we empathize with their pain when they are clearly suffering.

This is surely why, as a society, we must turn a blind eye to meat production. We prefer to pretend that it is not happening. The fear and even foreknowledge of cattle as they are sent to the slaughterhouse is one of the most haunting aspects of our modern industrialized economies. Those who eat meat prefer not to think about such things. But the fact remains that domestic animals slaughtered at abattoirs exhibit emotional reactions not dissimilar to those of human beings condemned to a horrible and meaningless death.

But is the emotion of fear and the experience of pain

confined to higher life-forms? This assumption is based upon the putative evidence of biological science. Yet there is no such conclusive evidence: rather, there are intimations to the contrary. Mainstream biology teaches us about progressively more complex organisms whose capacity to register pain or to have "feelings" is contingent upon their degree of neural development. A crab, a dragonfly, a parasitical worm, a bacterium, all rank far lower on the scale of neural development than a horse. Plants are supposed to be lacking in the nervous systems possessed by animals, and inorganic materials, such as stone or metal, are assumed to be inert, feelingless and dead. Conventional biology teaches us that higher life-forms have more complex nervous systems and that their capacity to "feel" is a mathematical function of their degree of neural development. Yet this cozy, neat, consensual notion is less than proven.

The great Indian scientist Sir Jagadis Chandra Bose was a contemporary of Albert Einstein. A physicist and physiologist, he became the pre-eminent plant physiologist of his day, and was at least fifty years ahead of his time.[33] Bose developed the most sophisticated, refined instruments of his day capable of registering and magnifying responses to externally applied electrical and mechanical stimulation. The degree of excitation produced in tissues was recorded on these devices. What Bose discovered was that plants have the same reactions as muscles to application of searing heat, sharp prodding, cutting, electrical current or exposure to toxic materials. Plants, despite having a fundamentally different structure to animal and human tissue, have similarities in behavioral physiology suggestive of neural reactions. This means that the sensitivity to pain and abuse we think of as placing us in a higher category than other animals, let alone plants, is based on erroneous assumptions.

Bose demonstrated—to the eventual acclaim of the scientific community—that plants have a sensitivity equal

NICHOLAS CORRIN, L.Ac.

to animal and human tissues. Even a carrot, when hooked up to electrical currents, was shown to respond no differently than human tissue would. Sentience, Bose concluded, is not confined to "higher" life-forms.

Even more strikingly, Bose discovered that metals also exhibit similar response characteristics. Experiments performed with iron oxide and tin demonstrated that these substances react in the same way as muscles do to exertion and sustained pressure. Metals will grow fatigued from exertion just like muscles, and will recuperate with rest, just as muscles do. Metals, in brief, possess the characteristics of animals. Metal fatigue can even be alleviated by gentle massage or bathing in warm water.

The boundary line between the organic and the inorganic, the sentient and the non-sentient, is nothing more than an assumption, a habit of the mind. In a lecture delivered to the International Congress of Physics in 1900, Bose declared that there is a "fundamental unity among the apparent diversity of nature".[34] If everything is to some degree sentient, and everything is to some degree vulnerable, what does this imply about the effects of our actions and behavior in the world? Could it be that many of our simplest, habitual actions cause a trembling to occur at unseen levels? Could it be that the way we go about things in our daily lives causes "human-like" reactions in matter? That sentience is all around us and in all things present, organic and inorganic?

In 1991, an issue of *Life Magazine* appeared with a picture of a great white shark on the front cover. The issue contained an article including recent data on the decline of shark populations and described sightings and encounters with the Great White. One part of this article stuck in my memory rather like a fishbone stuck in the throat. Earlier that year, two divers had spotted a Great White cruising off the southeastern seaboard of the USA. This was not too many years after the smash box-office hits of the Jaws series in the eighties. When this particular Great White became aware of the divers, it made a swift about turn and sped off into the distance, releasing behind it a cloud of excrement that also functioned as a kind of smokescreen. This image of the archetypal arch predator of the oceans evacuating its bowels in a reflex of apparent terror struck me deeply, and has remained with me ever since.

A number of questions arose in my mind. What caused the Great White to be so apprehensive about humans? What biological mechanism did it have at its disposal to both express its apparent terror and to obscure its route of retreat? What creatures, other than the killer whale, did it have to fear? And surely, its encounters with predatorial man would have been of too recent an occurrence to cause it to develop the biological response mechanisms for a perceived deadly threat? Or again, could this possibly be Lamarckian evolution working in the present moment? The shark loses control of its bowels as it senses the threat of the human. Very rapidly, this incontinence evolves into a controllable form of "smokescreen" to be released in the presence of the new super-predator... Great White Man.

A central tenet of orthodox evolution theory is that biological change is the result of a species' adaptation over time to random genetic mutations. In the nineteenth century, the French biologist Lamarck proposed that learned experiences could be transferred from parents to offspring, thus influencing evolution. Lamarck has been derided, even vilified by the scientific community for his thesis. Yet recent studies of lizards have shown that when the mother gives birth to her young in the vicinity of dangerous snakes, her young will have longer legs than those born in a less risky environment.

One conclusion to be drawn from this would be that the mother lizard's capacity to sense and "analyze" danger translates into her reproductive organs and through this means,

NICHOLAS CORRIN, L.Ac.

re-configures the DNA of her young. Fear, in this case, is a sophisticated surveillance system capable of reading levels of external threat and, on that basis, re-ordering genetic material.

Rupert Sheldrake's theories of morphogenetic fields may be helpful in answering these questions raised by the response of the Great White. If there is a field of consciousness in which all members of a particular species are, so to speak, embedded, then any member of that species will have access to information held in the field. Since sharks in general have become the hunted rather than the hunters in relation to man, the organizing field in which this species exists will hold current information as to the dangers of encounters with humans.

The field may also morphogenetically trigger evolutionary changes within the species that foster its survival. That is, the organizing field of the Great White shark species will carry coded warnings regarding humans that are accessible to any member of that species. Such codes could also be understood as energetic triggers for genetic adaptations in species.

To return to our question regarding the emotion of fear. We can infer from the sudden flight of the Great White shark that it is possibly motivated by fear of man. But we cannot say how exactly the consciousness of the shark experiences this condition of fear.

Since the dawn of the scientific age, Western man has come to believe that he alone is possessed of feelings, let alone "knowledge," and that lower life-forms are simply bio-mechanisms which operate on reflexes. Plants are even lower down the scale, and rocks and minerals are simply inert substances worthy only of being extracted and utilized by humans.

Before the advent of science, Christianity had relegated animals, plants, rocks and everything non-human to the role of extras, denying them souls and therefore fundamental rights. This has been a terrible error of so-called civilization which has now been brought into question through the extreme destabilization of nature in current times.

It may be that we are slowly waking up to a sense of fraternity with all that lives around and about us, from animals to plants to the Earth itself with its precious load of minerals and ores, riches there not for exploitation—as we have tended to assume in the Industrial Age—as much as for borrowing from the Earth so as to give it a "return" on its raw materials through the manufacture of higher shapes and forms. In that scenario, civilization would develop organically out of an attitude of reverence and love for nature. Many ancient versions of such a civilization have left scattered relics for us to ponder, from places such as Machu Picchu in Peru to Stonehenge to the autochthonous cities of Southern India.

Once we stop acting as though we alone have specialized access to higher states of understanding due to our evolved nervous systems, we can begin again to share the earth in a spiritual way with our brother and sister life-forms whether sharks, zebras, clouds or rock-pools. Levels of consciousness, beyond those we customarily acknowledge, integrate all living beings, including perhaps sub-atomic particles such as neutrinos and quarks. Such levels of consciousness can only be recognized when we let go of the assumptions of the intellect and cultivate meditation and reverence. By this means only can we come to sense the mysterious oneness that runs through all existence and of which we are only a small, and by no means the central example.

It is the human mind which has decided that advanced sentience can only occur within complex nervous systems. But if consciousness is a spiritual and energetic field transcending discrete physical structures, such views will not advance us very far. On the contrary, these views will prevent us from accessing information encoded within the phenomenological experience of other living creatures.

NICHOLAS CORRIN, L.Ac.

THE ORIGIN OF FEAR

Fear is a natural part of childhood, and the child's imagination discovers monsters in the wardrobe and witches hiding in the attic, waiting to attack. Do we undergo the experience of fear while still *in utero*? Today, there is evidence that this may well be the case on some basic energetic and cellular levels that could drastically influence our later life experiences.

Through the umbilical cord pass not only nutrients from the mother's blood which build the growing tissues of the fetus, but also chemical messenger cells secreted by her endocrine and nervous systems, not to mention environmental toxins circulating within the maternal bloodstream. For example, if the mother is in a chronic state of stress whilst pregnant, her sympathetic nervous system will be dominant, triggering the so-called fight-or-flight state. Adrenal hormones which activate this state will then flow through the umbilical cord into the fetus, directing its emphasis away from the brain and visceral organs towards the skeletal muscles. The growth patterns of the fetus will then have been imprinted by the nervous condition of the mother.

In the fight-or-flight state, blood-borne nutrients are shifted away from the internal organs to reinforce the body's physical strength, which may then be called upon in a perceived emergency. When this occurs, the inner functions of digestion, thinking and immunity are effectively curtailed because the priority is keeping the muscles ready for action.

More blood to the muscles means less blood to the brain and internal organs. If this shunt is sustained long enough during pregnancy, the fetus may go on to develop a weakened digestive system or central nervous system as a result.

We know too, of course, that drugs and other chemicals can pass into the fetus by the same route, compromising its health in serious ways. The latest research shows that most degenerative disease begins in the womb and is triggered by fetal exposure to toxins. It used to be believed that the placenta functioned as a kind of filter, but we now know this to be untrue. If fetal DNA can be damaged by toxins and drugs, it is also highly susceptible to being modeled by states of mind accompanying those drugs, indeed by any and all chronic emotional states of the mother.

Especially during the last trimester of pregnancy, the fetus is absorbing the external environment via the blood chemistry of its container, the mother. It lives at the very center of the mother, occupying the central nexus of her body, the womb. It lives a protected life, secure from outside threat, shielded and fed from within, bathed by warm uterine waters. Yet in truth it is far from secure and its environment is anything but impermeable by the harsh and toxic exterior airs. Most likely it is from these fetal experiences and their formative imprint on our psyche that our very sense of security originates. But precisely because the fetus is the passive recipient of the mother's state of mind, her own feelings of fear and anxiety travel inward and influence her child even before birth.

One of my personal memories from early childhood is of waking up in the middle of the night and calling out for my mother. "Mummy," I cried, "there is a germ in my bed!" Hearing adults talk about germs must have ignited my imagination. A germ, so tiny as to be invisible, was strongly evocative of menace from the outside and from the unknown. It was almost an emblem of fear itself, something you can't put your finger on but it is coming after you and it knows how to get inside you. Later, when I chose to study alternative medicine, I had much occasion to reflect on the collective phobias our society generates towards bugs and now,

NICHOLAS CORRIN, L.Ac.

superbugs. For sure, germs are real, yet they are strongly amplified by tendencies to fear that we carry in our psyches. Ironically, fear debilitates the immune system giving germs a stronger foothold.

This has worked to the advantage of the colossal pharmaceutical industry and its dominance over mainstream medicine: fear of "the germ" goads people to resort to medications and vaccines with dangerous side-effects rather than to carefully enhance their own immune systems through good nutrition, exercise and herbs. The approach of natural medicine is based on trust in the body's recuperative powers. Unfortunately, mainstream medicine is actually built on the cultivation of fear, claiming itself to be our only guarantor of safety. Such a medicine sells itself as "security," all the while generating fear and dependency in the population.

Drugs are the tool used to keep people in this state of fearful dependency. While it is undeniable that anti-biotics, for example, have saved countless human lives, today there is a plethora of drugs of all types that have deleterious effects on both the bodies and minds of the population. If we try to examine why and how this has come to be, it is clear that a good part of the reason lies in the corporate cultivation of our primal fears.

FEAR IN INFANCY

But when does a human first truly experience fear? I have speculated that, on some level, the fetus may well register fear states in the mother via hormonal messengers passing through the umbilical cord. This is, of course, not to conclude that the fetus would experience fear in the way that we know it. But the imprint of this "state" will surely affect growth processes, and fetal DNA may be modulated by the emotional and affective states of the mother. During the Renaissance, pregnant women were advised to contemplate beautiful works of art during their term and to avoid gazing upon ugly, deformed things. It was believed at that time that the beauty of the child could be influenced by the objects the mother gazed upon. Later in history, these beliefs came to be derided as sentimentality and silliness. However, we may be missing the point here. I am not suggesting that it is possible to shape one's pre-natal child's form merely by what one chooses to look at. (We now have genetic engineering tools instead to indulge our desires for designer children). Nonetheless, the fetus will, in some slowly unfolding biochemical sense, come to "mirror" aspects of the mother's state of mind. Such coding may later pre-dispose the child to develop similar imbalances or disease states to those affecting the mother. We still know very little about this process.

Fear is experienced in the context of separateness, vulnerability and aloneness. This is well expressed in the old adage, "Safety in numbers." The fetus and indeed the new born infant will not yet have developed any sense of a separate self: the mother's body is the universe, and it exists, literally, at the center of this universe. After birth, the newborn continues to identify with the mother's body as an unbroken field in which no separateness pertains.

However, a new shadowy element of disconnection and disquietude will have already entered into this field. Where there was once just water, there is now the phenomenon of spatial distance, what we might call the air element creating a divide between mother and infant. The baby can be held, coddled, breast-fed or, alternatively, placed in its crib by itself where its body will start to register the unpleasant experience of being away from the mother (ejected from the universe). It starts to experience the world as the space of absence and lack. This is not yet become fear, but the beginnings of fear have been laid down in the surrounding emptiness.

Many months will still have to pass before the infant truly disengages its sense of self from the mother's body and

NICHOLAS CORRIN, L.Ac.

from the surrounding environment. The cognitive development of a separate body and a separate self ego is a gradual process. Only once it has at least partially developed can we really begin to speak about the phenomenon of fear as an experience of consciousness.

THE FACE OF FEAR

If we look into a baby's face, it is impossible to find fear written there. The features of a baby's face cannot accommodate the expression of fear. Joy is altogether another matter. Everybody has seen the undiluted expressions of joy beaming out of a baby's face, much like the sun suddenly breaking out from behind the clouds. Yet a newborn's face can also look immensely calm, introverted and serious. I remember, as a seven year old boy, observing my new baby brother and being struck how much he resembled a wise old man with wrinkled brow, wrapped up in his own reflections.

For those who take a metaphysical perspective on life, the body is merely a vehicle or house for the soul. The soul incarnates into a particular body for its time of residency on earth. Prior to birth, the disembodied soul inhabits the realms of Light and Spirit. These are formless realms, where consciousness exists as a great ocean, with less distinct differentiation occurring than in that life we experience as individual human beings.

Suppose we assume that there is no fear present in the realms the soul inhabits prior to birth. There, the individual soul is interwoven into the great universal fabric, like a thread in an immense tapestry. Only through incarnation into a physical body does a sense of separateness and independence ensue. This is ultimately an illusion that comes with the possession of a separate body. The soul remains a thread in a vast tapestry, but it has become submerged beneath the fiction of a separate personality and a separate identity, and it no longer realizes its integral relationship with the web of existence. An individual body gives rise to the illusion that all bodies are equally separate and independent.

The incarnation process itself involves a process of forgetting. When the soul re-incarnates, its memory of previous existences must be washed clean. There are, of course, documented exceptions to this deletion of past life recall which, effectively, prove the rule.[35] The forgetting is essential: if we remembered significant portions of our past lives, it would be extremely difficult to engage in the present one.

When a soul incarnates into a newborn, that soul is still relatively close to the spiritual realm from where the soul has just emerged. The newborn's state of consciousness still swims in an ocean of oneness, an undifferentiated zone of connection, trust and joy. At the same time, its new bodily impulses drive it to a state of want: it wants milk, it wants warmth, it wants touch, it wants... what it does not have immediate access to. If it does not instantly receive these things that it wants, it cries. Precisely because it has been enclosed in a physical body, a state of wanting has been established. This is an inevitable part of the incarnation process itself.

"To want" has two meanings in English: to desire and to lack. So wanting generates a space or gap between what is desired and the source of that desire, the infant. As we grow older, this space or gap becomes more and more firmly entrenched until we come to experience it almost as the core of life itself: we are constantly in pursuit of what we do not have, and our minds are fundamentally preoccupied with acquiring what we feel we lack.

But this is not yet fear. Fear is actually the opposite of trust, and for fear to take residence in a child, trust must be broken. This kind of fear is subtly different from the child's fear of ghosts and monsters. It is the fear of not being loved, of not being adequate. This is such an important aspect of growing up that we need now to look into this quite closely.

NICHOLAS CORRIN, L.Ac.

THE INITIAL TRAUMA

We typically think of death as the ultimate trauma, while we imagine birth to be a pleasant, joyful experience. Yet although it is common for humans to die in pain, there has also been testimony from large numbers of people who have undergone "near death" experiences characterized by light, blissful states from which they have been reluctant to return. Many of these accounts are similar and describe passing though a tunnel into fields of light where they are welcomed and embraced by a warm presence.

By contrast we have, as far as I know, no such memories or accounts from people depicting birth in a similar way. Rather, it has been understood for some time that departing the womb and entering daylight can be a difficult experience, and one that can leave emotional scars later in life. Both birth and death appear to involve canals or tunnels. One is material, the birth canal; the other immaterial, the death canal.

For a brief period of our existence as embryos, we all develop tails and gills, recapitulating the ancient past of our species as sea creatures swimming in the oceans. Consider that life emerged from the oceans, and through the drive and curiosity that impels evolution, struggled out of one element and into another: from the water on to the land. We all repeat these dramatic rites of initiation at birth.

When the mother's waters break we must navigate our way out the birth canal and on to "dry land." This is an event that symbolically repeats what occurred for our primitive ancestors many millions of years ago. However, there is an important difference. For them it occurred gradually, over hundreds of thousands of years; whereas for us, it occurs suddenly, in a matter of mere hours.

Birth can be understood then as a trauma because we have been taken from a state of wholeness in the womb where we are essentially one with our enveloping environment, the mother, into a degree of separateness. We enter the world screaming for good reason! Growing up is a procedure which gradually develops our independence and, with it, our sense of separateness.

Development into an individual, the process of individuation, is unquestionably a good thing, possibly even the main thrust behind being, yet it carries behind it a kind of shadow which can produce disease in mind and body. This is the shadow caused by splitting off from one's greater, undifferentiated sense of self and it is characterized by a primal state of fear and by the failure to feel loved.

Beyond the physical dynamics of birth, another trauma awaits us in our early years, and it is this second trauma that is usually the crucial one in our development. At some time during infancy or early childhood, the majority of us get deflected from our true self. We learn to replace it with an acceptable self, one that is pleasing to our parents or teachers and eventually to society at large. We learn to forget who we really are. This can happen in a myriad of ways.

Eventually, later in life, we suffer the sense of loss that comes with profound disconnection. Many of us are not even aware of experiencing this sense of loss, so deeply have we been covered over with an assumed self, a mask. But usually, for most of us, the mask does not fit perfectly and tensions arise. The positive side of all this is that due to these tensions, an opening is created and a return to true self can be attempted by the individual.

NICHOLAS CORRIN, L.Ac.

THE FLOW AND THE VORTEX

My mother loved children—she would have given anything for me to be one.—Groucho Marx

Before birth we exist in the spirit realm. We exist as souls in a world not subject to space and time. When we incarnate we enter the physical realm, which is the realm of time and space, or more precisely, spacetime. Once we have entered a physical body we retain a link with our non-physical origins. This link may be completely forgotten by us or perhaps dimly remembered. It can be cultivated by us if we so choose.

We may view ourselves as consisting of an upturned cone of energy. At the bottom is our physical form, our narrowest, densest form of consciousness. At the top is our spiritual form which expands up and outwards towards infinity. The incarnation process can be understood as a descent from top to bottom. The life process which is engaged with our personal evolution can be understood as an ascent from bottom to top. Energy spirals upward and downward through this cone, conjoining the earthbound world of life with the great unknowns beyond space and time.

Once we enter the material world we have entered space and time. From conception, the cells of the embryo divide and multiply into surrounding space through the process we call time. Time can be understood as the flow of a river; and life itself as the river water. We each sit inside a tiny boat on this river water, navigating along its sinuous course towards the sea, all the while trying to stay afloat. The edges of the ocean into which the estuary will ultimately pour signify death; this will be the termination of our lives and it will require us to plunge into the fearsome unknown, perhaps into nothingness.

In ideal circumstances, there would be no obstacles in the way of our little boat and we would sail smoothly through without capsizing. But in reality, obstacles do appear, like rocks in the middle of the river. Our parents, from whom we seek protection and unconditional love, do not always provide these for us. Parents carry their own unresolved problems and issues and unwittingly inflict these on their children. What results is that the child's expectation of unconditional love is thwarted.

This can take a variety of forms from extreme abuse and child rape to simply a matter of a few harsh words carelessly spoken, or the mocking of something the child says, or a show of indifference. A child is a sensitive being and once it senses that something about it is not acceptable or lovable, it will try to bury this aspect; it will start to see love and being loved as a matter of conditions and negotiations. In brief, it will start to shut down aspects of itself and it will begin to wear masks, the masks of adaptation.

This entire process can be represented by rocks in the river. When large rocks stand in the midst of a river bed, they divide the flow, creating vortices in the current. This is exactly what occurs to the child's psyche, as parts of it get obstructed and, instead of flowing straight onward, get caught up in a vortex of disturbance which can last an entire lifetime, all the way to death.

The spin of the vortex becomes a negative belief pattern in the child's psyche, programming it for life unless this vortex is later on seen through and resolved. The essence of the primary vortex can usually be reduced to something as basic as, "I am not worthy of love." "I am not good enough to be happy or successful." "I don't have it in me to realize my dreams." "No matter what, there will be something wrong with me." "I am not like other people, I lack something essential." These basic programs can be further reduced to one single basic program which runs, "I AM NOT."

NICHOLAS CORRIN, L.Ac.

The primary vortex will cause secondary vortices to form. This is also a natural phenomenon occurring in flowing bodies of water.[36]

Because the self is a process in time, it is equivalent to the flow of a river and so the same dynamics apply. When a primary vortex has occurred in childhood, this will generate secondary spins later in life.

This can easily be explained. The first vortex is identifiable as the first trauma:

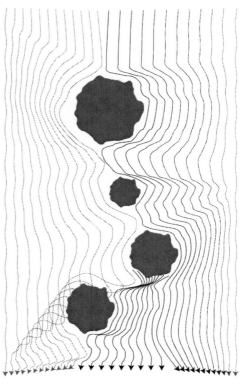

Rocks create vortices [Fig.9].

the moment or period when a child's heart is first hurt, that is, when it realizes that it is not loved completely and unconditionally. As a result, it no longer completely trusts, it becomes wary and it detaches itself progressively from aspects of itself that might meet with disapproval or dislike. It creates a shadow aspect which it locks away in a basement part of its being.

The obstruction in the river has actually caused a split. Now the individual proceeds through life with its rudder at a tangent, having adapted away from its authentic self. It tries to conform and work with this assumed self but there will always be friction from deep within, creating secondary vortices as the person's life plays out from the position of the masked self. The masked self is generated out of the split-off self.

The solution for the split-off, unhappy person is to reclaim their authentic sense of self: to re-enter the flow prior to obstructions. This will entail understanding how they themselves have contributed to the problems and disappointments they have encountered without, of course, understanding why; it is because deep down within them there exists a core of negative belief which can be expressed most simply as, "I AM NOT." They have allowed life to proceed from this filter of negation. They have unconsciously directed life to disappoint them; or perhaps they have sought to exact vengeance on life for the bad hand they were dealt. If a person is able to see through this negative conditioning and let go of it, then replace it with a positive vision, a great freedom can well up.

THE INNER PRISON

We come to imprison ourselves through an internal penal code, an internal judiciary and an internal police. Early in life we realize that certain aspects of ourselves are more acceptable than others. This is obviously because some aspects of our behavior are praised by our parents and teachers, while others get scolded and punished. Sadly, we may continue to punish ourselves on an unconscious level throughout our lives for instincts that are really quite innocent and natural.

The damage done to children may occur with the best of intentions on the part of parents who simply lack the self-awareness to see better. Or it may occur because of a darker shadow within the parent that seeks to compensate itself sexually upon the child for damage within the parent's own psyche. It has astonished me in my practice to see how many

NICHOLAS CORRIN, L.Ac.

examples there are in this society of people who have undergone sexual abuse as children.

In non-Western, traditional societies where a strict religious morality prevails, children and women often bear the brunt of harsh, insensitive treatment. They may have to become the scapegoats for the men's unconscious feelings of guilt and self-loathing. This is worst in societies which have a fundamentalist influence. The consequences of such repression and brutality affect not just the local society itself but the world at large, as we have come to realize with the recent epidemics of terrorism and suicide bombings.

Even growing up in a Western, democratic society does not mean that the obstacle of guilt is a minor one. In the Freudian analysis of the psyche, the unconscious mind becomes the repository of drives and instincts that are considered shameful by the conscious mind (represented by the ego.) Nonetheless, they do not disappear simply because they are repressed. On the contrary, they tend to grow stronger in the dark. A veil of shame and guilt hangs over us, according to Freud.

If we look elsewhere than Freud and consider Carl Jung's perspective on the role of archetypes in the human unconscious, we can see how guilt has cut a deep groove in the psyche of societies. In the West, the influence of Catholicism has been very powerful, generating the archetype of the Penitent. Also from the Judeo-Christian tradition we have the archetypes of the Fallen Angel and the First Sinners, Adam and Eve, that inhabit our psyches, promoting currents of self-condemnation and self-destructiveness. This need to condemn seems, on current evidence, to be even stronger in the Moslem societies. In the East, the idea of *karma* as punishment rather than learning has had a similar effect. When karma is internalized as a legal ledger, the archetype of the Inner Judge is brought forth.

Our secular, Western, consumer societies raise us in a

very confusing way. On the one hand, they encourage us to be competitive and self-seeking yet also require us to be compliant to a perpetual deluge of advertising. In effect, they are training us to succumb to artificial cravings which distract us away from self-reflection and self-knowledge. On the other hand, by means of a hand-me-down religious morality constellated in the unconscious, they admonish us for our "selfishness" and instill shame and self-loathing at our core; such feelings we bury deep inside where, we hope, no-one can see them. If our instinct is towards finding our own path rather than conforming, we have to negotiate the unconscious archetypes of guilt which may likely surface.

Many of us, conformist or non-conformist, find ourselves trapped in the consciousness of the Victim. The Victim is a powerful archetype in the world and it holds the reins to much of the nasty, insane political violence that now confronts us daily, with one of its epicenters in the Middle East. Yet the Victim lives also in mild-mannered suburbia in houses surrounded by green lawns and white picket fences. Whosoever, deep inside, feels themselves wronged by life and impotent to change their lot is in thrall to the Victim.

The Victim sometimes will form an alliance with the Judge, who castigates us inwardly, or else finds fault constantly with others, regardless of their intentions. We can also see a very dangerous alliance between the Victim, the Judge, the Warrior and the Executioner emerging as a toxic psychological cocktail out of streams of fundamentalism and political extremism in the war-torn Middle East. But we would be wrong to conclude that the archetypes at play in these acts of violence are essentially different from the ones at play in our own lives.

The Jesuits used to say, "Give me a child younger than the age of seven, and it will be mine for life." Children are very easily trained away from themselves. Because children are so malleable, traditionally there has been a tendency

NICHOLAS CORRIN, L.Ac.

amongst adults (parents, teachers, institutions) to want to mold them like clay figurines. What the adults have been seeking to do, unconsciously, is to imprint their system of values on to the defenseless child. Very often, unresolved aspects of the parent's own self will be projected on to the child, and the child will be forced, so to speak, to carry the can of the parent's disappointments and unfulfilled dreams. In this way, even a loving parent can unconsciously mold their children like putty into shapes that are at odds with the blueprint existing within the child itself.

Each person, we can say, has a specific "shape" that represents who they are in their "wholeness." This blueprint is the identity of the soul, not the superficial personality, with which it often comes into conflict. The superficial personality is the result of upbringing and adaptive habits and tendencies. The child comes into the family as an independent being, not just as an extension of the parents, not just an extension of blood, genes and family history. When this recognition is blocked, and when the individual fails to recover it fully, their power to flourish in the world is severely compromised.

It must be added that in recent years, fearful of causing damage, many parents have shied away from imposing anything on their children. They speak to their kids like little adults, reasoning with them and consulting them as equals. This leaves the children starved of the role playing and modeling they need for a healthy development.

Children need the powerful and decisive presence of adults who occupy a mythical zone of power, protection, knowledge and love. When parents abdicate from this zone, it can have a depleting effect on the children. Any absence by the parents can inflict damage on the child, and the tradition of the "absent father" has, for decades, caused emotional scars, especially in males who then repeat this absence, unconsciously hurting their own female partners, their wives and children. Children require a supportive presence, one which trains them towards becoming themselves, not towards splitting themselves up into acceptable and unacceptable parts. Later in life, a heavy price may have to be paid for such self-neglect.

At a deeper level than human psychology is the level of the soul. This soul is not merely human, it is planetary and it is cosmic. Our self–realization on a personal level is only part of our Self-realization on a spiritual level. The same yearning to become exists in all things, from animals to landscapes, from weather systems to galaxies. There is a principle of "becoming" that moves through all planetary and even galactic nature, whereby phenomena seek to express what they are, which is a particular form of the cosmic Self, the cosmic Soul. On that level, even rocks and clouds are seeking to "express themselves," for everything that moves outwardly also moves inwardly in a wordless pursuit of something greater and more expanded than the outward form. Human beings are made of the same materials as fields, trees, mountains, stars and nebulae, and are subject to the same influx of cosmic energies. The great dance of life and death seeks awakening in us, seeks to awaken us but on its terms, not on our personal ones.

This means that the freedom to develop one's innate nature requires us to be in tune with the cosmos itself. And to have this obstructed is to obstruct the unfolding of the cosmos, the Tao, or whatever term we wish to apply. We ought not to disparage the importance of our small existence and the shape we give to it, for the consequences of our choices may reverberate further afield than we realize.

FEAR AND THE SHADOW

Fear could be called the first emotion though it might more accurately be thought of as a primal state that reigns

NICHOLAS CORRIN, L.Ac.

in much of the natural world, a state even *before* emotions occur. It is, as we have already seen, the sense any creature or species can have that its survival is threatened. For an individual human being, it can be the sense that being oneself endangers one's survival, and that therefore this self must be disguised or masked. When we perceive a strong psychological pressure coming from the outside, this could lead to our *acomodador*. The accommodating point is the point at which we decide to give in; and giving in is a way not just of wearing the mask, but of beginning to identify with it. We pretend to be other than who we are so that we will not be harmed or overwhelmed with difficulties. It is a position similar to camouflage in nature which, we have mentioned, could be understood as part of a "morphology of fear." The problem for us is that when we consistently accommodate in this way, our spiritual power leaks away from us since we have failed to accept the challenge of being "ourselves."

We also place a filtering screen in front of our own eyes. When we accommodate to the world, we wall off parts of ourselves from ourselves, dis-indentifying from them and these then become our shadow aspects. According to Carl Jung, re-integrating the shadow aspect of the self is vital for health and growth, what he calls the process of individuation.

The shadow is formed at the same time as the *persona*, which is the acceptable part of the *ego*, in Jung's perspective. The *persona* is the mask we turn towards the world and towards our inner eye. The disowned part, of which we are ashamed, becomes our shadow aspect. The problem with the shadow is that it won't go away. Unless we come to terms with it, it will rule us "from the underground." In such a way can human beings become tyrants, killers, rapists, monsters. Even without such violent extremes of the shadow world, anything we disown of ourselves (anything we are ashamed to be identified with) will be repressed, and from underneath our superficial consciousness will constantly enforce a pressure, like mounting steam or gas. What happens, inevitably, is that we will start to project our "shadow" on to others.

For example, people who have repressed their own angry side will usually see angry behavior exhibited by others, and be strongly disapproving of it. People who have repressed their submissive, weak side will frequently "see" weakness all around them, even when there is none really there. Projection is almost a kind of hallucination: we become convinced that we are seeing something which really only exists inside our own heads.

The good news is that when we welcome back to us our repressed shadow aspects, we grow internally. By acknowledging our darker side, we are less in thrall to it. Instead of being carried off by a dark river, we develop the skill to navigate skillfully, even elegantly, through dangerous waters. Assimilating the shadow is really only a first step towards returning to the source. Because it is a first step, it is perhaps the most vital. Until we have come to terms with our own shadow, we will always be acting from an unreal position of repression and judgment. We will turn this unconsciously held judgment on to others, ever creating more instability and turbulence in the world.

How to recognize your own shadow? After all, this is something you have deliberately concealed even from your own eyes! If we observe types of behavior that are constantly pressing the wrong buttons in us, usually this provides us with a clue as to what we have denied in ourselves. The button activates our own repressed qualities that we have projected out on to others. When we are always finding fault with others, it is because we have found fault with ourselves but won't or can't admit it. Because we have narrowed ourselves down, and are constantly policing the borders of what is "legal" and legitimate in our sense of self, we hurl the same energy outward at others, attacking them for the very

NICHOLAS CORRIN, L.Ac.

attributes we fail to acknowledge in ourselves.

But if we listen to the voices of our shadow aspects, we can learn from them. And as we listen to them, they can reveal themselves to be helpers not enemies. For example, many people have a good deal of repressed anger. They have dis-identified with their own anger, rejecting it as bad or wrong. They try to appear decent, nice, compliant, respectful. But an angry fire simmers inside. This simmering fire is dangerous and destructive because nobody is tending to it. But if they spoke to their own anger, face to face, they might realize it was there to help not hinder them. It can teach them, not only why it came to be part of who they are, but why it can be an ally rather than an enemy.

For example, there are many situations in life where we are faced with manipulative or lazy people who are trying to ride on our backs. If these people sense our angry side coming up, they will jump away, as though from a fire which burns. Our inner fire, when used in this way as an elemental energy, can be of great benefit even to others because it can see to it that the right thing is done, and done in a timely fashion. Anger is not intrinsically a bad thing; it can only be used badly.

We could say the same for softness. Some people refuse any trace of vulnerability or tenderness in the mask they present to the world. They may pour scorn on such quali-ties, seeing them as nothing but weakness. But in their hearts they may well be searching to re-unite with the very aspects of themselves they have judged to be despicable. Being soft and gentle can also serve one well in the world, and serve others. The fiery side of us and the watery side of us both belong to the complementary nature of energy itself.

We create internal injustice when we ban parts of our-selves based upon prejudice. When we rule out parts of who we are because they are not socially acceptable, we take away our own rights, imprisoning or exiling parts of who we are, without right of appeal. These rejected aspects then retaliate by gaining the force of archetypes which are the expression of a primal psychic energy that is like a great wind blowing through us. When, instead, we turn to our shadow face to face, speak to it and listen to it, we actually become more human, more integrated with the whole of existence, and our shadow can become a living partner with its own wisdom to impart rather than a saboteur.

BROTHER LIGHT AND SISTER NIGHT

Above us, in the middle of the deep, black night, there hovers a river of light: the Milky Way. Unlike our earthly rivers, the Milky Way has neither banks nor boats nor does it flow inexorably into the ocean. The Milky Way is its own ocean, yet it perches almost as a mere afterthought on far greater oceans of blackness. These oceans of blackness extend not just around it but behind it, and not one of us can say where these infinite fields must end.

Dark matter makes up the majority of the known universe. What is dark matter? It is matter that does not register to the eye and to the senses. Invisible, occult, it yet appears to be the main material out of which the unknowable, creative forces shaped our universe. Like anything dark (night, shadows, death, evil) it escapes our comprehension. Human beings are creatures of the daylight. Lacking any effective night vision—in contrast to many of our fellow mammals, birds and insects—we become most vulnerable, least confident, after nightfall. Shapes lose their reassuring contours, and all the ghosts and monsters of childhood re-emerge from long hibernation in our adult psyches, ready to strike fear in us once more. Night is the mother of panic and terror. For it is only when we can see clearly what lies around us that we humans feel secure.

NICHOLAS CORRIN, L.Ac.

It is good not to feel secure. Security, when it becomes too habitual, is toxic. Like chloroform, it brings about a loss of consciousness.

It is the very beauty of this strange, endless blackness that provides the Milky Way with its gentle aura. There it hangs, like an outstretched hammock of peace and longing, strung between great branches of the tree of night: the river of light flowing through branches of the tree of night.

CASE HISTORIES

KAREN

Karen, a charming young woman in her early thirties with a successful career in business administration, initially came into my office seeking acupuncture treatment for whiplash following an automobile accident. However, it soon became clear that her trauma ran much deeper. Karen could hardly bear to be looked at directly in the eye. Though physically attractive, Karen was severely overweight, had been for many years, and had a history of binging and alcohol abuse. Above all, she was addicted to wheat products. This was a true addiction because, in her case, wheat was both extremely disturbing to her metabolism and had effects on her brain chemistry similar to a narcotic. In fact, wheat was toxic to her.

In the course of treatment it transpired that, as a child, her father had had a habit of walking down the corridor outside her bedroom and whacking his leather belt against the wall prior to giving her a beating. She had lived in utter terror of this sound. She had never been able to properly accept herself after this experience, and secretly sought solace in food which she would consume alone in her bedroom, in a kind of alternate world she was constructing for herself. Later on, in adulthood, though very competent at work and caring and generous towards others, she was unable to turn these attributes towards herself; she would grow agitated and anxious whenever she received a compliment. It somehow had become necessary for her to disbelieve in her own intrinsic validity as a person.

Karen slowly improved from a condition of extreme anxiety to one of increasing calm and first signs of self-confidence, though she struggled with wheat as with an inner demon. She was able to advance by connecting her sense of self to the source. This she did largely through contact with nature and through painting, especially colorful, circular forms which brought her back energetically into a state of inclusion with the rest of life. Karen went on to leave her career in business administration and go back to school to study psychology. Her many empathetic gifts and natural healing talents eventually found a way to express themselves to her and re-configure her life in a joyful, expansive direction. Since that time, she has moved on to a successful practice as a clinical psychologist.

It is very interesting to note that Karen's father had himself been traumatized by a leather strap as a child. His own father (Karen's grandfather), a policeman, used to take his young son out into the countryside on weekends. One day, they climbed up a water tower and gazed down together at the ground below. Karen's grandfather undid his leather belt, strapped it around the boy, and dangled his son upside down over the abyss below. Who knows what caused him to try such a thing? All we can say is that the scars traveled down over the generations like ripples spreading out over water.

NICHOLAS CORRIN, L.Ac.

LANCE

Lance, a well-dressed, silver haired man in his early seventies, was a realtor specializing in commercial property. Although Lance had a very polished smile and suave, outgoing demeanor, there was also something diffident about him, as though he were a fugitive, constantly in hiding. It turned out that Lance, married to the same woman for over forty years and now a grandfather, had been leading a double life the entire time, a life of homosexual liaisons, orgies and occasionally also illicit drugs such as crack cocaine.

It transpired that Lance had been sexually preyed upon twice in his youth: first by an elder, male cousin, and later by a summer camp mentor. Lance maintained that these events, and the appetites they stimulated in him in response, had deflected him from a normal sexual life into the life of a covert, highly promiscuous homosexual.

Perhaps because of his advancing age, Lance was now experiencing great anxiety, for his sexual appetites had not diminished even though his body had aged. Lance wished desperately to be at peace with himself and with his secret existence. As a church going Christian, he had always admonished himself for his "illicit," other life, yet in his heart he seemed to embrace it in the spirit of hedonism and rebelliousness. He was caught in a tangle of confusion and uncertainty as to how he ought to "play out" his remaining years. And he was terrified of aging and death. He knew his life had somehow been hollow, and something from deep within him kept him urgently in search of a human love he had never been able to fully experience.

During treatment, this awareness of his need for love and to be loved became far clearer, pulsing out from his own heart center. After months of progress, however, he ceased treatment. Perhaps the prospect of facing down his fears was too challenging for him, and he had actually come to settle for the entrapment of his double-life, squeaky clean on the surface, squalid underneath. But in his heart of hearts he knew he had closed the doors on peace, and his conscience would forever eat away at him.

TWO CASES INVOLVING THE ABDOMEN

The abdomen with the navel at its center is, as we have seen in a previous section, a highly charged zone. When the abdomen is struck in childhood this can leave lifelong energetic "scars," particularly in boys.

I know of at least two middle-aged men who were thumped there as kids. One of them, Mike, was punched in the belly by an older boy at the age of ten. He still feels pain there to this day, though now over fifty. The pain comes up whenever he feels depressed, down on himself, or is unsure how to react to a situation.

The other man, Ken, was punched in the upper abdomen, in the region of his liver by his elder brother when Ken was eight. Not only does he still feel pain and discomfort there forty years later, but he has also accumulated a great deal of repressed anger and hatefulness towards the world. Such emotions are compatible with a liver that has been damaged on an energetic level. Ken has never taken charge of himself effectively, has never been successful in business or in relationships, and he appears plugged up with bile just as a liver would be that could not release its normal secretions.

The abdomen is governed by the solar plexus chakra, which is the chakra of fire. The solar plexus conditions both our intuitive abilities and our outward going personality. It is, for these reasons, the subtle organ governing our personal power in the world. It is, energetically speaking, the seat of the ego. If it is damaged or misaligned, personal power will not develop in a healthy way. A person's ability to act effectively in the world will be impeded, and they may well

NICHOLAS CORRIN, L.Ac.

compensate with bitterness or expression of repressed anger and prejudice.

TWO CHILD CASES INVOLVING THE ABDOMEN

Lino, a slender, intelligent boy of seven, was having difficulties focusing at school. His parents had divorced about two years earlier and it was clear that Lino's experience of that split had been traumatic. His mother had custody, but Lino would frequently spend the weekends with his father.

One night, Lino's dad, who was most likely a good man at heart but eaten up with his own frustrations and misfortune, had forced his young son to take a bath in very hot water even though this had scalded the child's skin. As a consequence of this, the child developed a phobia surrounding authority and spoken commands: most specifically, he was terrified of action movies and school principals. Clearly, an authoritarian figure, or action figure barking out orders gelled with the image the child had formed in his own mind of his dad and that he needed, for obvious reasons, to project away from him.

For treatment, I placed an electrode supplying a minute, micro-amp charge to Lino's navel while asking him to hold in his mind's eye images of what he was most afraid of. These fears were quickly eliminated by discharge. The micro-amp stimulation appears to zap the crystallized coding of the fear at the level of the child's abdomen.

In a related case Stephen, a stocky eleven year old boy, suffered from distractedness at school and anxiety attacks at home. In Stephen's case, fear had crystallized into arachnophobia. Although it took more than one zapping over a period of months Stephen moved from being terrified of the very thought of spiders to being able to approach them and even play with them.

CINDY

Cindy was a forty year old attorney with a good, though high stress job at a law firm. But Cindy's personal life was a trail of woe, with one unsatisfactory relationship following another and with no end in sight. "They always end up abandoning me," she lamented, as though this were part of her strange, unhappy destiny. It turned out that Cindy's mother had suffered a stroke whilst giving birth to her daughter.

As a newborn, Cindy had been kept apart from her mother for many weeks before being able to make physical contact with her. Later in life, her mother informed Cindy about the circumstances of the stroke, leaving her daughter to accumulate feelings of guilt and even doubting her right to have come into the world at all.

As Cindy slowly gained ground in herself, she realized that she had always loved elephants and wanted to do something to make their lives better. When she was researching tours to elephant refuges in various countries, she met and formed a relationship with a man who, for the first time in her life, was not about to abandon her. He moved across country to live with her. Cindy stopped drinking and over eating, left her job for a more pleasant office and made her first trip to an elephant sanctuary in Thailand.

LILY

Lily was a five year old girl who had been adopted from an orphanage in China by American parents. Lily would often fly into uncontrollable rages, kicking out at her sister, parents or the pet dog, Rollo. She would throw things on the floor and often refused to go to bed, screaming furiously. For treatment, I would have her lay on the floor of my office and gently rotate my hand in a clockwise direction over her

NICHOLAS CORRIN, L.Ac.

abdomen whilst softly placing my other hand upon her fore-head. In a matter of moments, she would fall into a deep, trance-like sleep. As she did so, her eyelids would flutter and her eyeballs would swivel upwards (just as in yoga practices aimed at stimulating the crown chakra). It was obvious to me that Lily's rages were based on fear and on the intense pain of disconnection and separation. Part of her wanted to check out of life and return to a pre-birth, pre-incarnate state of being. Gradually, Lily's rages began to soften and mellow. Though still a fiery character at heart, she became more humorous and patient; eventually she stopped checking out as she began to feel loved and accepted by her new family.

NICHOLAS CORRIN, L.Ac.

EXERCISES and MEDITATIONS

The following exercises and meditations have been designed to help you absorb the ideas in this section, and apply them to your own life.

PRACTICE FEARLESSNESS

Create an image within yourself of a safety handle. You can reach up to this with your mind's eye at any time and you will be safe. Also imagine a spherical shield of light that surrounds your body and will protect you from any harm. Keep these very clear and strong in your imagination. Whenever you must enter a situation which you find scary or threatening, keep a part of your attention on these images. Tell yourself that you will not slip into anxiety, that these two things will keep you safe from all harm. Watch your confidence grow as you succeed with this technique.

PRACTICE SELF-TRUST

Place your trust in yourself, telling yourself that you will find ways to solve problems and find solutions. Tell yourself that by becoming calm and quiet, the solutions will present themselves. Keep reminding yourself of this as though you were talking to a child in your care: that child is yourself, and you are guiding him/her away from fear back towards self-confidence and an unshakeable sense of inner value.

ALTERNATE NOSTRIL BREATHING

1) Sit in a comfortable position, making sure your spine is straight and your chin tucked in slightly. Imagine a silver thread connecting the top of your head to the sky above you.

2) Fold in the index and middle fingers of your right hand so that they touch the palm, but keep the ring and pinky fingers plus your thumb extended.

3) Raise your right hand to touch your nose. Touch your left nostril with the pad of your right ring finger, and touch the right nostril with the pad of your right thumb.

4) Empty your lungs and then press both nostrils closed.

5) Release your thumb slightly so that your right nostril can open, then breathe in fully and deeply through this nostril until your lungs are full. (Your other nostril must be closed).

6) Now press the right nostril closed and open the left nostril.

7) Exhale fully through the left nostril until your lungs are completely empty.

8) Now inhale again through the left nostril keeping the right nostril closed.

9) Close the left nostril again as you exhale through the right nostril.

10) Continue doing this circulation for several minutes, evenly balancing the right and left sides of your system.

There are many variations on this exercise. This is just the

NICHOLAS CORRIN, L.Ac.

basic form. If you do it correctly, you will immediately notice a calming and balancing effect as the right and left sides of your brain become more integrated.

HEALING FLOWER MEDITATION

1) Sit in a quiet place where you won't be disturbed. Take a comfortable position with your spine in an upright position.

2) Close your eyes.

3) Scan your brain with your mind's eye and see the two prongs of the amygdala glowing red. Watch as they cool down like embers until the red glow has disappeared.

4) Now focus on the central region of your brain where the hypothalamus lies.

5) Start to imagine a pool of beautiful, deep blue water there, sparkling with brilliant points of light.

6) Now see an incredibly beautiful flower take shape there, floating on the sparkling, deep blue water.

7) Smell the intoxicating scent of the flower and feel this scent drift into every part of your body.

8) Relax deeply into the presence of the flower and allow its beautiful colors to shine everywhere inside you, and its scent to penetrate every cell with healing energy.

9) If there is a part of you that is sick or ailing, send extra energy there from the flower. Send its healing scent and colors.

10) Stay completely focused in this meditation for as long as you can.

11) Slowly open your eyes, feeling refreshed and strengthened. Give thanks to the healing flower that emerged within you.

The power of this meditation is due to the special role the hypothalamus plays in brain and body secretions. Remember that the hypothalamus governs the pituitary gland and through it, both the endocrine system and the autonomic nervous system. This makes the hypothalamus, in effect, a kind of supercomputer. It tells the pituitary gland to set about secreting bio-chemicals to the cells through the "factories" of the endocrine and nervous systems. In this way, the flower meditation works towards generating internally all the chemicals your body needs to heal. To be effective, this meditation must be done with deep focus and intent, and repeated as often as necessary.

FINDING YOUR SILENT QUESTIONS

This exercise will help you to clarify what troublesome questions you may well be putting to yourself beneath the threshold of daily consciousness. For example, it might be, "Why do I always feel unimportant?" "Why don't people respect me?" "Am I bound to fail over and over?" "Why do I never get what I really want?" "Why am I not loved for who I am?" "Why am I so unattractive?" "Why am I so unnecessary to others?" If you listen carefully inside, questions such as these will probably emerge. They represent cracks in your foundation, places where fear and self-hatred are fermenting. Locating them will enable you to begin to repair them.

1) Sit down in a quiet, comfortable environment where you will not be disturbed. Keep your spine erect and close your eyes.

NICHOLAS CORRIN, L.Ac.

2) *Slow down your breathing: focus on deep, rhythmic inhalations and exhalations.*

3) *Imagine a place where you feel happy and relaxed. Go there in your mind.*

4) *Imagine a person, or perhaps a pet that loves you and makes you feel good. Smile inwardly to that person or pet.*

5) *Relax into yourself. Release tensions from your entire body and let them sink into the earth. Breathe in light energy from your crown and exhale dusty, dark energy through the soles of your feet.*

6) *Now listen attentively for those inner questions that are always going on beneath the surface of your consciousness. What are they? What are the questions you are repeatedly asking yourself?*

7) *Find the questions in your gut, not in your head. They are not mental questions, they are gut questions.*

8) *Now bring the questions forward and up. Shape them into short, clear sentences. They will "ring true" as you say them if they are really from your gut.*

9) *Write down this question or questions in a notebook that you have set aside for your inner work.*

ASSIMILATING
THE SHADOW SELF

This meditation is a guided visualization, and should be practiced regularly until you have recognized and re-assimilated disowned aspects of self. The visualization consists of two segments. Segment one should be done first, followed by segment two. Segment one can be practiced regularly by itself, but segment two should always be preceded by segment one.

SEGMENT 1

1) Find a calm, clean and well-ventilated space. Sit either cross-legged on the floor, or on the edge of a stool with your spine erect, chin tucked slightly in. Keep your shoulders relaxed. Relax your entire body. Close your eyes. Now focus on the point between the eyebrows, the 3rd eye. Become conscious of this point.

2) Now visualize a tall, multi-story building. It is modern, the architecture is sleek, and the building has many floors. It is also empty, there is not a soul to be seen inside. You walk through the glass revolving doors, across the marble floor of the lobby to the elevators. Enter one of the waiting elevators and press the button at the top right, RG (Roof Garden). The elevator will carry you up swiftly past 10, 20, 30, 40, 50, 60, 69 floors. One level above the 69th floor you will exit. This is the roof garden. It is the most delightful scene, full of lush, unusual vegetation, flowers of every sort, sandy pathways which wind around fountains and tiny, intricate canals, and birds flitting between the bushes. Overhead, the sky is bright, with light cottony clouds carried by strong, high winds. You can hear just the faintest drone from the city down below. Now you notice a large, flat boulder, shaped like a rounded bench. You sit down here. Now, you notice a fire in front of you, burning in a brazier. It is a sacred fire. You feel elated, expectant. Now, you sense a presence by your right side. You cannot see anyone there, but you can FEEL someone's presence. It slowly dawns on you that this is your higher self. You feel protected and loved for what you are. You feel the presence of a guide. Silently, you greet this "Stranger" and ask for guidance. How can I free myself of my pain? (... my frustrations, my blockages, my feelings of hopelessness and resignation...?)

Listen to what emerges as a quiet voice of guidance deep within your consciousness. Your higher self is the same as your innate intuition, and will provide you the answers you seek.

3) Say goodbye to the presence beside you, exit the roof garden, descend the elevator and re-enter the buzz of the streets outside.

4) At this point, it is a good idea to write down, in a special notebook, all the thoughts and feelings which have just occurred within you during this visualization.

SEGMENT 2

1) Re-enter the multi-story building and walk across the lobby to the elevators. Retain the sense of your higher self as though you were not alone, but accompanied by your mysterious, protective guide. Enter the elevator and now descend to the bottom floor. The elevator now rapidly descends down through many basement levels and underground parking levels until it stops at the lowest floor. Glancing up, you see that this floor has the same initial as the first letter of your first name. Exit the elevator. You find yourself in a dim, industrial sort of space, smelling of damp, chemicals, petroleum and some faint type of unpleasant human odors. Suddenly you remind yourself that you have come here to pay a visit to YOURSELF. You call out your own name. Now you make out some sort of human figure hunched over in the background. You make your way over to it. As you get closer, the figure looks disturbingly familiar. You realize it is you, but in the worst possible shape. The look in the person's eyes may be violent or even insane. Address this creature again, using your own name. Allow your consciousness to accept that this is a part of you that you least accept, that you wish for no-one to ever witness, not even yourself. Observe how this part of yourself looks back at you. Now try to find the words within yourself to describe this "you" and what its state of mind is. Don't flinch. Try to observe accurately and see what it is experiencing.

2) Now ask your higher self to come to your assistance. Watch while your higher self emerges out of the shadowy light and walks over to the wretched figure. Watch how your higher self stands there patiently, perhaps placing his/her hand on to your lower self, perhaps embracing the lower self, if this is permitted.

3) Leave these two together in the basement, re-enter the elevator, ascend to the lobby, and walk back out into the sunlit street.

4) At this point, it is advisable to write down in your notebook all thoughts and feelings that occurred within you during this visualization.

NOTE: these two visualizations can be repeated numerous times until you have identified which parts of you disgust you, which are the parts that you have disowned and tried to keep hidden. As you begin to feel a reconciliation with these rejected bits of you, it will slowly lead you to a greater understanding both of yourself and of others, and to a more relaxed way of being in the world.

NICHOLAS CORRIN, L.Ac.

PART 4

LOVE: CONNECTING TO SACRED POWER

NICHOLAS CORRIN, L.Ac.

LOVE LIBERATES

The nameless is the beginning of heaven and earth.
—Lao Tzu

A t the very center of our chests there is a mystical point. In India, this point has been called the *hridaya*. Hridaya means our "spiritual heart." It is an energy vortex beyond language, beyond names, beyond naming, beyond mind. This point is understood to be our essence, a point of origin through which all the energies necessary to sustain us flow from the mysterious heart of the universe itself. Our physical structure, our physiology, our breath, emotions, desires, thoughts and goals—everything that makes us what we are depends on this one point. There is more silent power in this one point than in the greatest mountain or deepest ocean. What flows through this point is the readiness of the universe to give life and to support life. Yet this point of origin in the heart is the same in all of us. Different as we are in form and character, deep inside we are all just expressions of one incomprehensible reality.

The energy that connects and sustains this reality is love. This energy produces every conceivable form: stars, clouds, storms, raindrops, bacteria, fish, horses, spiders and man. Human beings are just one manifestation of the energy. We are beneficiaries of this love energy simply by virtue of our existence.

Love is not an emotion; it is the original energy that

gave birth to the cosmos, to the planet and to all of life. It is the strongest energy there is: there is nothing stronger than love. This phenomenon of love is not something that can be quantified, demonstrated scientifically or analyzed for its constituent parts in a laboratory because this type of love cannot be understood by the intellect. It cannot be understood from a point outside itself: it can, however, be accessed by any who so choose.

Perhaps the best way to experience this love is through nature. We are not speaking about enthusiasm or enjoyment of nature, we are speaking about something very elusive but extraordinarily powerful which can be sensed there, a presence. Nature, after all, is the source of all life and therefore of all the feelings and ideas we come up with, including scientific ideas and even spiritual ideas. Nature supports and nourishes every conceivable life-form and organizes them into environments and eco-systems of boggling complexity. Yet when we spend time away from our daily routines in this natural complexity, we derive a sense of peace and inspiration, because there is a paradoxical simplicity to it all which derives from a feeling of oneness.

This presence is not something that can really be put into words without framing it, and thereby distorting it. Lao Tzu said the same thing about the Tao, and in fact, Love and Tao have much in common and perhaps are even the same mystery given different names.

Anything truly mysterious is liberating. Mystery liberates because it takes us away from our normal daily preoccupations which are really, at bottom, so humdrum, repetitive and uninspired. When we discover something mysterious we are freed from this entrapment in mundane, run-of-the-mill living. Much of so-called normal life is actually rather like being a fly stuck on flypaper. Because we are so engaged in our personal struggles and concerns, we become glued down by them and lose our innate capacities of movement, let

NICHOLAS CORRIN, L.Ac.

alone flight. But mystery, particularly when it is experienced in the context of nature, restores our attention to something greater and finer, and our spirits are able to breathe again.

Fear blinds us to all of this as it keeps us locked in our own concerns and needs. With fear, we are always in need of something to patch up our broken walls or our inner emptiness. With love, we are free to give and to receive. Love which has no conditions is not a demand, but a willingness to be grateful for life's experiences and to care for others as oneself. These "others" are not just other people, but also other species and forms including the elements themselves: air, water, fire and earth. To be "in love" with the world is to sense its mystery and its beauty, and to be able to absorb the powerful energies that will stream into us if we open to receive them. The light breathing exercises in the previous chapter are methods that work to align us with those cosmic powers of love and healing, and to use them for our own healing or personal fulfillment, or to help others by radiating good energy outwards.

EVOLUTION AND LOVE

Love cannot be confined—neither can it be defined. To attempt to grasp love would be like attempting to grasp water flowing out of a fountain. It may be drunk but not held. And, like water which moves through everything, rising as steam, falling as precipitation or as innumerable pristine, individual crystals, love is that silent power passing through us. Love is fluidity itself.

Love is inherently paradoxical: to love is to be drawn to something or to someone, passionately. And yet it is also to lay no claim to that object or person. It is to allow them perfect freedom. And love is also bound up with knowledge, with the desire to know. The pursuit of knowledge is an aspect of love, for love always seeks greater understanding. But "knowledge" which encloses reality, just like possessive "love" which holds down a person, is incompatible with what we are speaking about. Such ways of being have more to do with ownership than with love. And they are rooted in fear: the fear of losing what one owns.

Love as we are describing it did not come to us on a silver platter. It was something that had to be refined over many million years of evolution. We still, somewhere at our core, carry distant memories from our pre-human days when we were small four-footed mammals much like rats scuttling fearfully in the shadows of the great thunder lizards; such beings towered over us like scaled trees, some endowed with rows of sharp teeth. We emerged but gradually and with much hardship through several periods of glaciation with temperatures dropping to unimaginable depths, and winds whistled across plains deeply packed with drifting snows as high as modern skyscrapers. No doubt we carry in our collective memories much reason for fear and caution.

And yet we are not governed by fear alone. As we evolved, a more refined sense came to flower in us just as the angiosperms with their dazzling colors and scents suddenly emerged out of the green monotony of the Cretaceous period. To love and to see deeply into things became part of human destiny. And to love and to see deeply are, perhaps, two ways of saying the same thing. But as a species, we seem to have lost our way.

We seem, as a species, to have become specialized in destruction and over-exploitation. Many of us know this but feel powerless to change anything. It seems as though we are collectively sliding towards the edge of the precipice. Greed, denial, complacency and violence characterize our age. But if it often seems we can do little to affect the world in a positive way, we can at least change how we react and how we

NICHOLAS CORRIN, L.Ac.

engage with things. If we maintain an inner connection with love for our brother and sister species, those already gone or soon to become extinct, perhaps this will register with the universe in ways we cannot possibly know or understand.

LOVE IS UNTAMEABLE

Love is an untamed force. When we try to control it, it destroys us. When we try to imprison it, it enslaves us. When we try to understand it, it leaves us feeling lost and confused.—Paolo Coelho

Anxiety, I have suggested, stems from feeling that time— past, present or future—is out of our control. Most people today suffer from what might be called chronic, low-grade anxiety. This is also why so many people are on medication or on recreational drugs, which amounts to the same thing, a chemical adjustment to stave off anxiety. The only way to go beyond anxiety is to embrace uncertainty.

To embrace uncertainty is to relax out of the need to control things. When we relax, we grow stronger. Why? Simply put, because in a relaxed state, energy will circulate, whereas in a tensed state, energy will stagnate. It will build up at focal points and generate pressure. Pressure build-up results in anxiety. And where there is anxiety, there is the need to control. It is a vicious cycle.

Living with uncertainty is living without security but with an open heart.

This force is on earth to make us happy, to bring us closer to God and to our neighbor, and yet, given the way that we love now, we enjoy one hour of anxiety for every minute of peace.[37]

Love and control are opposites. Love cannot be controlled: to control it is to kill it or be killed by it. There is a wildness to love like the wildness of the wind, like the wilderness itself, full of strange sounds, colors, scents and textures. Love, in a deeper sense, is life itself, the Shape-shifter, the Disturber, the Dreamer, the Creator, the Destroyer. It is never the Placator or the Compromiser.

Letting go, in the sense this book intends, means opening to love as an uncontrollable yet spiritual energy. The power of letting go means allowing love to become the navigating force of life. Love and water are irrevocably linked: love is the wind that blows over the oceans, the clouds that form over their blue horizon, the ships that set sail into the terrible vastness of the sea and also the strange creatures that inhabit its depths.

If all life arose from the oceans, love is that force in us that seeks to return there; a return to something unconfined, deep, untameable and ultimately unknowable.

LOVE AND DARK FORCES

Yet there is also a dark force at work in the universe, an aspect to things that appears to be the opposite of love. We find this darkness all around and within us. We accumulate more of this darkness if we turn our backs on the rights of other beings and treat them as tools for our own satisfaction. Hatred is typically a mixture of fear, pride and rage that is capable of exacting terrible vengeance, or worse, genocide, as we have seen in Rwanda, Bosnia, or under the Nazi regime in Germany. Our capacity to hate and to maim is surely at least as great as our capacity to love.

The history of human destructiveness is terrible and immense. Not only have we tortured and enslaved one other,

NICHOLAS CORRIN, L.Ac.

we have decimated entire species, ravaged ecosystems and polluted the stratosphere. Our meat and poultry industries alone should shame us into becoming vegetarian. To give but one example: as part of routine process in the U.S. beef and veal industry, young calves are taken away from their mothers when still at a suckling age. They are kept in small containers deprived of light and fed a weakened, depleted form of milk from which iron and other nutrients have been removed.

When killed, the calf's flesh has that pale pink color so beguilingly attractive to consumers. In the supermarket, the label on the veal package states, "Milk-Fed." This conjures up rosy, sentimental pictures of a young calf happily raised by its mother in some far-away farmyard. The real truth is barbaric and inhumane. This is but one example of how our consumer society based on *packaging and processing* is, in some respects, more uncivilized than its predecessors of centuries ago.

Love and awareness go together, as love and mystery go together. Living in denial is an option for all of us but it will only result in dark forces gaining the upper hand if all we do is look the other way. Love is the opposite of fear because it is also courageous; and courage is required if we are to look at things as they actually are so that we can change them for the better. Our very word courage comes from the Latin word for heart, *cor*.

The universe consists of light and darkness, but there are two kinds of darkness. One is the rich, mysterious, velvety darkness of the earth and of the night itself. This is the type of darkness that allows the stars to shine. But there also exists another kind of darkness and that is the absence of light. This is an "empty" form of darkness, and this is really the same as what we traditionally have called evil. When our hearts turn away from the evidence of the light, or fall into apathy and indifference, the vortex of absence is ready to come spiraling into the empty spaces. In the end, our fate as a species will depend on what our capacity to love has been.

However, each one of us who maintains an overall state of love in the heart is somehow sustaining the entire species on some small, invisible level. Things are not simply what they appear to be at first glance, as we now well know from the strange characteristics of the quantum world.

SCIENCE, FIRE AND THE HUMAN LIGHT BODY

According to quantum mechanics, the reality of things behind the illusion of solid appearances is composed of myriad, minute bursts of energy called quanta. These are analogous to pulsations of light and a photon of light is released with each interaction. The pulses occur as discrete events, not as part of a continuous outpouring. So the energetic "fabric" of reality could be said to be made up of pulses of light, not a constant flow of energy, like a river.

Think of a roll of celluloid film inside a movie camera: each image is discrete and bounded by a frame. The light source in the camera sends "bursts" of light through the celluloid, because each photographic image on the roll is framed in black which effectively interrupts the "flow" of light and illuminates each image as a discrete event. Yet as the images are projected on to the screen, what we perceive are continuous forms in movement, the movies. Now imagine the familiar night sky but with all the trillions of stars flickering on and off in innumerable combinations, permutations and sequences. Out of these multi-dimensional sequences of flickering energy, patterns and macro-forms start to appear and then subside. These patterns form what we experience as perceptual reality.

NICHOLAS CORRIN, L.Ac.

What is true on a scientific level, however, is not necessarily true on a mythic level. Science has focused on interpreting physical reality and yet there is also a spiritual or mythic dimension which can only be apprehended "inwardly." The spiritual and the scientific are not mutually exclusive, but they pertain to different frames of reference. On a mythic level, it may not be accurate to speak of quanta but rather of simultaneity, where everything is somehow happening "at the same time" and everything is intimately connected.

Nevertheless, the idea that the universe and all that it holds is essentially composed of energy conforms to both a scientific and a mythico-spiritual perspective. And this energy has a close relationship with light. In Einstein's equation, the speed of light is the one constant in a relative universe and, as we have seen, at the quantum level, photons are constantly being emitted as part of innumerable energy exchanges. Yet the idea that nothing travels faster than light may not in fact be accurate: in superluminal theory, there is the idea of information traveling faster than the known speed of light. This information may, in fact, be composed of *tachyon*s, a different "form" of light than the particles of light we call photons.[38]

Ancient traditions both religious and philosophical have placed Light and Fire at the source of creation.[39] In the Bible, God says, "Let there be light," and Moses encounters the holy spirit in the form of a burning bush which is not consumed. And in the Egyptian Book of the Dead, the god *Osiris* who represents death, resurrection and eternity, describes himself as, "The Great One, the son of the Great One. I am Fire, the son of Fire."

In the ancient Vedic writings of India, amongst the world's oldest texts, Fire is described as the source of everything past, present and future. This holy fire is one with the light of the universe. The Vedas tell us how the manifest universe is basically a kind of ash (*bhasma*) cast off by the deathless, cosmic fire (*agni*) as it burns beyond the level of our perceptions. In other words, out of light comes substance; out of vibrational energy, comes matter. Another way of putting this would be to say that all matter is really just light slowed down to compact density. Energy vibrating at very high frequencies can get slowed down to such an extent that it becomes dense enough to "materialize." In this way, light rays produce physical forms.

Such a theory can be supported by referring to quantum interactions: when a high energy photon (a cosmic ray) approaches a heavy atomic nucleus, the photon will apparently transform into two, mirror image particles. One of these particles is matter, the other, antimatter, an electron and a positron. This "new" particle pair that results from the influence of the heavy nucleus upon the cosmic ray corresponds to what we think of as matter. It possesses the attributes of mass and inertia (properties that photons do not have). Thus we can see that density and inertia have the capacity to turn a ray of light into an extension of themselves. We could also suggest that when these physical forms have been generated out of light they "forget" that they once were light. They have entered the domain of illusion, the realm of *Maya*. In brief, physical reality is a residue (or after-effect) of spiritual luminescence.

If we reflect on it, what makes us "alive" is a kind of inner fire. Our digestive processes are metabolic fire operating within our bodies, allowing us to move, act and speak. Even our thoughts are a type of fire, burning the fuel of experience and generating the light of perception and insight. The ancient *rishis* of India considered consciousness itself to be the light of pure awareness. They named this *chidjyoti* in Sanskrit. When we gain a little more awareness we inch closer to the light source of the universe. And to be enlightened is simply to allow the universal consciousness to shine through

　　　　　　　　　　　　NICHOLAS CORRIN, L.Ac.

you without obstruction. Not that this is a very simple act to master!

Since we were produced by the universe and are made of the same fundamental materials and energies as everything else, the human body is, quite obviously, made of light. Many ancient cultures recognized this tenet. In the ancient Greek city of the Sun, Heliopolis, solar temples were constructed and used for medicine. The architects devised ways to break up natural sunlight into its various colors (frequencies) in order to treat different illnesses.[40] Today, contemporary application of light therapy is still based on the understanding that monochromatic frequencies (single hues) are the key to healing.[41] Furthermore, research conducted by German physicist Dr. Fritz Albert Popp has demonstrated that our cells actually communicate with each other using photons –in other words, pulses of light generated from within the body. This bio-photonic mode of intercellular communication appears to be more primary than the bio-chemical route.[42] Popp's research corroborates the theories of subtle anatomy upon which vibrational medicine is based.[43] It also confirms the ancient esoteric theories which speak of an energy body consisting of light; this "body" is actually a kind of template organizing and maintaining our physical cellular structures.

Our eyes are extraordinarily sensitive to light. Nerve endings in the eye will be activated by as few as five or six photons striking the retina.[44] This is all it takes for the nervous system to register the presence of light! This does not, of course, imply that the conscious mind "sees" light composed of just five or six photons. With five photons striking the retina, the mind will only "see" darkness yet the body itself will "see" light. This, if you think about it, is an extraordinary fact: the body is, literally, more illuminated than the mind.

The physical body is, ultimately, constructed out of light

since its principal nutrition is plant material, either directly, or indirectly through the consumption of meat. Plants, as we know, create carbohydrates out of sunlight through the process of photosynthesis. But human cells themselves exhibit a remarkable faculty of photosynthesis in the phenomenon known as "photo-repair." If a cell is exposed to high intensity UV light under laboratory conditions such that 99% of the cell is destroyed, including its nucleus with the cell's DNA, the cell can be almost completely restored simply by exposing it to the same frequency of light at low intensity.[45]

Biologist Bruce Lipton has demonstrated that the brain of the cell is in fact the cell membrane rather than the nucleus and there appears to be another as yet unexplained biomechanism whereby exposure to light can restore cellular integrity, apparently by tapping into some kind of memory or recall phenomenon.[46] Such cellular memory obviously does not exist within the "real" space of the physical cell, but is somehow co-existent with the waves of ultraviolet light that have the capacity both to destroy and to restore that cell.

German biophysicist Fritz Popp discovered low intensity biophoton emission occurring in the body and concluded through years of research that these photons "switch on" molecular reactions within cells. In other words, specific light frequencies generated from within the body appear to organize and coordinate the functions of cellular proteins with different frequencies stimulating different molecular reactions. Later research by Stuart Hameroff, an anesthesiologist from Arizona, suggests that within dendrites (tiny filaments that form connecting meshes between neurons in the brain,) photons are constantly being transmitted via microtubules. The light passing though these microtubules somehow functions according to quantum processes such that every neuron in the brain could somehow be aware of what was occurring "globally" within the brain. The passage of photons through the microtubules correlated with vibrational fields that al-

NICHOLAS CORRIN, L.Ac.

lowed different parts of the brain to "log on" to these fields and "download" information via quantum processes.[47]

The discoveries of Popp, in particular, point to light as the organizing principle of the physical body. Conventionally speaking, science has not been able to account for the distribution and differentiation of cells in the body: that is, how does a cell "know" it should become a stomach cell or liver cell; and how does it know where exactly to "place" itself as the fetus is growing and cells are rapidly dividing? Or for that matter, in the adult body, where cells die off and cell replacements occur rhythmically as a matter of course? (Red blood cells have a lifespan of 120 days, while your entire GI lining is replaced every 72 hours). What gives cells their ability to know at what address they are supposed to live, and how to get there?

Something causes this intelligence to go awry, as in the case of cancer, where cells are produced which no longer have a particular form consistent with a particular organ or tissue of the body but are "undifferentiated", which is to say faceless and functionless, bedding down in the body and feeding off its nutrients. The cause appears to have something to do with light, which is the language whereby cells know what to become and where to reside.

When the internal regulatory system monitoring emissions of this inner body light malfunctions, the health of the physical structures can be compromised, even destroyed. Too many bio-photons produced correlates with ill-health, according to Popp's research. This excessive emission of bio-photons suggests a correlation with inflammatory processes, hypertrophy, or cancer. Conversely, when the inner body is calm, only the necessary, most economical amount of light signals are emitted and good physical health is maintained: there is no disregulation of internal processes.

This coordinating and orchestrating activity of photons in the body meshes with concepts from Ayurvedic Medicine about our energy body. This "body" is a subtle counterpart to our physical structure, closely interwoven with it but composed of a more refined material, what we call the life-force or *prana*. In the Ayurvedic and Yogic systems of thought, this energy body is known as the Pranic Sheath, the *Pranamaya Kosha*. Through this sheath vital currents of energy flow, most specifically through distinct conduits called nadis (from the root *nad*, which means to flow). This vital energy is known as *prana* in India, and *chi* in China. In the Chinese paradigm, the acupuncture meridians effectively conform to an "energy body" that overlaps and sustains the physical body. *Prana* and *chi* are, in this context, similar notions. Problems in the energy body lead to physical or psychological illness. Conversely, treatment to re-harmonize the energy body can restore the physical body to health.

If viewed clairvoyantly through the third eye, this energy body can be seen as a field of light overlapping the physical form. Distinct flows of current can be seen to operate within it. Popp's work on the activity of bio-photons provides a scientific perspective that appears to support ancient theories regarding subtle anatomy. However, we should remind ourselves of the deeper, evolutionary meaning attributed to light in traditional ideas from India and other ancient cultures. According to Ayurvedic theory, our very essence is a form of fire, or light. Our faculty of perception represents a kind of fire just as our digestive system is a "fire" that cooks the food we ingest, allowing it to nourish the "light" of our consciousness. Fire breaks things down, transforms them and allows energy to be re-constituted at higher levels. In a healthy digestive system, enzymes and stomach acids "burn" food, separating out minerals and amino-acids and delivering these nutrients to the cells for maintenance and repair. The archetype behind the process of digestion and its relation to consciousness is represented by the phoenix rising from the ashes.

NICHOLAS CORRIN, L.Ac.

Let's focus a little more on this idea of perception as Fire and Light. Just as stomach juices and pancreatic enzymes break down food and convert it, so the penetrating flames of perception break down the "stuff" of experience and re-constitute it into feelings and ideas. Our fires of perception, however, can burn clean or they can produce a great deal of smoke. Smoke here is an indicator of illusion, possessive-ness and self-centeredness. The more the ego holds sway over perception, the more smoke will be produced. The less the ego is in control, the brighter and cleaner the fire. If the light of the mind is clear and strong enough, it will produce actions and thoughts in tune with the fires of the cosmos. Such is living in wisdom. This is another way of describing the love principle: respect for all life and reverence for the earth, whose dark body is the female, inviolable counterpart to the light of spirit.

WE ARE ALL COMPOSED OF LIGHT

We have seen how we can be deflected from self-accep-tance early in life by "rocks" and "dams" that obstruct the flow of the river. As children, we gazed up at our parents seeking unconditional love, protection and support. This expectation may have been shattered in numerous ways, through harsh words, anger, blame, neglect or downright abuse. If we did not experience unconditional love from our family, we may then expect to receive—and to give to oth-ers—only conditional forms of love, the type we are "famil-iar" with. Within our core, our self-love has fault-lines and many of us will seek for external means to compensate for this inner weakening of our power.

In this way, we come to use others and the world at large in the attempt to fill a void within. We may be quite unaware of doing this; or we may unconsciously deprive ourselves of happiness and success because an inner sense of unworthiness incites us into self-sabotage. In either scenario, the fault-lines in our sense of self will have impeded us from connecting fully with our deepest aspects, our soul and sense of purpose.

To re-connect with these aspects requires that we first of all let go of the certainties we have believed in thus far, which are really illusions that have led us into states of unhappiness or confusion. Only by entering the river of uncertainty can we begin to free ourselves of old, fixed, unconscious beliefs that have kept us trapped and limited us accordingly. But once we find the courage to embrace uncertainty, we can start to re-align with the vital flows of the cosmos and grow receptive to its powers of growth and abundance.

To re-connect it is helpful to recognize one fact about yourself that is basic yet very hard to "see," and that is that we are made of light. We have discussed how the universe itself must be understood as a vibratory field of energy, fire, or light. The same holds true for you and me. Around our tangible, physical forms, we extend further out as "light bodies," which link us up with wider subtly vibrating fields around us. Our light bodies can become dirty, blocked or diseased, just as our physical bodies do if we do not take good care of them. Negative feelings about ourselves and about life correspond to patches of murkiness that occur in our non-physical structures.

We actually consist of interpenetrating envelopes, or subtle "sheaths." These subtle sheaths, envelopes or fields can be seen by those who have developed a more sensitive type of sight, one that relies upon the Third Eye rather than the physical eyes. A few people are born with this capability. Others can acquire it through meditations and energy practices, such as the light energy exercises described in this book.

NICHOLAS CORRIN, L.Ac.

However, it is also possible to "read" these non-physical envelopes in other ways. For example, if you lightly rake your hand over somebody's head and body about 3-6" above the skin surface, you may start to feel differences in temperature, or consistency. Certain areas may feel cold, tingly or sticky. These sensations correspond to disturbances in the light fields surrounding the physical body. Often they also correlate with tissue pathology at a physical level. Where there is something wrong—blocked, damaged, or diseased— there is a corresponding change in the brightness of the light bodies. This manifests electrically as vortices of ion efflux streaming out of the physical body over areas of pain, trauma or tissue pathology. They also can be detected by means of reticulated magnet beams, crystals or other types of subtle, resonating instruments.[48]

These patches of darkness reflect problems in the physical body, or else they correlate with mental or emotional negativity held in the mind and its corresponding subtle sheaths. Such blockages of psycho-emotional energy flow impede or deregulate the circulation of blood and other nutrients within our actual physical bodies, leading to pain or disease. The longer these darkened patches remain present in our light bodies, the greater the chance of a physical illness developing out of them. Murky, stagnant energy on levels of emotional and mental consciousness needs to be identified and transformed if we are to succeed in re-connecting to our sacred source: Earth, planetary Soul, and the Cosmos itself. Today, there are many forms of alternative medicine available to us which can help release these dark, unhealthy patches. A fairly comprehensive overview of such types of medicine can be found in *Vibrational Medicine*, by Dr. Richard Gerber.

THE DANGERS OF
WORSHIPPING THE LIGHT

To bring more light into one's system is also to become less heavy. Dark energy is heavy and stagnant, whereas light energy is the reverse: weightless and expansive. Remember that photons—physical particles of light—have neither mass nor inertia.

There are many ways of making oneself "lighter." However, one mistake that is commonly made by people who attempt to do this is that they fall into the trap of idolatry. For them, light becomes the Golden Calf. This is a very common issue today amongst all sorts of New Age "seekers." However, it has always been around. It is a type of perversion that besets people who start to consider themselves to be more "spiritual" than others. Self-styled spiritual people easily fall into the mold of racists and colonialists. By identifying with the "Light", they reject the "Dark." They fail to see that darkness is complementary to light, just as heaviness and gravity are complementary to weightlessness and to flight. I call such people "Light Consumers" but they usually like to refer to themselves as "Light Workers." This is such an important point that I need to make it quite emphatically: *To seek to become one with the light will only lead you into the dark.*

Why is this? What goes wrong? Surely it cannot be a bad thing to seek to be more illuminated? No, but separating light from dark is like separating day from night and sun from moon. Would you not say that the consequences of such a separation would be catastrophic?

The negative aspect of darkness is an absence of light,

or an obstruction of light. An example of this would be a room with no windows. Or a closed heart, indifferent to the feelings of others. Or a controlling, dishonest mind, attempting to prevent people from seeing things in their own way, a different way than the interpretation you are imposing upon them. The positive aspect of darkness is a complement to light. Without its complement, light would die, so darkness in this sense is a necessary and vital part of light. For example, if the night were not dark, we would never have seen the stars. Perhaps we would imagine that the sky was just an empty field of blue, with nothing in it.

White is expansive and contains all known colors. Black is contractive, but also contains all known colors. In this respect, darkness represents absorption of experience, while light represents transformation of experience. The two can in no way be separated.

Cruelty and even madness lie along the path of those who inwardly separate light from dark. The terrible history of religious bigotry is testament to this. And we see it menacing the world today in the form of renascent fundamentalism. So making yourself lighter can have nothing to do with rejecting the dark, for part of that dark is inseparable from and equal to the light. Heaviness is also inseparable from lightness. To deny weight and gravity is to deny the ground of life itself: it is to deny the Earth.

MAKING YOURSELF LIGHTER

The solution to these problems is to be grounded. To be grounded means to be real, not puffed up with fantasies of self-importance. And it means an attitude of reverence and patience towards the Earth. To be grounded means to be one with the Earth. It means not to be in denial of one's physical nature and physical needs. It means to spend time with animals, birds, plants and rocks and to listen to the wind, the rain and to the sound of the waves. To be grounded is to remember that being human is intimately bound up with all other forms of life that surround us.

Once we are grounded, we can begin to remove those dark patches and stains that may exist in our light bodies, adversely affecting our health and thwarting our mental and emotional wellbeing. But if we are not grounded in this earthly sense, those stains will never truly go away: they will always return in one form or another.

There is a positive aspect to weight: it connects us with the sanity of the Earth, with the humor and warmth of the soil and the strength of the mountains, valleys and plains. It protects us from anxiety and spaciness. It also promotes healing: NASA found that when their astronauts suffered health problems or minor injuries on their space missions, their bodies were very slow to heal. In the absence of gravity, normal cellular healing does not occur properly. This was one of the reasons for NASA's research into the healing aspects of red light, most specifically red light with a 660 nanometer frequency.[49] Such a frequency has been found to accelerate healing in human cells and to counteract absence of a gravitational field. Interestingly, there seems to be a correspondence between this particular frequency of light and the effects of gravity. It may be that this red is precisely the frequency of the Root Chakra that re-charges the blood and restores the physical tissues.

Once grounding has been established, lightness is really a matter of letting go. We are light when we have no excess baggage, nothing dragging us down. But of course, this is far easier said than done. So how do we lighten the load? One way is to learn how to breathe in light. Such techniques make use of energy centers which correspond to acupuncture points and chakras, and which link up with energy channels

NICHOLAS CORRIN, L.Ac.

running through the interior of the body.

There are several key points of entry for cosmic energy. These include the soles of the feet, the fingertips and palms, a point between the eyebrows, and a point on the crown of the head. These points on the head correspond to the Third Eye chakra and the Crown chakra respectively. There are seven main chakras each of which absorb energy from the universe and also emit it back from within our core. However, for the purposes of conscious breathing of light, only the palms, soles, the Third Eye and Crown chakras need to be used. Please refer to the specific exercises at the end of this section.

Remember that energy is a form of light and light itself is energy. But the light we see with the eyes—ordinary light which is the visible portion of the electromagnetic spectrum—is not the kind of light we breathe in through the energy centers. This special kind of light is of a different sort and can only be accessed through intention and visualization. It is drawn from the higher conscious fields of the cosmos, and when we draw it into our systems, we can use it to flush out and transform negative emotions and beliefs that are impeding us. The source of this light energy is inexhaustible and available to all. To draw it into ourselves we have to use the mind and the inner eye: together, the combination of mind and inner eye can guide fresh energy into our systems and guide stale or toxic energy down and out. But to have a real effect, these practices need to be done regularly.

A VIBRATIONAL UNIVERSE

The source of everything is vibration. Our bodies recognize this more easily than our minds do. When we bathe in the sea, our bodies respond to the rise and fall of the waves. A sea without waves would be surreal, almost unimaginable. Why? Because waves are the vital sign of life in the ocean, the very pulse of its life-force, just as we have a pulsing of our blood signifying life in the heart. And if we raise a conch to our ear, we can listen to that roar of the body's inner oceans, sensing that we are but part of those great vibratory oceans of wind and water that surround the land on which we live. We hear their presence in us, reminding us of where we came from.

Many creatures such as gulls and rays mirror by their forms the wave-filled environments in which they move, almost as though they were forms dreamed up by the water and by the air so that these elements might express the pulsations of energy that unceasingly course through them. Theodor Schwenk has shown us, in his fascinating work, *Sensitive Chaos*, how the physical structure of many animals precisely describes the play of air and water, both these elements being constantly moved internally by rhythmic waves and pulsations.

The oscillation of waveforms whether visible, audible, invisible or inaudible, corresponds to the idea of space itself. Space itself is composed of vibrations. Space, we can say, is an ocean of energy. This ocean is without known boundaries or limits and its waves extend everywhere: there is no place that they are not. Nor do they travel in one direction only; according to Einstein, light waves travel both into the future and into the past. Space is not empty in a classical sense. It is only a perceptual and philosophical conditioning that causes us to "see" emptiness around us.

We have already discussed how space was not originally seen as empty. Space was originally equated with the ether, that non-physical matrix that binds and sustains everything in the universe. Ether was not so much a substance, it was a field of possibilities, much like the Zero Point Field spoken of today.[50]

Our idea of the cosmic ether probably originated in India with its philosophy of five elements composing the manifest

NICHOLAS CORRIN, L.Ac.

universe: earth, water, fire, air and ether, in decreasing levels of density. The Sanskrit word for ether is *akasha*. This *akasha* fills the apparent emptiness of space with "a limitless reservoir of sound and thought vibrations, and is endowed with supreme intelligence."[51] This concept goes back at least as far as the *Kurma Purana*, compiled in the fifth century BC, which describes a great radiant Being from which emanate all imaginable rays and vibrations, both those perceptible to our senses and those beyond the reach of our perceptions.

Conventional scientific understanding repudiates the notion of such an ether and pours scorn on it. But recent advances in theoretical physics show us a universe that is interconnected in countless ways, allowing for interactions which are "non-local", which is to say, without any mechanical interaction. The concept of a universal field of inexhaustible energy and unfathomable complexity has been studied in depth by physicists such as Hal Puthoff, and the prospect of extracting free energy from the field is very real. If we were successful in developing the means to do so, it might become possible for man to travel extraordinary distances through the interstellar spaces, in the wake of Captain Kirk and the Starship Enterprise.[52]

If the idea of space as filled with sonar vibrations sounds far-fetched to some, we should be aware that, even today, astronomers study the structure of distant stars using the science of asteroseismology. This involves the use of detectors capable of reading acoustic ripples that move like winds across the surface of stellar bodies. In a sense, these ripples are comparable to the sonar waves sent out by whales, except, of course, that whales use sound to communicate with each other, whereas stars, at least as far as we understand at the present time, do no such thing. Whale sounds are sonar ripples that travel through ocean water in order to reach the ear of other whales. Such ripples can speak across great distances, much like long distance telephone calls. The stellar waves can be compared to these whale sounds, not because they are a direct medium of communication, but because they are acoustic and convey information. Using asteroseismology, scientists are able to translate these ripples into precise data regarding the stars' age, exact mass and chemical composition. The sounds of the stars could, in this respect, be compared to the rings inside tree trunks, and also to the lines and wrinkles on a human face.

In astro-physical terms, the universe is itself understood to be a gigantic field of vibrating plasma. This plasma, essentially a precursor state to matter, forms nodal concentrations as a result of gravitational forces. Sonic booms are emitted as a result of these nodal contractions, disturbing the entire cosmic field and giving rise to stars and galaxies.[53] These stellar bodies then emit light which is the visible expression of the original force that went into their making. Thus sound and light—radiance—can be seen as the very basis for all cosmic form. That radiance we can experience equally as sound or as light. Sound and light are simply two perceptual ways of registering the same basic reality.

The symbiotic relationship between light and sound is known as *sonoluminescence*.

THREE ASPECTS OF SOUND

Sound into Light: SONOLUMINESCENCE

Experiments have been conducted in which water has been strongly bombarded by sonar waves over a period of time. As a result of this impact, bubbles form within the water. These bubbles swiftly implode, releasing a flurry of photons, visible as a flash of light.[54] In other words, via the medium of water, it may be possible to convert sound into light, possibly through the rapid ionization of water mole-

NICHOLAS CORRIN, L.Ac.

cules. There have also been numerous anecdotal accounts of visitors taken inside caves in Tibet by Buddhist monks. At first, the visitors could see nothing, as the cave interiors were utterly lightless.

However, once the monks had started to play on singing bowls, quartz "lamps" hanging from the walls of the caves gradually began to glow, emitting bright light much like lanterns such that the cave interior became illuminated with all their contents now clearly visible to the eye. Jonathan Goldman, a well-known pioneer in sacred and meditative use of sound, recounts entering a pitch dark cave in Palenque, New Mexico with a group of other people. When he was asked to begin toning (which is the chanting of specific tones felt to be in resonance with the local environment,) the cave interior grew progressively lighter to the point where people's faces emerged in considerable detail from the previous penumbra.[55]

Sound into Matter: PENETRATIVE SOUND

Sound waves are capable of stimulating physical structures, even of re-configuring them at a molecular level. Today, the use of ultrasound is commonplace in medicine. High frequency ultrasound can readily be focused into a beam, like laser light. And just as easily, again like lasers, this beam of sound can burn human tissue. Infrasound, on the other hand, which occurs below the lower threshold of human hearing, which is 30 Hz, is also capable of disturbing biological processes, even of atomizing water molecules.[56] The application of infrasound to water can send ripples through it such that its local temperature rises suddenly to very high levels, ripping the molecules apart and generating vapor. Thus, sonar waves which are either above or below the threshold of human hearing have energetic properties which enable them to interact with matter, either creatively or destructively.

Sound into Space: RADIANT SOUND

When we listen to non-melodic, modal sound, inner spaces open up within us. These "inner spaces" are the "emptiness", or the "air" surrounding our thoughts and feelings. This inner emptiness, however, is not empty in a barren sense. It is the vast potential of the unknown that we each carry within us, and probably corresponds to the 90% of the brain that we tend to leave inactive. These inner spaces are much like the outer spaces of the cosmos: they lead, ever expanding, into the infinite. Mysterious and perhaps frightening too, they represent absolute freedom and potentiality. Our inner spaces are our personal interface with the nameless and formless cosmos itself.

Meditative music, which is non-melodic and based on shifting, swaying repetition and microtones is very close to the soundscapes of nature. The sounds unclutter our minds of habitual daily thoughts, and our consciousness can then loosen from its typical limitations and habits. Thus, sound can bring light into us by expanding our normal consciousness. Sound itself is radiant. In fact we are receiving such radiance all the time, but it is below—or rather, above—the threshold of our consciousness.

The ancient Greeks called this "The Music of the Spheres", by which they meant a kind of harmonious radiation emitted by the heavenly bodies as these traveled in their orbits. In Renaissance Italy, this idea was developed by philosophers such as Marsilio Ficino. The great art that flourished at that time would have been unthinkable without the ideas that supported it. The great creativity of the Renaissance was understood to be linked to the Cosmic Mind and Cosmic Soul. Cultures like ours, which have lost all sense of our existence within an intelligent cosmos, make it

NICHOLAS CORRIN, L.Ac.

very difficult for people to connect to these higher energies. However slowly, things are changing as the human species is forced to face up to its precarious position on the planet and its possible demise. Now more than ever, we need to renew our higher capacities to link up with the cosmos that bore us.

THE SOUNDS OF CONSCIOUSNESS

When great Nature sighs, we hear the winds

Which, noiseless in themselves

Awaken voices from other beings,

Blowing on them

From every opening

Loud voices sound. Have you not heard

This rush of tones?

—From "The Way of Chuang Tzu," interpreted by Thomas Merton

———•———

Not I, not I, but the wind that blows through me.

From "Song of the Man Who Has Come Through"
—D.H.Lawrence

The Taoists distinguished between music made by man and the "music" made by Nature. They preferred the music of Nature. Sounds emitted by Nature have a very different effect on us than manmade sounds, however beautiful and harmonious these might be. A chorus of frogs, for example, has a particular, mesmerizing quality very different from a tune or a melody. The same is true of crickets and cicadas, or of water in its diverse forms as rain, ocean or rivers. Even the silent hush of snow falling has a powerful "sonorous" effect on us.

Non-melodic sound can open up our consciousness in quite a different manner than songs, tunes, melodies or symphonies. Melodies and lyrics concentrate our emotional attention, streamlining it in a particular direction. Listening to music of this type, we tend to be "carried away." This is why music is the most immediately accessible and also the most enrapturing of the arts, because music touches us most directly at our emotional center and captivates us. Listening to music is cathartic because our buried emotions can find release there. Listening then becomes a sort of journey made of strong, directed feelings.

By contrast, the rhythmic, non-melodic sounds of nature calm us by dissolving our sense of self. They are more like the modal music of India, classical *ragas*. *Ragas* have neither the chord series nor the melodic structures of traditional Western music.[57] Some contemporary, modal, meditative music such as the work of David Parsons, also invokes spatial, non-emotional effects, and is strongly influenced by Buddhism. Instead of directing our attention strongly in one emotional direction via the melody, such sounds generate a shifting expanse of textures and microtones without specific melodic shapes.

Listening to this type of sound, our edges gradually unwind, as though the linear contours of our form were unraveling; we expand into fluctuating fields of sonorous vibration. Because the reality of all that exists is, beneath appearances, composed of vibrational fields, listening to such soundscapes can open up our consciousness to a deeper connection with reality.

Sound is our most fundamental sensory "plug-in" to vibration since we are capable of detecting it through our auditory system. Listening to the wind is, as Thomas Merton's

NICHOLAS CORRIN, L.Ac.

rendition of Chuang Tzu shows, a way of perceiving how the dynamic and intangible energy of life is carried by the wind, and as it moves it brings out the particular characteristics of the forms it blows through. Thus every part of nature exposed to the wind becomes a wind instrument contributing its own particular refrain. What could be more perfect an example of this than birds, which seem to have embodied the wind within themselves, not only in their aerial capacities, but in the sounds which blow through their larynx like a kind of personal refraction of the breath of life, a single possible song drawn from the wide, limitless and unfettered expanse of air and space?

Our singular call rings out, as air from the lungs is compressed through the vocal cords and expressed out through our windpipe. We humans identify ourselves with language and with the power of speech, yet we fail to reflect that, ultimately, it is the air itself that speaks through us. We only give shape to it. The human larynx contains vocal cords through which our thoughts and emotions ex-press themselves, but they actually emerge from our mouths as ripples of air. These ripples become disturbances in the all encompassing energy field which retains and records all information.

The content of our speech is, really, a matter of commotion in the air, a type of personal wind we put out. And what we put out as speech imprints itself on the physical air as sound waves, but equally so on the subtle "air" of the enveloping universal field known to science as the Zero Point Field.

If the winds are really representations of the cosmic life force expressing itself as it blows across rocks, gulleys, over miles of ocean waves and through the throats of birds, what does this tell us about human speech? Human speech can be as natural as linen or as synthetic as viscose. It can be as beneficial as fruit or as toxic as pesticide. This has less to do with the actual words used and more to do with the tone and inflection of utterance. For the tone and inflection of what we say is at least as meaningful as the semantic content. And it is these qualities, not the semantic content, that shape the air into specific vibrations, specific ripples of intent.

Because we humans have come to believe ourselves sole possessors of speech, we have lost the fine sense of being able to hear non-semantic meaning. Accordingly, our voices have become dull and synthetic. Just spend some time paying close attention to the sound of people's voices rather than to "what" they are saying. Pay attention to the quality of the sound, the quality of the voice as opposed to the words themselves. Listen to the "ring" and "tone" of voices around you in terms of texture and resonance. In this way, you can begin to attune yourself to the vibrational quality of people's consciousness.

It is possible to know "where" someone is coming from, what their real intentions are, how masked and how open, how sincere they are, how respectful or disrespectful, how caring of others, how generous or mean, merely from the sound of the voice, for this is the music of the wind as it passes through the human larynx. Today many people's voices seem to have become hard and generic, like plastic. But this actually only reflects the outer shell they carry around with them as a social identity and as a way to mask their inner self, which is vulnerable and starved of attention.

This "outer shell voice" we hear so much around us today seems to evoke many of the synthetic materials and artificial aspects of contemporary life. It is a voice favored and, one can say, perfected, by the media who use it as their vehicle of choice for delivering their so-called information, much if not most of which is, as we know, mis-information. It is a kind of alloy voice that somehow expresses the indifference, insensitivity, denial and greed that are the hallmarks of mainstream consumer culture and that threaten to bring down the entire human species along with innumer-

NICHOLAS CORRIN, L.Ac.

able plant and animal species, as the sacred terrain of nature is devoured to feed the stupid cravings of unreflective souls. The glass of the human mirror can become so cracked as to reflect nothing at all.

Yet there are days when I awaken at dawn to the sounds of a solitary bird. As my mind slowly focuses on the song of this unidentified bird (for my mind does not seek to name it, and therefore to kill it,) repeated multiple times between rhythmic intervals of silence, I feel as though the entire meaning of life has somehow been compressed into these few, avian syllables. How can this be? It is the magic of paying attention to the "other". When we really listen, without pre-conception or prejudice, a revelation occurs. It is the revelation of mystery, which is also the revelation of relationship. This state of mind is alien to most adults but not to children. For children, who naturally pay attention without the filters of self-regard, the sense of the "other" is also the sense of the "friend" or what we might call the "guest". The guest is the sacred presence inhabiting each and every form of life. Children do not conceptualize this, but they recognize it. Adults do neither.

Contemporary, urbanized adults no longer recognize the Guest. However, this has not always been the case. In tribal, pre-literate cultures, the sounds of other species have been heard as speech equal to the speech of humankind. For the *Koyukon* of northwest Alaska, for example, birdsongs are utterances filled with meaning. Indeed, they consider their own language to be the same in essence as the language of all other species and natural formations such as rocks, clouds, rivers and lakes. The *Koyukon* believe that there was once a time when all sentient creatures shared a common society, and humans moved back and forth into and out of the plant and animal kingdoms as shape-shifting presences in a fluid reality. This was the so-called "Distant Time", a magical form of time which is not locked into the deep past, but which interpenetrates with the present in much the same way as the "Dreamtime" of the Australian aborigines. Similar traditional beliefs existed in the ancient Mediterranean cultures and among Eskimo peoples:

"In the very earliest time,
when both people and animals lived on earth,
a person could become an animal if he wanted to
and an animal could become a human being.
Sometimes they were people
And sometimes animals
And there was no difference.
All spoke the same language."
-Traditional Inuit Poem [58]

Such was a world where the human and the more-than-human interpenetrated, and language was a common energy field linking the two. Today, if humans have turned their backs on the language of nature, nature has perhaps reciprocated and no longer is willing to engage with us in the same way. For example, the *Koyukon*, so attentive to the messages of the birds, have observed that the robin's song is not what it used to be. "The robins don't say their song plainly anymore—they only say it halfway, like a kid would when it is learning."[59]

Yet if we, as a species, have tragically and catastrophically disconnected ourselves from our common ground and our common language with nature, all the doors have surely not been closed. But to find doors that are still open requires us to revision the natural world as imbued with spirit and with inner meaning. And to recognize that human survival depends as much on this soul aspect of nature as on any raw materials or physical nutrition we might draw out of her.

NICHOLAS CORRIN, L.Ac.

THE SPEECH OF NATURE

Nature always speaks to us, but we don't always hear what she is saying. Perhaps we stopped listening to her subtle speech a long time ago. Now, it seems, we only "pick up" on her tirades: earthquakes, holes in the ozone, melting ice-caps, rising sea levels, shifting ocean currents, rising temperatures, sudden species extinctions, and new diseases. It is as though we must be screamed at to bring us to attention. Civilization, so-called, has made us deaf. Deaf to the speech of nature, and it is to this "speech" that we must bring our full, alert listening if the human species is not to wreck the entire planet. Five major, across the board extinctions appear to have occurred at various times during the four billion year life of the Earth. There is a general consensus amongst scientists that these extinctions were caused by meteorites or comets slamming into the planet. One of the most recent studies concludes that a sixth major extinction is now well under way, and its cause this time is not extraterrestrial, "it is caused by one animal organism—man."[60] We might refine this point and say that it is caused by one animal organism's failure to listen.

Man has not always been such a poor listener. In David Abram's profound study, *The Spell of the Sensuous*, the author explores how the development of written, alphabetic language ushered in a condition of separation between humans and the natural realm. The written word is based on abstract, alphabetic signs on a blank page, exactly what you are looking at right now. We have been used to this alphabetic code for so long that it is hard for us to see how it has ended up exiling human beings from our ancient, sensorial connectedness with nature. With the alphabet, writing was made possible, and with writing came ideas and abstractions.

When this occurred, we ceased to regard nature as our teacher and guide. We began to treat nature as mere backdrop, the "space" of raw materials, territories to be seized, exploited, lain waste to, prettified, or manipulated. But not *listened to.* If we consider how indigenous, oral cultures have listened to nature, we suddenly realize how divorced our species has become from the matrix from which we emerged: the natural realm.

Before writing appeared, indigenous peoples communicated—not, like us, through abstract signs bearing no direct correspondence with anything real—but through sounds and gestures modeled on the sounds and movements of animals, plants and weather. These were not simply abstract signs or signals, they always referred back to something within nature itself, sounds and movements exuded by the enveloping realm of brooks; whispering trees; the buzz and hum of insect-wing; or from the crackling of fire, or sheets of ice; or the hoot of a great horned owl, shaping the motionless night airs into invisible tapestries of content, rich with inner meaning. Human speech was modeled on nature's speech such that it was almost an echo of this original speech. We can say that human speech was made of the same "sound-substance" as nature's speech. In the Bible, we find the often quoted phrase from St. Paul, "In the beginning was the Word and the Word was with God and the Word was God." In the Vedic and Tantric traditions from India, this creative "word" is associated with the great goddess, thus with nature and with earth, rather than with sky and the male principle.[61] Indigenous peoples without holy scriptures have lived this idea directly by intuiting the creative "word" in the sounds emanating from nature. If we return again to the root meaning of nature as a giving birth, we can see some trans-cultural essence which establishes nature, female divinity, sound, meaning, nurture and wholeness in one mysterious formula.

This understanding allowed pre-literate peoples to com-

NICHOLAS CORRIN, L.Ac.

municate telepathically with animals, plants and even weather, skills which were crucial for their survival but which also grounded them psychologically in the natural realm. Humans were constantly reminded by the speech of nature not to over-step their bounds when interacting with other life-forms, thus maintaining an ecological equilibrium, a state which may also be called natural democracy. Such daily communication with nature also meant that indigenous peoples never felt alone the way civilized man does. For there is no "emptiness" around them as there is around us, and indigenous man does not feel the need to fill the airwaves with his own noise to drown out the silence.

Civilization could be defined in many ways, but one less complimentary one might be "something which produces a great deal of noise." And noise can be understood in physical terms as electromagnetic waves passing through space and causing interference patterns. So, for example, today we have the phenomenon of cell-phone telecommunications towers emitting potent waves, which interfere with the natural fields of trees, causing large swathes of vegetation to wither and die on the hillside. Such negligence would have been severely admonished in an oral, indigenous culture. Everything that lives is due respect, for everything that lives has speech. When man started to regard himself as the only creature possessed of language, he separated himself from nature at the center point of his brain. Human beings, through our assumption of special rights due to our unique ownership of language, have allowed ourselves for centuries to treat nature as deaf, dumb and blind, to the point where we have become mad enough to attempt to re-write nature's genetic codes.

Isolation and meaninglessness are shadows cast by contemporary people, like the shadows cast by solitary trees in a wasteland. Modern culture, for all its great teeming cities, bright lights and incessant buzz of fiber-optic communications, spawns depression and anxiety. How so? Because the individual cannot experience her/himself as part of an integrated web. The arrival of the internet and the creation of hyperspace have actually pointed to a deeper human need that is unfulfilled: the need to feel part of the web of existence, where the many parts are somehow in communication with one another, and where there is an underlying order and oneness, a cosmos. For indigenous peoples, such a lack did not exist. They were part of nature and vice versa. All around, whether from the forests, the sky, the hills, whether through dreams, stories, or encounters, messages are relayed from the spiritual realm, the invisible realm that runs through everything and unites everything. The sudden appearance of a particular animal by the forest's edge, the flight direction of a hawk, the unusual shape of a cloud overhead, the soft smell of a first snowfall and the precise orientation of a bear's footprints on the white "page" of the landscape are all indications streaming in. It is a language of sounds and signs, audible and visible. And this information is interpreted because it will lead to success in hunting or foraging. But at the same time, it provides the constant reminder of human inclusion within nature and the realm of spirit, purpose and meaning.

And us? We are also the recipients of information streaming in: emails, voice-mails and text messages. They, also, are audible and visible pieces of information. But they refer exclusively to the human realm. This flow of information is highly specific to us and originates in the abstract nature of the alphabet itself. Clearly, there is something missing in all this.

MANTRA: SACRED SPEECH

What is missing is the sense of the sacred. Indigenous people live all their five senses through this special sense. Their sensory awareness, so much more acute and refined

NICHOLAS CORRIN, L.Ac.

than ours, is founded upon this one super-sense. This super-sense is an awareness of *presence* running through all things, or what David Abrams calls, "the more-than-human" realm. By contrast, our civilization, as it stutters forwards into a new millennium has for centuries oriented itself towards human mastery over the natural and cosmic realms. We are always trying to shrink things down so that they fit inside the human brain. It is a poor fit, perhaps because there really is not that much room in there after all.

Several cultural traditions associate speech with creation itself. The Biblical phrase, "In the beginning was the Word," equates divine speech with the origin of all things. In India, the Vedic tradition asserts an identical notion: speech gives rise to the things of the world. There is a sort of "breath" or "wind" behind things, behind forms. Behind our word tree, there is the tree itself. But behind the form of the tree, there is a sacred sound or vibration, a kind of mysterious "naming", or utterance which gives rise to the physical form of the tree. And so with all things, ourselves included. There is a mysterious background to us, whereby we are "spoken" into existence. Spoken and also "called." This means that our particular life has behind it a deeper level of meaning, a meaning that is strangely connected with sound as its source.

In some literate cultures, the very alphabets are considered to be sacred repositories. This is the case with Hebrew and with Sanskrit: each letter of these alphabets is imbued with mysterious powers. In Sanskrit, the letters of the alphabet are thought to compose the very "body" of the Goddess behind creation. Sometimes they are spoken of as a garland of flowers adorning her neck and throat. Even the written forms of these letters contain cosmic energy, and have been used to transmit healing over a distance to many thousands of people.[62] In the past, poets and singers were considered highly important people as they were able to control cosmic energies flowing through words and sounds. In early Irish society, poets were engaged in warfare and occupied a position superior in some ways to that of the commanders, as they used their lyrics to awaken storms, waves and other natural forces to topple the enemy's advance. Even today, the stuff of psychological warfare is done through words. And when we set words to music, who cannot be swept away easily by the emotive power inherent in song?

But we have forgotten what our ancestors felt so deeply: every word is sacred and carries consequences. In ancient China, where writing on paper was first developed, no scrap of paper with any calligraphy on it was ever left lying around. There were men whose specific job it was to go around collecting any such fragment. This was more than litter control. They felt that the speech transcribed on to the paper was filled with power, it was somehow alive, and therefore dangerous. Such caution is almost unimaginable to us: we seem to be drowning in a flood of words, news columns, magazines, emails, text mails, voicemails, never mind the unending chatter in our own heads...The truth is silence is also a part of sound, its inner heart. And when we reconnect with silence, we can also reconnect with the powers inherent in sound and in speech.

For every word we utter and every sound we make, there is, potentially, a background of immense depth, like the ocean beneath the ship. Our own speech can be attuned to the depth of the ocean or it can ignore it, treating it as mere surface. The power of *mantra* joins us to these sacred depths that flow through speech once a spiritual connection has been made in the heart. Chanting *mantras*, whether out loud or silently in the mind, establishes this connection. For this reason, *mantra* is used for both healing and for the transformation of consciousness.

All *mantras* originate in one original, transcendent *mantra*, OM. This is the key sound within all *mantras*, the seed in the seeds, for OM is the first of the *bija mantras*,

NICHOLAS CORRIN, L.Ac.

or seed sounds. In the spiritual traditions of India, there are seed sounds which give rise to the universe, just as there are seeds which give rise to plants and trees, and also to humans. There are a number of these seed sounds which are called *shakti mantras*, and which are associated very closely with the Divine Feminine powers of creation. Most of these *mantras* are based on the "ee" vowel sound.

All speech—including *mantra*—has three components. Intention, the thought we have in our minds and which we seek to express. Energy, which moves our breath internally through our vocal chords. And sound itself, which results from the vibrating streams of air that flow from our mouths, having passed through our larynx where they have been shaped into speech. So speech is a flow of intentional energy traveling through the air. It begins with intention and ends with audible sound. As with anything, if we focus and deepen this process, the effects will be far greater. Our speech can become like a living river instead of a leaking faucet!

In order to use mantra well, we need to align the sounds with the breath. It is very important to bring the breath deep down into the core of the body. As you inhale, use your mind to bring the breath all the way down to your lower abdomen, and even to the base of your spine. Before you start focusing on any particular sounds, practice this kind of breathing—which must be done with the lungs and the mind together. The energy will be sent wherever the mind directs it. Energy travels where attention goes; this is particularly true of the breath, which represents our internal flow of energy. The more you practice bringing your energy inward and downward as you inhale, the calmer and stronger you will become, and the more success you will have with all the exercises in this book.

The following seven sounds are some of the main *shakti mantras* and have specific benefits associated with them. As they stem from the powers of the goddess or divine feminine principle, to use them effectively you must enter an initial state of receptivity and reverence. Such a state of mind is one of abandoning control and welcoming in. It is consistent with what I have called the feminine side of power, and it is a main theme of this entire book, running cover to cover. Breathe slowly and deeply and then choose from amongst the following mantras and repeat the sound over and over, focusing upon its inner meaning. At first, you can chant the sound very softly, under your breath. Then, gradually, you can continue chanting in silence, just using your mind to shape the sound.

To be effective, mantra must be repeated many times over. Less is not more, more is more. Find a quiet place where you will not be disturbed, concentrate on the sounds. Think of it as learning to play a musical instrument. With regular practice you will become proficient.

SHRIM (pronounced *Shreem.*) Generates calm. Brings abundance and prosperity.

KRIM (pronounced *Kreem.*) Stimulates the life force. Increases the bio-electrical energy in the body. Good for initiative, and for the shaping of goals and intentions.

KLIM (pronounced *Kleem.*) The complementary sound to KRIM. Stimulates the bio-magnetic energy. Helps draw to you that which you are seeking.

TRIM (pronounced *Treem.*) A fiery mantra. Burns a path through obstacles and negative forces coming from outside.

GUM (pronounced like chewing *Gum.*) Also good for clearing obstacles.

DUM (pronounced *Doom.*) A protective mantra, it counteracts fear.

HRIM (pronounced *Hreem*). A very deep mantra, like OM. It strengthens the heart, promotes inner clarity and increases our powers of attraction.

The art and science of mantra is vast. It is best to find proper guidance from a teacher or other knowledgeable person. However, there are various good books explaining how to use mantra in more detail. If you wish for a more detailed approach, please consult "Healing Mantras" by Thomas Ashley-Farrand.[63]

HUNTING WITH LOVE... AND WITHOUT IT

Even at the earliest stages of human development there must have been a bifurcation in the heart, an interplay of light and dark forces. This was an inevitable corollary of the free will that came along with the development of the frontal lobes. Together with free will came something we would call conscience. Man's brain had grown too large for him to participate any longer as an equal in the animal world: now he was partly above and partly below his animal peers. Mankind as a species had emerged from the womb of animal consciousness, and the protective waters of pure instinct had broken. We were now, in a very real sense, on our own, somewhere in the middle realm between heaven and earth. The Greeks would later call this middle realm the *metaxy,* and they would associate it with the soul.[64]

The soul is an interaction of light and dark forces. This is its elemental makeup. Spirit is actually the highest vibration within the soul, the highest aspiration of the soul. But it is the soul that determines our actual inner lives because it is there that we make our real choices. We usually call these choices good and evil, but these terms must be understood not only in a socially driven sense, but also in a cosmic one. Here the dualism involves love or the absence of love, which we have correlated so far with error and with fear. The history of our relationship with hunting has much to teach us in this regard.

Before the first great cities were built and the first true civilizations were created, primitive man was a hunter and gatherer. During the last Ice Age, we were cave dwellers and relied upon hunting wild game for food. But hunting was not just for our physical survival, it was also for spiritual food. We shed blood to eat, but also to take in the mysterious life spirit into our system: for most early human societies, God was identified with food. So hunting was not entirely different from communing with the universe in a "spiritual" way.

Food gives life. Without food, as any animal knows, life stops. Food is the mysterious life giver in the guise of plants or flesh. This was how it was understood by early man's symbol producing mind. And because there was a sanctity about food, there was room for potential transgression if the spiritual presence in food was not honored. Man saw animals feeding off plants and off each other. There was no need for animals to perform cleansing rituals because they were intrinsically part of the divine presence: the gods lived under the guise of animal forms. But man felt himself to be different. God did not live in his form. This idea would only occur to man much later on after man had extracted himself from such close proximity with nature. At the beginning, there were stirrings in him of conscience, for he was partly a spectator, partly a guest, and, in part, an interloper. He was already, in some ways, much more powerful than animals, but also far weaker. He was not yet himself a god; he was the beneficiary of the plenty provided by the gods. So he needed to pay homage to them, and to pay his respects for what they offered and for the life they allowed him.

My first encounter with hunting was as a boy on vacation in southern France. I had wandered down a leafy trail and

NICHOLAS CORRIN, L.Ac.

found myself in a small copse. It was a beautiful October day, crisp yet warm, blue and golden. After their exposure to the sun during the long summer months, the leaves had a touch of dryness to them, and fluttered almost like gilded paper in the light breeze. Presently, I came upon a number of local men, squatting amidst the undergrowth. An odd maze of camouflaged corridors had been rigged up with twigs and branches so as to conceal the movements of those inside. Dappled light similar to what you would expect to see in an impressionist painting filtered down and played on the ruddy faces of the silent men. I also noticed some strange cables and pulleys that had been attached to various trees.

Craning up, I saw what at first sight I took to be birds perched amongst the uppermost branches. Slowly, it dawned on me that these were in fact decoys, whose mechanical wings could be made to move by means of the cables and pulleys. I asked one of the men what this set up was for. "It's the *palombiere*," he told me, adding, "This is *palombe* season." Palombe is French for "wood pigeon" but I did not know that this beautiful, medieval looking bird migrated south over the Pyrenees in fall, headed for Spain and North Africa. The predatory ambush devised by these squat, taciturn men beneath the cover of their burrows on such an idyllic day shocked me. I watched one of the men pull on a cable and I could see one of the decoys above raise its wings as if alighting on a branch.

The thought of those migrating wood pigeons being deceived and then shot down in numbers in this way disturbed me profoundly. I imagined the soaring elegance of their flight, their courage in traversing many hundreds of miles over mountains and sea, guided by some internal compass that kept them in mysterious alliance with the seasons and the turning world. Then I imagined them gunned down, cooked, and eaten.

However, there was probably still a small residue here,

a warped fragment of the original reverence for the god in the eaten. Trapping and killing the birds was a way for those men to capture not just a food source, but some of the wild energy and poetry of nature itself. This has always been an aspect of hunting and explains its allure to the present day.

But if we consider modern examples of hunting as a tribal way of life, such as exist in indigenous societies, we see that there is a genuine identification that occurs between hunter and prey. Without shotguns, the indigenous hunter must gather close to his quarry, not just on a physical level, but also on a deeper level as he closely studies the habits and movements of animals, to the point of even copying their cries and movements, and by "apprenticing himself to those animals he would kill".[65]

It is customary for such hunters to speak modestly and respectfully about their goals. For example, "The most you should say is that you'll try to catch a fish, or better yet, don't say anything at all".[66] This is due to reverence for a kind of spiritual solidarity with the species preyed upon, an understanding that humans are only one part of the tapestry of nature; and that the animals themselves, at some level, offer their own so that humans may eat. In brief, there is a primitive but genuine understanding there of a "love" force binding hunter and hunted together in a type of soul compact. Ecology is spiritual as much as physical, and hunting, for indigenous peoples, might in fact be more "loving" than the vegetarianism of clean-thinking modern people in their artificial environments.

Historically speaking, kings and aristocracy have gone after the finest and most exotic prey, as though thereby to acquire the premium attributes of nature with which to adorn themselves. In such places as China, many strange and wonderful species were rendered extinct in this way. In Africa, the safari became the European profiteer's take on this same theme.

NICHOLAS CORRIN, L.Ac.

Another, and even darker aspect of hunting is mostly concerned with numbers and economic value. In such cases, animals have not been the only quarry. We typically associate the practice of headhunting with cannibalistic tribes. But in the nineteenth century there was a brisk trade in the sale of shrunken heads to British Navy men at berth in Tasmania. Local tribes would meticulously "prepare" select victims from amongst their own servant classes for decapitation so that the heads could be processed and sold to the sailors who would take them back home as curios, or sell them on again. What underpinned this gruesome commerce was gain in what was, effectively, an early version of the global economy.

As a young child, I would travel frequently with my family to Switzerland, which is where my grandparents lived. We would often go to spend an afternoon at the Halwilersee, a large lake in the German speaking part of the country. We would usually spend our time swimming, sunbathing or picnicking, and occasionally we would take a small ferry boat over to the other side of the lake. I remember one day we did this and as we disembarked on to the small jetty, there was a solitary man fishing. He had a huge plastic bag next to him, the size of a garbage can. It was already half-filled with fish; as I stepped down on to the slatted wooden boards of the jetty, he removed yet another gasping mouth from off his line, tossing it nonchalantly into the plastic bag. There it cavorted and flipped on top of the heap. I now noticed that many of the fish that composed this heap beneath were not dead yet, but were slowly squirming with various degrees of residual energy. Their silver and black bodies shone with a kind of sad, metallic beauty, and there were smears of blood visible all over the interior side of the bag and about their mouths and gills. Already another fish was being removed off the end of the line and thrown into the bag. Small child that I was, I was struck into consternation at this scene. The red smears over the black and silver, the sheer excess of numbers in the bag, the monotonous gestures and facial expression of the fisherman, plus his apparent complete absorption in what he was doing left me with feelings of disgust and horror.

During the span of the eighteenth century, the so called Age of Enlightenment, it has been estimated that approximately sixty billion herring were caught by human beings fishing in the North Sea.[67] Today, as many are now aware, many species of what were still, until quite recently, commonly found fish such as Chilean sea bass and cod, are now on the endangered list. The industrialization of fishing which is, after all, a type of hunting, has allowed a deeper shadow to pass from our actions and be thrown back on to nature. Instead of reciprocating the bounty that nature has offered us, we have contrived to decimate it.

THE HUNTER OF BELIEFS

He who has conquered doubt and fear has conquered failure.—James Allen, from *As A Man Thinketh*

Nevertheless, there is a mystery to the act of hunting. Nature is inconceivable without the animal as hunter, and her entrancing beauty and splendor depend as much upon the lion as upon the lamb in its peaceful fields of swaying grass. The great blue heron, one leg raised, beak and eye held in perfect equipoise above the slurring waters; or the flame of a cheetah, burning its trail across the savannah to bring down a gazelle; or the devastating plunge of an osprey to land a fish. These are but a few examples of the wildness of the Life force: a mysterious fusion of beauty and violence as energy pirouettes through the natural realm like a tornado.

NICHOLAS CORRIN, L.Ac.

Were it not for the hunter, might it be that everything in nature would degenerate into a kind of torpor? It may well be that a fat, indolent world take the place of wild nature, if the predators were removed. And ecology itself would unravel, like a great tapestry whose threads were coming apart. We are seeing these sorts of imbalances in our own time, after the wholesale destruction of natural predators and their habitats. Only a few years ago, in Southern California, I entered a suburban park only to be warned by the warden that there was a group of mountain lions camped out by a group of trees. The big cats had abandoned their normal caution around human beings. Had they given up, sensing their demise was near? Each year, the warden told me, these cougars had to cross at least four major freeways to reach their breeding grounds. Most of them did not make it. And with each year, more housing developments went up, less open land was left. I felt the wrenching sadness of the endgame.

Yet if we can do little by ourselves to come to the assistance of natural predators, we can at least emulate their attributes as we engage with our own psyches. In the Toltec tradition, of which Dr. Miguel Ruiz is a principal modern exponent, we are guided to track down all negative beliefs we may have accumulated over the years, beliefs that have limited us and damaged our true potential.[68] Becoming a "Hunter of Beliefs" involves tracking and slaying ideas that have made a home inside us from an earlier period in our lives.[69] At one time, these confining beliefs were necessary, enabling us to survive in a critical period, but they have long outlived their purpose and become toxic. In essence, we originally accommodated to painful situations by telling ourselves we were somehow deficient or inadequate. This became an inner programming: we programmed ourselves in the negative. "I am not," and "I cannot," are the core archetypes of this negative self-programming. It is this negativity that needs to be hunted down.

Becoming a Hunter of Beliefs means pursuit of the "prey" of unconsciously held, damaging beliefs. It means observing the subtle fluctuations in our moods, and tracking the negative self-talk that lies just below the surface of consciousness. We may need to stalk ourselves so that we can get past our camouflages, defenses and denial mechanisms that protect this concealed negativity. All of this requires endurance, persistence, skill, acuity of vision and, last but not least, patience, all attributes of a natural hunter.

So, as we face outwardly toward the world, we can act to protect the weak and the endangered. As we face inward, so long as we are thwarted by unconsciously held negativity, we must tap into the natural instincts of the hunter. Limiting ideas about ourselves that often produce depression later in life were typically formed in childhood, and are known in Ruiz's approach as, "The First Dream".[70] In this Toltec tradition, the First Dream, once seen through and removed, must be replaced by "The Second Dream". This is when we consciously design our lives not on the basis of lack, but on the basis of self-confidence and self-belief. In the last section of this book, we will explore the concept of magnetizing intention and see how, through techniques of highly focused attention, we can emit charged images of the contents of our Second Dream.

ST. FRANCIS OF ASSISI AND STORIES OF ANTS

Like Gautama, who would become the Buddha, St. Francis of Assisi was born into wealth and privilege. Yet he gave all this up to live in proximity and solidarity with the poor, animals, nature and with God. What drove him to abandon accepted social values for such a life? It was something stronger, a voice, experienced personally, of divine

NICHOLAS CORRIN, L.Ac.

summons. To "feel the call" is not, I think, that rare that only saints or buddhas experience it. It is just that there are competing voices in us. Most of us feel drawn in different directions at the same time: the human heart is complex and full of contradictions. Brutality, egotism and indifference co-exist with self-sacrifice and great tenderness. The human heart is a battlefield—and a debating room—where opposing tendencies play out. Ultimately, these tendencies are composed of light and dark forces, but it is not always so clear what is light and what is dark.

St. Francis was viewed by the ecclesiastical authorities of his day as a social activist and an agitator. The Church was worried that he—and others like him who appeared to have abandoned the hierarchical values of feudal society—threatened the social and political order. The church authorities were afraid that Francis would ignite a revolt amongst the poor against the rich, powerful church and its allies in the upper classes.

But Francis was moved by things they could not possibly relate to, let alone understand. It is quite possible that, had he been born in a later period of history, he would have been institutionalized with the criminally insane. For Francis regarded the whole of nature as his family. He spoke not just to humans but to animals and to birds. He considered the elements such as wind and rain to be our brothers and sisters, for he intuited consciousness in them that was linked to the divine: spirit was in everything, even rocks, clouds and forests. There was nowhere God was not. To harm anything, therefore, was to harm God. Gentleness was a way of serving God and recognizing His presence in all things.

Yet if we look closely at what goes on in nature, we don't find a friendly world that reassures us everything is going to be okay. I will never forget one time I was walking with a friend along a sandy trail on a hillside near Santa Fe, New Mexico. The sun was low in the sky, and dusk was soon to fall. The air was thick with the scent of pinon and juniper trees. We paused to look down at a large mound of red, dusty earth, where thousands of ants were engaged in scurrying along long, interweaving lines, much like a miniature version of busy urban traffic, with movement in both directions. Then we spotted an odd tug of war going on in the midst of all this commotion. A large beetle had somehow strayed into this city of the ants, and a single ant, less than a quarter the size of the beetle, had grabbed hold of it and was trying to drag it up the hill. The beetle was pulling away in the other direction, but neither creature had the edge in strength, and the combat shifted now this way, now that but with neither party breaking away or giving up. Surprisingly, the streams of ants passed by this gargantuan struggle without paying any notice at all until, completely out of the blue, five or six other ants suddenly joined forces with the first and latched on to the beetle. Now its fate was a forgone conclusion: it was summarily dragged uphill into the heart of the citadel where it would meet its end in a manner neither of us wished to witness.

Years later, I read an account by Sundar Singh of his travels in Tibet. Singh, who died in 1929, was well-known in his day as India's most famous convert to Christianity. Like Francis before him, he abandoned a comfortable home at the age of sixteen to lead a pauper's life as a wandering holy man. He sought nothing for himself other than to teach to others his mystical encounters with Jesus, whom he called his Master. Once, in a village in Tibet called Rasar, Sundar was summoned by the chief lama and accused of heresy because of his preaching.[71] In a manner that brought back to me the scene on the anthill in New Mexico, Sundar was seized by a local mob and stripped naked. He was taken and thrown into a dry well which was then covered over with a stone lid. Inside the well, Sundar discovered that he was not alone: he had landed on top of a mass of rotting bodies. In

NICHOLAS CORRIN, L.Ac.

the pitch darkness, his hands reached out and felt decomposing flesh and raw bone. The stench was almost unbearable. After an uncertain period of time in this hellhole—perhaps two or three days—Sundar heard a grating sound above, and found that the lid had been unlocked and was being dragged aside. A rope was let down into the well and an unseen voice ordered him to take hold of it and haul himself up. He did so, and soon lay gasping on the ground above, whilst he heard the lid being closed again. There was no-one around to be seen.

The next day, Sundar was again dragged before the chief lama and made to give an account of his escape. Furious, the lama ordered an immediate search for the man who had taken the only key to the stone lid. However, he was astounded to discover that this very key hung from his own belt. The lama himself was the only person in possession of a key to the dry well. Enraged and terrified, he commanded Sundar to leave the village forthwith. In Sundar's view, it was his "Master" who had come to the well to release him.

Sundar also speaks about a Sufi mystic who had set out on a journey with a load of wheat. Several days into his trip, he opened his bags only to find a number of ants amongst the wheat. The Sufi pondered what course of action he now must take. Overwhelmed with concern for the lost ants, he decided to return home to take the ants back to their original colony.[72]

What sort of a universe do we inhabit where we can watch ants haul off and dismember a beetle that has blundered down the wrong path, and also find a man who is willing to turn back and walk for several days on foot just to return a few ants to their original home?

THE MATRIX

Everything that exists derives from the same source, the same mysterious origin. Human beings are part of the Earth, which is part of the solar system which, in turn, is part of our galaxy, itself a small part of the universe. There exists an unbroken continuum through it all from the tiniest portion to the greatest. And the very constituents of our bodies, the chemical elements that compose us are the selfsame elements that make up the macro-structures of nature: mountains, rivers, rocks, clouds, fields and forests. The laws of their physical and chemical interactions are the same, regardless of where they are to be found, in volcanic lava, in sea turtles or in ourselves. We are made of the same stuff as earth, dew and snow not only because we share the same chemical building blocks, but because the same energies course through us: we are all subject to the same universal dynamics, whether animate or inanimate. The mysterious interplay of waves and elementary particles goes on within all forms, structuring them and unraveling them. And the life giving or destructive winds we find outside also blow and echo through our nervous systems, as an inner wind of thoughts, emotions and reflexes.

Both material forms and the energy that activates them depend upon the existence of a matrix which has been referred to variously as ether, bio-plasm or unifying field. A useful analogy for the way physical forms merge out of this organizing matrix is the example of crystals forming out of the mother liquor.[73]

This holds true on an incredibly fast level with electrons and protons, and on a vastly slower level with complex structures such as human beings. Length and brevity of du-

NICHOLAS CORRIN, L.Ac.

ration are merely relative. However, all structures somehow "crystallize" for a while out of the mother substance, which is an organizing matrix that signifies much more than our concept of matter. The Vedic sciences from ancient India call this matrix *Prakriti*.

It is very important for us to understand the difference between the concept of the Prakriti matrix and the concept of matter. The idea of matter is essentially inert and passive like clay. But the idea of a living matrix contains not just the basis for physical form, it contains the organizing intelligence that binds form together; and it contains the possibility of all combinations and even the possibility of experience itself. It is somewhat like the idea of a quantum soup: everything and anything can be drawn out of it, the way all biological life forms that we know of emerged out of the primal oceans. This means that if we direct our focused attention upon this matrix of potentiality, we can creatively draw up out of it the potentials that reside within it. In a very real sense, everything is already there, including past and future.

Einstein came to a similar conclusion when he observed that time flows in two directions, and that the future exists simultaneously with the past. All possibilities exist "within the ether", and great inventions are really nothing but great discoveries. Nothing is thought up or created independently by mankind. Whether we consider great works of art or great scientific breakthroughs, both originate in a state of inspiration in which the consciousness of the individual is able to "plug-in" to a higher source, and draw the information down. All the individual does is "give shape to" this information.

We all do this from time to time, in various ways. It may be through dreams, sudden insights or "brainwaves." Our "plug-in" may not be to something that we would consider of earth shattering importance, but the world does not work by dictating that some things or some people are more important than others: everything, in a sense, is equally important.

If we could align ourselves more effectively and trustingly with the source of insight in the organizing field, we could participate more joyfully in the process of life. The human imagination is a vast and undervalued instrument. It is perhaps the vital tool that can help our species avoid extinction and improve life on earth for all.

Nature performs the act of drawing forms out of its own potential in a continuous stream. This is in accord with its core meaning of "giving birth." Physicist David Bohm speaks about the natural processes as processes of in-form-ation.[74] In Bohm's theory, there exists what he calls an "implicate order" which is an organized field of potential that has yet to become manifest as form. The process of in-form-ation at a cosmic level is really about making explicit or actual what is latent. This concept has been applied to the individual and the idea of specific purpose by the Jungian psychologist, Richard Whitmont. We each have a life which encloses a specific "form", or "shape." This form represents our purpose for being here, so there are certain experiences we are required to live through and grow from. High level energy is running into our systems from its implicate source, impelling us to explore life in certain very individual ways. If we cannot, or will not, metabolize these currents of energy—if we fail to meet our inner life challenges—we most likely will fall sick, according to Whitmont. Illness then becomes the result of energetic congestion or inflammation which starts to break down the integrity of the physical body. From this perspective, healing has everything to do with who we actually are and why we are here. Activating self-awareness becomes the key to getting well.

NICHOLAS CORRIN, L.Ac.

ENTERING THE SOURCE

When a bird glides silently overhead barely moving its wings or when, beneath the ocean's surface, seaweed fronds sway lazily with the pull of inner currents, these creatures are simply melding with the swirling energies of their environments. They are surrendering control so as to live their lives pleasantly and well. They are letting go. But their way of letting go is not exactly passive. It is in between active and passive. It is passive-active: that is, by surrendering outer control to the surrounding environmental energies, animals and plants are able to "extract" particular kinds of dynamic which they can use to their advantage. This type of extraction through blending is the opposite of human, industrial action which is performed by imposing from the outside, by coercing. Human industrial extraction of energy relies on male, active power. Obvious examples are coal mines, oil refineries and nuclear reactors. Natural extraction (of potential energy) relies on female, receptive power. Obvious examples are solar power, wind turbines and less well known are the recently developed free energy technologies using magnets or zero-point field research. When we spend time in nature, we are constantly being exposed to examples of this receptive power without being aware of it. This is why spending time in nature is so calming, so rejuvenating and yes, so empowering for human beings.

A perfect example of this is a red-tailed hawk I watched a few days ago. I was taking a long walk in a park in Seattle with a friend. The park fronts the Puget Sound, and you can look down from the tree-lined cliff at a spit of grey beach that angles out toward the distant Pacific. Though still early in the day, the light was already failing, as it was not long past winter solstice. A flash of rust colored wings moved overhead, a little above the wintry tangle of branches, then positioned itself in mid air directly above a bramble covered incline sloping downward to the grey spit below. The air was blowing quite hard; many trees had recently been felled or damaged by gale force winds. Yet the hawk "sat" there, in all this windy turbulence, as though it had moved into—or even become—the eye of the storm. It was not moving a single feather, let alone exerting a muscle. How did it do this?

If you looked closely, you could see that the hawk had curved its body into a concave sculpture. It held its wings like two incurling airplane wings, while its legs thrust forward strongly from its pelvis so as to create a sort of hollow, smooth tank of space in front of its torso. Its head and neck were arched forward and then down, generating some kind of counterflow. Clearly, this was masterful aeronautic engineering. The hawk's profound natural instincts had allowed it to tap into the forces of the wind so as to master them, so as to be supported effortlessly. It had turned nature on its head, so to speak. Or it had mined the hidden potential that always lies behind the surface of things. It had, more precisely, yielded so as to be able to transform outer adversity into its opposite, all through minute bodily adjustments. It was a perfect display of receptive power. And it was this receptive power coupled with the hawk's active intelligence that gave it the prowess to hunt from its magnificent vantage point.

The river trout has mastered this skill to such an extent that it can remain perfectly still in the midst of swiftly rushing waters. If you observe trout that "sit" as stationary as the hawk, in the onrush of a powerful current, you wonder, how is this possible? Callum Coats, in his book detailing the amazing discoveries and inventions of Viktor Schauberger, explains by what means the trout is able to do this. As the downstream current sweeps by the body of the fish, small eddies and vortices are created along the trout's flanks. This is because the individual water particles start to accelerate

NICHOLAS CORRIN, L.Ac.

when they hit resistance, causing turbulence. What occurs then is a series of eddies along both sides of the trout, spinning in an opposite direction to the downstream current. The trout's brilliant native intelligence somehow mastered this advanced principle of hydrological dynamics. How so, you ask? By finding its power through submitting to the flow, just like the Old Man in the Ganges. This is what I mean by the passive-active mode. We can all apply this passive-active approach to life and circumstance. The power of letting go is precisely this. By attuning oneself to what is actually present, what is actually there swirling around you (not what your confused, absent, inattentive mind thinks is there), you can be carried by a hidden world of energy that is innately flexible and supportive of life.

In fact, the trout can do far more than remain stationary in rapid downstream currents. It can dart, quick as a flash, against the flow of water. When you hold a stick above the water where the trout is "sitting," motionless in the river, it will immediately surge upstream to remove itself from danger. Why upstream, and how is it able to do this? It goes against the flow because this way it can retain control and not be swept away. It is able to do this merely by pumping its gills. Pumping its gills increases the spring of the vortical eddies of water along its flanks and so powers its thrust upstream. It moves effortlessly, yet with the acceleration of a Ferrari. Is this not a most amazing phenomenon, that it has figured out a way to *be swum* by the river in a direction completely opposite to the one the river is demanding? Remember, it is using almost none of its own energy. It is simply utilizing the river's free energy.[75] The trout has used evolution to learn, not just how to swim, but how to be swum. And not just to be swum, but to be swum in a manner and direction of its own choosing. It has turned the river into both a limousine and a chauffeur. In a word, it has accessed the power of the source.

We humans do not inhabit the same rivers that trout do. Yet we inhabit the same river of life. When the little old man leapt into the raging waters of the nascent Ganges, he was leaping into the source, not with fear but with confidence. Can we do what he did? Can we do what the trout does? Why not? Both the stationary trout and the old man have somehow mastered the river's currents, not by fighting them, not by overpowering them, but by uniting with them. If we could learn to unite ourselves seamlessly with the river of life, might we not be able to remain unharmed in the midst of adversity and turmoil? Or be carried in the best possible direction, though it might appear outwardly unlikely, not to say impossible?

Where does the impossible exist, except in our own minds? If birds and fish refuse to use the word impossible, should we humans be the first to engage it? Does that make us special? Obviously not. All human achievements have broken the boundaries of what previously was considered impossible. From the invention of the radio to Roger Bannister's first sub-four minute mile, what happened to old ideas that this type of thing could not be done? They went the way of flat earth theory.

The essence of the type of power we are examining here I am calling *passive-active.* It is like something beyond, above, and prior to *yin* and *yang.* In ancient Chinese philosophy, both *yin* and *yang* devolved out of the *Tai Ji*, the "Great Ultimate", which transcends them both. Living our lives in a passive-active way is to stay in touch with the Great Ultimate, or, if you prefer, with Spirit. In the English language we have two so-called voices, which are modes of using verbs. These voices are called the "active" and the "passive." The active voice is used when we do something to something. For example, "I opened the door." The passive voice is used when something is done to something by someone. For example, "The door was opened by Jane." This choice between

NICHOLAS CORRIN, L.Ac.

active and passive, presented by our language, makes the world seem a very either-or place. Either you are the doer, or you get things done to you. Either you are the boss, or you are an employee. Either you are on top, or your partner is on top. It is an either-or world and essentially, an artificial and a mechanically driven one.

Interestingly, ancient languages such as Sanskrit and classical Greek made much use of another voice, the "third voice", which is somewhere between active and passive. Not exactly doing, and not exactly being done to. We don't see that much of this in English, but one example would be, "Flowers bloom in the spring time." This is passive-active. The flowers don't act on the spring, but they aren't just made to bloom by the spring either. They somehow engage with the forces of spring, so as to bloom. They tap into the potential energies of spring in order to manifest their potential. This is the way of the passive-active mode. It is surely no coincidence that in ancient India and Greece, there was a far greater connection and reverence for the forces of nature, and there was an understanding of the spiritual oneness that ran through it. This is why those languages were modeled on these very understandings.

Adopting a passive-active way, the third voice, could also be described as becoming light, as opposed to dense, inert and heavy. And becoming light could also be described as becoming soft. Softness is the essence of the internal martial arts, where the adversary's violence is turned back against him. Photons, as we have seen, have neither mass nor inertia. In a way, then, light particles are "soft" and yielding, whereas physical particles may be said to be hard and insistent, since they possess both mass and inertia. If we are really made out of light, could we not then become more like photons, which is to say, more like water, pliant and yielding, yet also intensely alive? Become the very river in which we swim, drawing its great strengths up into us?

All the exercises included in this book have been designed to enable you to engage with your softness and lightness, so as to engage the strength they will release, a strength far greater than the hard strength of brute force.

A UNIVERSE
FIT TO LIVE IN

Ultimately, if we are to move away from fear into love, we must recognize the universe as fit to live in. Traditionally, humans have always seen the universe in three ways: benign, malign or neutral. Tribal societies with a shamanic basis honor the otherness of creation and see humans as but a part of a great, mysterious whole. Through shamans, they negotiate with the spirit realm in both its light and dark aspects. Both benign and malign forces may be summoned up, or unwittingly offended. Christianity combines benign and malign in the concepts of good and evil (or Christ and the Devil). Generally speaking, religions see light at the basis of creation, but both dark and light forces at work in the heart of mankind. Organized religions theoretically place the powers of light higher than the powers of darkness, but historically have tended to strongly emphasize the pervasive influence of the dark side, making believers prone to feelings of guilt and shame, or even prompting them to violence and bloodshed. It is astonishing how many malign acts human beings have committed in the name of a benign god. By contrast, in the last century, science and philosophy offered us a neutral universe which was neither benign nor malign, but indifferent to us as to our hopes and fears: a universe of swirling gases, molecules and subatomic particles, but with no conscience and no god at the center of it.

But a benign universe does not have to mean "good" in the sense we conventionally think of it. It means benign on

NICHOLAS CORRIN, L.Ac.

its own terms, which we must somehow accept and surrender to. This was God's message when He spoke out of the whirlwind to Job. If we humans did not create the universe, who are we to judge what is right and wrong within it? We can only judge our own human actions, according to the conscience we carry in our hearts.

For example, if one man murders another, we can say he is guilty. But if someone dies of an infectious disease, are we going to call the bacteria that killed him guilty? Or if a storm at sea sinks a ship, is the storm guilty? Of course not. We only have a sense of guilt in us because we know we have freedom of choice. That freedom consists in either listening to conscience in the heart, or ignoring it and acting with disregard for other forms of life, both human and non-human.

If we look within, without the need to dominate, use, or make others pay for our difficulties, we find compassion, tolerance, and hope as well as the desire for freedom, justice and understanding. We may also discover instincts for creativity, and a hunger for beauty and mystery. In silence of the heart, nature speaks directly to us, and we have a different way of evaluating life. We sense that the meaning of life is wrapped up with the digestion of experience, and with learning to love and to see more deeply into things. In the heart too, there is courage, which can only exist in the face of challenges and obstacles. Sometimes these obstacles are too severe or harsh to be overcome, but the courage in the human heart survives somehow. A friendly universe could be one that somehow placed these searchings and qualities at the center of the human heart. In that place, there may be what we could call a spiritual language, or code, representing the ultimate intentions of the cosmos.

In our Western heritage, we have long separated mind from body and spirit from matter. In fact, our overriding tendency has been to analyze everything and break it down into separate bits and pieces. This has allowed us to gain immense mechanical and industrial control over the physical world, but somehow we have lost the essence of life in the process. It has also brought the planet to a state of desperate breakdown and depletion. In brief, our collective actions and our technology have issued from the command center of the head, without regard for the heart. From such a point of view, the heart is nothing more than a pump to supply fuel (oxygen and nutrients) to the human system.

In the Eastern heritage, there has been a very different idea about the heart and the mind. Both ancient China and India considered the heart, not the head, to be the true center of consciousness. In the West, we would consider "thinking with the heart" to be all about emotion and sentimentality, but this is not what they meant at all. In fact, it is not the physical heart they were referring to, it is really an energetic zone that overlays the physical heart but extends beyond it. It is through this zone that we can access a deeper way of knowing. It is through here, actually, that we can best align ourselves with the consciousness of the universe. We can call this area our spiritual heart. And if the universe is spiritual at the core, we can resonate in harmony with the universe if we acknowledge the spiritual heart. The spiritual heart can be understood as our plug-in to a less tangible representation of reality.

NICHOLAS CORRIN, L.Ac.

EXERCISES
AND MEDITATIONS

*The following exercises and meditations have been
designed to help you absorb the ideas in this section, and
apply them to your own life.*

PRACTICE COMPASSION

*Simply approach others with compassion, knowing that
they are ultimately fearful and in need of love, just as you
are. Be the first one to be loving and compassionate. Be
this way even to people you don't like. Tap into your own
capacity to be kind and compassionate. You will be surprised
how people respond. What you give out to others you will
receive back. Don't be fearful of the results, and don't do this
with any expectation of reward. Simply maintain an open,
compassionate heart.*

CONNECT WITH WILDNESS

*Make sure to spend time out of doors, under the open sky.
Watch the birds fly past, and feel the wind. Look at the wild
aspects of nature close by you and connect with them. Pay
attention to the intense vitality that is there. As you do so,
allow yourself to re-connect with this. Think about the
horizon and all the different landscapes, people, animals,
cities, rivers and mountains that lie beyond it. Expand your
senses as you walk outside, dreaming of other lands and
experiences. Now draw all this back into your heart, feeling
it grow stronger, wilder, more alive.*

SEARCHING FOR YOUR UNDERGROUND BELIEFS

1) Sit down in a quiet, comfortable environment where you will not be disturbed. Keep your spine erect and close your eyes.

2) Slow down your breathing: focus on deep, rhythmic inhalations and exhalations.

3) Now visualize a spiral of light forming around your body. This light spiral is a protective capsule that will enable you to go anywhere without danger or harm.

4) Now slowly relax into yourself. Allow yourself to simply be present with those "underground" feelings you carry deep inside about life, about yourself. Don't judge: simply be present with these thoughts and feelings, even the most painful ones.

5) Allow yourself to sink into this world of your inner thoughts. As though you were drifting down through space and time in your protective capsule, search for those core beliefs that you hold about yourself, and about life. Once you have a sense of them, form them into a sentence or two, and say these words out loud to yourself, softly but clearly.

6) Now, with eyes still closed, "rise" back upwards in your capsule. Slowly open your eyes. What you have said out loud is the essence of the unconscious program of belief that has been driving all your actions.

7) Write down this sentence or sentences in a notebook that you have set aside for your inner work.

NICHOLAS CORRIN, L.Ac.

ACTIVATING
THE SPIRITUAL HEART

1) Sit, or lie down on your back in a quiet place. If you choose to lie down, make sure your body is relaxed and positioned symmetrically, with your arms outstretched by your sides, palms open and face up. It is best to do this meditation in a shaded or darkened area.

2) Close your eyes and slow down your breathing.

3) Feel your body grow dark, like a landscape at dusk.

4) Now sense a small flame emerge at the very center of your heart.

5) See this small flame take on your exact shape: it is like a tiny living replica of you at the center of your heart, made of flame.

6) Watch this tiny figure of flame meditating at the center of your heart.

7) Allow all your doubts, fears, and regrets to roll in towards this living flame and disappear into it.

8) Watch the glow from this tiny figure of flame shine outward beyond your dark body and into the night, all the way into the deep sky beyond.

9) Feel the tremendous power of love and compassion at the center of your heart.

10) Stay with this visualization, slowing down more and more, just watching this tiny you of flame, this tiny you that is meditating at the center of your heart.

OPENING THE HEART

1) Sit in a quiet place where you won't be disturbed.

2) Sit either on the edge of a stool with your knees bent at right angles, or cross-legged on the floor, (or in lotus position). Use a cushion to sit on if this makes you more comfortable.

3) Make sure your spine is erect, and your pelvis is evenly balanced.

4) Rest your arms on your thighs, palms face up by your knees. Keep your shoulders, elbows, wrists and fingers fully relaxed.

5) Close your eyes. Breathe slowly and deeply.

6) As you inhale, breathe up energy from the ground into your heart, and then exhale it from your heart through your open palms.

7) Visualize this exhaled energy from your heart spreading outwards like a bright vapor.

8) Continue breathing in and out like this until your heart feels alive and expanded. Feel a tingling in your heart as the energy pulses through it. Feel yourself like a living fountain, pouring forth generous energy from your heart. Feel your entire chest grow bright, expansive and free.

9) When you feel you are done, touch your heart with one hand, then place both palms over your navel for several slow breaths and allow yourself to be centered back in your navel area.

10) Slowly open your eyes and get up.

NICHOLAS CORRIN, L.Ac.

FLUSHING WITH GOLDEN LIGHT

1) Find a calm, clean and well-ventilated space. Sit on the edge of a stool with your spine erect, chin tucked slightly in. Keep your shoulders relaxed. Relax your entire body.

2) Close your eyes. Now focus on the point between the eyebrows, the 3rd eye. Become conscious of this point.

3) Now think of something pleasant which brings a smile to your face: it could be a dearly loved person, animal, place or memory, or something you love to do. Breathe in the sense of joyfulness.

4) Now, as you inhale deeply, visualize a stream of golden light entering through your 3rd eye point and circling into your brain. As you exhale, see the haze of golden light filter down through your torso, becoming greyer as it descends. As you complete your exhale, watch the now grey, ashen light stream out from the base of your torso, and through your feet almost like ash. Continue a few times until the light stops getting grey and exits still bright and golden. As you gradually cleanse your inner self of toxic negativity, the grey will be flushed out and the golden light will be absorbed.

5) You may now choose to repeat step four with the following areas: Heart, Lungs, Liver, Stomach, Reproductive organs, Bladder, Colon. If not, simply continue on to step 6.

6) Finish by placing your hands over your navel. Breathe slowly down there for two minutes.

7) Gradually open your eyes and greet the light of the room.

ABSORBING EARTH ENERGY

1) *Sit (preferably outside in good weather) on the edge of a stool, bench or large stone.*

2) *Make sure your spine is erect and your thighs are perpendicular to your calves (the knees should form a right-angle).*

3) *Close your eyes and focus on the earth underfoot. Let your energy sink down through your legs and feet, like deep roots penetrating into the earth. Become conscious of two glowing points on the soles of your feet (these points are about 2/3 of the distance from the tip of the heel to the toes). Visualize these points strongly. Now see a cable of energy descending from these points deep into the Earth.*

4) *Now place your arms into an L shape. (Your elbows should form right-angles with the palms facing downward). Visualize glowing points at the center of your palms. See cables of energy descending from these points on your hands deep under the earth.*

5) *Now, breathing slowly and deeply, with each inhale "pull" energy up from under the earth via the cables running into your feet and into your hands. At the culmination of each inhale, collect and concentrate this energy in the center of your lower abdomen, in the area of your energetic womb, the Dan Tian. Also contract the anal sphincter upon inhalation.*

　　　　　　　　　NICHOLAS CORRIN, L.Ac.

6) *Exhale slowly, relaxing the anal sphincter, and mentally watching a glowing ball of energy forming at the center of your Dan Tian.*

7) *Continue the same process in exactly the same sequence.*

8) *When you have finished, slowly open the eyes, greet the day, greet the daylight and the air around you, and slowly stand up and return to your activities.*

NICHOLAS CORRIN, L.Ac.

PART 5

HEALING YOURSELF, HEALING THE WORLD

NICHOLAS CORRIN, L.Ac.

THE HEALING SECRET: BE BOTH DYNAMIC AND CALM

It is necessary to be still, and activity should emerge from this stillness, like the concentric ripples from a stone tossed into a lake. Stillness is that feminine side of power we have already spoken about. That stillness, that receptivity is the only way to stay on course. How can you navigate successfully if you do not know how to negotiate the winds? If you carry too much wind in yourself, too much chaotic activity within, then your power will constantly leak away and eventually you will be blown off course. You may even capsize. However, by abandoning the need to control, you can tap into a deeper instinct, one which aligns us internally with the forces of nature, with the turbulence of life itself, ever changing, ever moving onward. When we become one with it, it can no longer destroy us. Yielding is not a giving in, it is a learning to respond intuitively, to adapt, to become flexible, to conquer through softness.

To be able to grow, to heal yourself, or to be a healing presence in the world, requires two things: inner calm and improved circulation. If you approach life in this way, you will stay focused and clear; you can then begin to take charge of your healing process rather than delegating it to someone else. This in itself is empowering, and therefore will start to bring good energy into your system. What might appear to be hopelessly complicated situations can now be approached with understanding, and therefore with greater confidence.

Inner calm is really equivalent to healthy circulation on a mental and emotional level, while healthy circulation is really equivalent to inner calm on a physical level. They are two sides of the same coin.

We can look at life problems and illness in the same way, using the same terms: any disease can be defined as absence of inner calm and disturbed circulation. Therefore, to restore calm and to harmonize circulation is to heal. Calmness and circulation are the two fundamental factors of health, and their absence is the fundamental basis of disease. Emotional problems destroy inner calm and eventually disrupt the normal, healthy functioning of the body's regulatory systems: respiratory, cardiovascular, muscular-skeletal, immune, lymphatic, urinary etc. Both number one killers of our time, cancer and heart disease, result from internal turmoil at a cellular level and from circulatory impediments where blood and oxygen are not flowing smoothly, or are being directed to the wrong cells to feed tumors instead of healthy tissue.

What is true of us is, of course, also true of nature and the environment. Ecology, as we have seen, is nature's way of preserving its multiple creatures in an interactive, cooperative way, so that all may thrive. In nature, there is a constant circulation of energy and nutrients, within species, between species and between individual members of an ecosystem and the ecosystem itself. The ecosystem preserves the equilibrium that allows life to occur within its parameters. If, for example, we step inside a woodland, we will find birds, insects, trees, mammals, ferns and other plant life, plus microorganisms breaking down dead structures, converting them back into nutrients. There is an amazing hub of activity going on. Yet we also sense a type of impeccable calm, a stillness that we drink in like nectar.

Nature today is not well, and this is the result of human negligence over a long period of time. The state of nature reflects back to us our own inner state as a species. If we

NICHOLAS CORRIN, L.Ac.

look into the problems that we have caused to nature and the environment, we can see very clearly what we have done wrong and what we need to change. Fortunately, nature has tremendous powers of recuperation, often underestimated by us when we see all the damage that has been done with the unleashing of global warming and its concomitant catastrophes. While this disruption of homeostatic harmony within nature is tragically real, and while pollution of air and water, mass extinction of species, disruption of major eco-systems, elimination of old growth forest, de-mineralization of soil and the spread of genetically modified organisms are now facts of life, we need to remind ourselves that nature is more than just what we perceive through the mind and through the senses. There are hidden powers within nature, just as there are within ourselves. Perhaps, with the right kind of focus and dedication, we can harness these types of energies both for our own personal healing and for the survival of planetary life as a whole. It will not be easy, but the possibilities are there. Potentiality, after all, is the bedrock of all that exists. When life force energy is directed purposefully, and with inner calm, then circulation can improve in such a dramatic way as to reverse what seemed irreversible. Imagination is the key, for imagination is our channel into the realms of possibility, the realms we all emerged from.

MIND OVER MATTER

Healing work performed on human beings, and, most specifically, healing through intention gives us hope that we might yet reverse the disastrous condition of the global environment in similar ways. It is worthwhile considering closely what might be involved in this type of healing action, since its application could theoretically be extended to assist in the recuperation and repair of the planet itself. Those of us who have been engaged in energetic healing know that there exist portals through which one can access currents to produce effects that science cannot yet explain. Whether you wish to experience such healing yourself, develop the skills to apply it, or simply wish to participate in transmitting healing vibrations to others and to the planet as a whole, the following few examples will give you some indication of what is, in fact, possible.

The healing described by Greg Braden, author of *The Isaiah Effect*, concerns a completely non-invasive treatment for a woman with cancer. In Braden's example, a woman with bladder cancer receives *Qi-Gong* therapy at Huxia Zhineng Qigong Clinic in Qinhuangdao, China.[76] Dressed in loose clothing, the patient is placed on a bed in the clinic. She lies on her back, face upwards. A nurse practitioner moves an ultrasound wand over the patient's abdomen. The wand is hooked up to a monitor upon which the tumor, approximately three inches in diameter, is clearly visible as a dark mass in the woman's abdomen. Now, three male practitioners stand behind the supine patient. They coordinate their focus to direct healing energy to the patient. Starting softly, but with volume and intensity gradually increasing, the three men repeat over and over in Chinese one single phrase which, roughly translated, means "already gone".[77] In a matter of seconds, the dark shape on the monitor corresponding to the tumor trembles, shrinks and then disappears altogether. The cancerous mass is gone.

This is a clear example of the elimination of a toxic physical structure by the power of directed thought alone. What is particularly interesting about this case is that here we see not just one healer, but three acting in unison. Their concerted energies appear to be more than just three times the power of one. The synergistic aspect of group meditation can greatly amplify effects well beyond the sum of the participants. Although radical healings such as this one are far from common, they do occur with more frequency than one

NICHOLAS CORRIN, L.Ac.

might suppose, and not only with life-threatening conditions. How can we explain this type of "miraculous" healing?

Qi-Gong—or any other effective meditative and spiritual technique to shift energy patterns—works by influencing the subtle, organizing field around a physical structure. Remember that living cells are organized and maintained by energetic fields. We have already referred to these fields as the Energy Body, Light Body or Energy Envelope.

The healer's energy interacts with the patient's field, which contains discordant factors corresponding to the tumor. The coherent energy streaming from the healer re-organizes the patient's field and, indirectly, causes the tumor to dissolve. The rapidity with which this phenomenon occurs in the case presented may appear to be utterly astonishing. However, such things are entirely possible. We need to realize that what we see as physical structures—for example, human cells—are not separate and distinct from the energy that supports them, nor from a kind of intelligence that flows through these fields. Ultimately, the intelligence that flows through all matter is cosmic consciousness, or the mind of God. But human thought, or rather, human awareness, can align itself with these fields and affect material structures accordingly. Such directed thought, or awareness, is power in both its masculine and feminine aspects. The masculine aspect is in the directed intention to heal. The feminine aspect is in the surrender to a higher power and the receptivity to the flow of that higher power. This synthesis of male and female aspects of power is necessary for such types of healing as this to occur.

It is a scientifically accepted fact that waves contain information. Unhealthy tissue emits unhealthy vibrations: waves which communicate the "content" of the state of the disease factor. Because thoughts, feelings and beliefs we hold are also emitted from us as waves corresponding to these mental states, our physical bodies will be the recipients of these waves, and will be modified accordingly—for better, or for worse. The coincidental relationship between cancer and human thought makes it clear that, to a certain statistically verifiable degree, tumors and their deadly effects are controlled by mental processes. For example, several studies have shown that death rates from cancer amongst the mentally ill and the mentally retarded are 25%-50% lower than those of the general population.[78] Clearly, mental normalcy is not an asset with cancer. How is this explicable? Could it be that the fear surrounding cancer—and therefore the medical diagnosis itself—cause a collapse of resistance in the patient, with ensuing fatality? That our culturally manipulated beliefs surrounding this disease, as much as the disease itself, are waylaying the capacities of the patient to fight back?

Typically, both the diagnosis and treatment of cancer (which now affects, at some point in their lives, one in two Americans,) instills tremendous fear in us. Cancer and its representative, the tumor, stand for the enemy within, the traitor, the terrorist, as well as the vicious, well-armed invader with a long trail of death and destruction in his wake, a sort of medical Genghis Khan. The very word cancer has us quivering at the might of the enemy. This, in essence, is the social programming we have absorbed regarding cancer in this society of ours that continues to produce more and more cancer, and that feeds us fear while allowing big business interests and the oncology industry to profit from that fear.[79] What if, by contrast, cancer is treated with love, not fear? Remember that the way we are describing love is not an emotion or merely a warm, consoling and caring human environment. Love is that primal energy and that ineffable, tender intelligence that supports and sustains each cell and component of every existing thing, animate or inanimate. To subscribe to love rather than to fear is to recognize one's essential affinities with everything else that exists in the universe, and also to recognize a compassionate kindness and

NICHOLAS CORRIN, L.Ac.

generosity that streams through life from the cosmos itself. This inner stream can be directed by the human will if we so choose.

If this is so, why do we find it so difficult to align ourselves with this supportive energy? It is because of the way we interpret things. The mind houses the Interpreter and the Interpreter tells us the story of "how it is." This aspect of the psyche cannot surrender its need to retain control—the most it can do is give in to resignation. Resignation in the face of a challenge and surrender to innate intelligence are not the same at all: indeed, they are opposite. One study of immune function in patients facing a life threatening disease (macrocytic hypochronic anemia) found that patients could be separated into three personality types based on analysis of their attitude to the disease and also their blood chemistry, which showed a correlation with attitude.[80] The three basic types are:

1) Resignation.
2) Non-directed struggle.
3) Purposeful action.

The first group became passive and non-combatant versus their disease. The second group became agitated. The third group took a focused response, marshalling their inner resources and aiming to prevail. Blood chemistry panels of all three groups show a much stronger immune response in the third group, with higher levels of white blood cells. Thus, a coherent, positive attitude from the mind can be mirrored at a cellular level, with the immune system reflecting the "mental structure" of the mind. How we choose to feel and what we choose to believe can significantly affect survival rates via its influence upon the immune system. This phenomenon is not restricted to disease, but applies to the whole of life. How we choose to interpret things, and, therefore, how we act as a consequence, is crucial in determining what will befall us. Fate is not something imposed on us like an iron glove. While there undoubtedly are exterior forces that threaten our well-being, we also have internal access to higher energies, if only we make ourselves receptive to them.

The extraordinary potential of focused positive thinking can be illustrated by the following two examples of spontaneous remission from "incurable" illness. In 1952, Dr. Robert Mason, an English physician used hypnosis to treat what he thought were warts on the skin of an adolescent boy. [81] The hypnosis was successful: during the first session, Mason concentrated on one arm, which recovered a normal, healthy looking skin. However, when Mason brought the boy to be seen by the referring surgeon, the surgeon told Mason that the boy was suffering, not from warts, but from congenital ichthyosis which is a deadly genetic anomaly, usually fatal. Mason went on to successfully heal the rest of the boy's skin. Thus, using hypnosis alone, the physician had successfully treated what had, up to that point, been considered an incurable, fatal disease. However, Mason was never able to replicate these results with other ichthyosis patients. Why was this so? The problem lay in Mason's own inability to truly believe in what he was doing. He lacked the faith to support his own work. Whilst, at the beginning, he thought he was applying hypnosis to a simple case of warts, his mind did not interfere with what he was doing. But later on, some deep skepticism from within his interpretive mind "scrambled" the information he was emitting to his patients, rendering his therapies useless. Without deep belief, good intentions are not enough. Belief itself is the "make-or-break-factor", not just in healing but in life, and what we allow into it. Allowing something to happen is an ancient form of wisdom, and one that eludes most of us as we block it off from within.

The second example concerns a patient in the last stages of lung cancer. [82] A man by the name of Wright, whilst

NICHOLAS CORRIN, L.Ac.

awaiting his end in a hospital, hears talk about a new wonder drug, Krebiozen, that is being tested on patients in his ward. He asks to be a recipient of the drug, but is turned down by the selection committee who consider him too close to death to be worth including. But Wright begs to be given a chance, the doctors relent, and Wright apparently receives an injection of the experimental medication. What Wright is not told, however, is that the injections contain merely placebo. Not wishing to squander this expensive new wonderdrug on a hopeless, terminal patient, the docs give him sugared water instead. In a matter of days, he is restored to full health, the multiple tumors dissolving away, "like snowballs on a hot stove." Meanwhile, none of the other less terminal patients who have received the real drug have shown any benefits whatsoever. Wright leaves the hospital and returns to normal health for two months. However, he eventually reads reports in the media questioning the efficacy of Krebiozen. This skepticism triggers a return of his illness, and the tumors reappear. Back in a hospital, the doctors tell Wright they are going to administer a new, far superior drug which has since become available. In reality, they inject him, once again, with a placebo of sugared water. As before, the tumors dissolve away like melting snow, and the patient returns to normal life. And then the same negative information comes his way a second time: after two months of vibrant health, he reads a report put out by the American Medical Association which describes Krebiozen as a "worthless drug in the treatment of cancer." Two days after reading this report, Wright is dead.

The case of Wright highlights the power of belief—both positive and negative—in influencing disease. The so-called placebo effect is typically disregarded as a trivial phenomenon by mainstream medicine. But the fact is that around 30% of patients in trials improve in double blind studies regardless of whether they have received a placebo or an actual drug.

It is indeed questionable whether many of the benefits associated with medications are in fact not due to the patients' belief in the medicine rather than to the chemical actions of the medicine itself. And again, we must apply this same principle beyond the field of health and illness. We must extend it to life: if we wish to receive the life we want, rather than to feel punished by disappointments and disillusionment, it is vital that we have some equivalent to the placebo effect. That is, we must be able to tap into some positive, non-conscious faith that life is supporting us rather than working against us. On that note, in studies by Larry LeShan on which attitude of mind will positively reinforce an individual's chance of survival by revitalizing the body and the immune system, LeShan concludes that it is the strong desire of the patient to "sing the unique song of his own personality".[83] By contrast, the fear of dying or the selfless urge to survive so as to be able to care for others do not produce the same responses from within the body that can lead to healing.

This last point is very interesting and important. It seems to indicate that only by embracing ourselves can we stimulate the body to shrug off disease. Altruistic intentions do not help the body when its survival is under threat from within. Could it be that life threatening disease often originates in a neglect of self at some basic level? And again, what is true in medicine surely is also true in life as a whole. To marshal the inner resources to break free from unhappy, confining circumstances in life, it is equally necessary to reclaim the right to "sing one's own song." Things go wrong for us when we deny our individual nature, and therefore our sense of purpose in being here. Our reason to be here is, after all, to be ourselves. Removal of the traumas and blockages that disturb this "being oneself" can be a real task. But it is this very task which gives meaning to our lives, and which can lead us into an ever deeper relationship with life itself.

NICHOLAS CORRIN, L.Ac.

MAKING YOUR MIND
LIKE A LASER

In the state of letting go, we can access power by becoming one with that power—precisely because we have ceased to struggle internally, we no longer impose ourselves as the source of that power. In Yoga, this is known as nirodha, a state of non-distraction, a state of zero disturbance. In Buddhism and Zen, this is known as becoming empty, or as No Mind, or as Original Mind. But it is not emptiness in a conventional sense at all. It simply means that all filters, all blockages have been removed.

If we enter a state like this, the life current will run through us in ways we cannot possibly comprehend rationally. In higher states, all sense of a separate self will disappear. However, even when this does not occur, the feeling of what one is changes from something narrow and sharp to something cloudlike.

It must be stressed, however, that this is not what is popularly understood as going with the flow. "Dead fish", a wise Irishman once pointed out, "go with the flow." Letting go is not becoming passive, it is raising awareness so as to allow something greater to unfold.

We can, in such a state, use the mind in a highly directed way, rather like a laser. Once the intention in your mind has been linked up with a deeper sense of what is real, and in some fundamental way, with what is right, then the mind can generate a stream of light from its thinking center. In essence, the pineal gland, which lies at the center of the brain's structure, will become internally activated, and a bio-photonic stream will be directed outwardly into space. Such a stream is, literally, a light stream generated out of your own brain and out of your own consciousness. As the atoms of the pineal gland become excited through focused attention, they emit photons outwardly from the third eye, which is the non-physical structure through which they spiral outwards towards their target. This was what occurred in the Chinese healing we have described earlier. Such an activation of the pineal gland is within reach of everybody, although it does require practice, and spiritual development.

We can compare such a use of the mind and of intention to a laser beam. A laser beam is made up of what are called coherent rays of light. The means that the light waves stay in sync as they travel, maintaining a parallel relationship in space. Ordinary light is incoherent: the crests of the light waves do not stay parallel, they diverge from each other. Daylight is incoherent, as is the light emitted by a normal, incandescent bulb; which is to say that lightwaves are dispersed in many directions.

LASER BEAMS: COHERENT LIGHT versus NON-COHERENT LIGHT

A good way to get a better sense of coherent rays of light is to form a mental image of five fighter jets. Imagine a group of five fighter jets streaming through the sky at high speed. Now imagine them swerving to the west, perfectly in sync, then swerving in the other direction, in impeccable unison. Such is laser light. This unison gives laser its tremendous power. Hot lasers are used to cut or cauterize, and have applications in industry, printing and surgery. Cold lasers are used in what is known as photobiostimulation.[84] This is an alternative medical procedure to restore damaged cells by stimulating cellular metabolism with light. If lasers, which are coherent rays of light directed in specific ways, can be used to these effects, just think what you might be able to

NICHOLAS CORRIN, L.Ac.

achieve if you made your mind like a laser!

In fact, using the mind like a laser is really an ancient idea. Techniques to use the mind this way are basic to yogic practices which stretch back some ten thousand years. In yogic theory, the everyday mind is made up of non-coherent waves, called *vrittis*. This non-coherence of our thoughts and emotions keeps most of us in a state of confusion and ignorance, unable to access our higher potentials. We react to external stimuli without much self-control. These external stimuli push our buttons in positive or negative ways, generating reactive emotions of craving, hatred, envy, disgust, anger, jealousy, bitterness, revenge, shame, boredom and so on, plus the thoughts and beliefs produced by such emotions. Yoga calls this typical human condition the state of distraction. The principal goal of yoga is not to bend the body into strange poses, it is to move our internal state from distraction into clarity. Clarity is a condition of inner light, and this requires the ability to focus the mind like a laser.

THE MAGNETIC POWER OF FOCUSED THOUGHT

Light can be produced from electricity, as we know. But we ourselves are electric. Electricity is not something that can only be derived from an exterior source such as an outlet or a battery. A human being—indeed, any living thing —is intrinsically electric, which is to say that it produces its own electrical charges. In our case, this is made obvious by EKGs and EEGs. Electricity is not only the product of mechanical processes, it is also the product of biological processes. Living matter has a kind of bio-electrical current running through it. Indeed, without this current, it would fall apart; it would immediately become entropic.

Electricity is also the product of mental processes: when

we think (when we have a "brainwave"), we often have a "flash" of inspiration. And this electrical nature of thought is well depicted in the proverbial light bulb going off. Somehow we have always understood that a bright idea equates with a surge of current in the brain: the brain is lit up by the power of inspired thought. What we do not generally acknowledge is that the light generated in and by the brain can stream outward, laser-like, in a focused beam of intention. By means of this beam, we can emit the image of what we seek, deep in our hearts. Once this image has been emitted with clarity and power, it will draw to it a corresponding response. Such a response occurs through the phenomenon of magnetism interacting with that plenum of possibilities, the zero-point field. This zero-point field, as we have already mentioned in a previous chapter, is the vibratory fullness hidden within what appears outwardly to be a featureless void of empty space.

It is a well accepted fact that wherever there is a magnetic field, an electrical potential will be generated, and vice versa. The electrical potential, or current, is aroused at a right angle to the flux direction of the magnetic field. In other words, electricity and magnetism have a symbiotic relationship where one is perpendicularly situated to the other's vector. This is known as the right hand rule of electrical induction.

If we apply this electromagnetic understanding to human beings, we can develop a corresponding model of how thought—specifically, waves of intention—reverberate outwards into the world, generating magnetic fields or as some people would call them, "attractor fields".[85] The brain is an electrically charged organ composed of neurons which deliver an action potential down the axon. Once it reaches the synaptic cleft, this "electricity" is transmitted to an adjacent neuron via synaptic neurochemicals. When we have thoughts and emotions, neurons convey electrical impulses through

NICHOLAS CORRIN, L.Ac.

various pathways within the brain's internal structures. Neurochemicals are secreted which correspond on a physical level to these transitory thoughts and feelings. Until quite recently, it was believed that such chemical events took place only within the brain itself. But less than twenty years ago, Candace Pert discovered that the very same neuro-chemicals found within the brain are also secreted from endocrine glands, from nerve plexuses and from immune cells distributed throughout the entire body: these protein components are today known as neuropeptides.[86] In fact, it became clear, as a result of Pert's research, that the central nervous system, the immune system and the endocrine system all communicate with each other by means of a common language, the language of neuropeptides, which Dr. Pert calls "molecules of emotion."

The timed secretion of neuropeptides throughout the body and the looped, repetitive pathways and junctions between neurons correspond, on a physical level, to the undercurrent of thoughts and emotions that we carry around daily as our unspoken beliefs. In a word, these are our fundamental attitudes about life and our place within it. They correspond to the programmed state of our inner consciousness, a state that lies below the threshold of normal awareness and is normally very difficult to observe, let alone to transform. However, it becomes less difficult if we allow that we are electromagnetic creatures in an electromagnetic world. If we refer to this electromagnetic model of the human being and its relationship with surrounding space, and if we concentrate our awareness on light as our fundamental essence, then we can begin to shift our inner programming and, simultaneously, to transform our outer conditions.

We have already referred to the pineal gland. The pineal is a tiny ductless gland situated in the central region of the brain, so called because of its similarity in size to a pine nut. In fact, its minute size belies its tremendous importance as a storehouse of coded information. The Mystery Schools of antiquity regarded the pineal as the repository of higher knowledge, a kind of super-compressed component able to link us up to higher dimensions of understanding. On a physiological level, the pineal is starting to be recognized as a vital part of the endocrine system, perhaps displacing the pituitary as the "master gland" of this system. It is highly responsive to light, and it supplies us with the hormone melatonin, without which we would not be able to sleep.

Close by the pineal is the ethmoid bone, one of the inner bones of the skull. The ethmoid bone contains within it small quantities of magnetite. Magnetite is a naturally occurring mineral that has magnetic qualities. When a substance responds to a magnetic influence without itself being fully transformed into a magnet, that substance is called paramagnetic. In fact the very clay of the earth is paramagnetic, as are we ourselves: our paramagnetic nature causes us to be held in the earth's magnetic field, and constantly nourished by it. The earth's magnetic flux streams from south to north, passing through our nervous systems, affecting our blood, autonomic nervous system and brain.

Magnetite is found in relatively high quantities in the skullbones of migratory birds. Since such birds have an uncanny ability to navigate their way through vast, forbidding distances, we can reasonably conclude that magnetite is an important part of their navigational equipment, for it appears to facilitate their orientation in space. Via the earth's magnetic field, migratory birds are able to orient their trajectory to very distant destinations, many thousands of miles away. In such a way, the seemingly impossible occurs: groups of tiny creatures find their way unerringly across endless deserts of sky, soaring over what is often inhospitable terrain, but driven on by some absolute sense of trust in the accuracy of their venture. Where could we possibly find a better metaphor for the fusion of risk and trust than migratory birds, with their

NICHOLAS CORRIN, L.Ac.

inner storehouse of magnetite?

We could also suggest that the very destinations of the birds call out to them through the language of magnetism, that silent language of the earth and of the air. The place towards which the birds are drawn on their epic journeys is the attractor field acting on the birds from a distance. In a sense, their futures call them forward: their place, not just within the spatial realm, but also within time, within the cycle of the seasons. It is the unfolding of their own futures that magnetizes them, pulling them onward across many thousands of miles. Not all of them will make it. But those that do offer us human beings a poetic metaphor for hope, for courage and for pushing the boundaries of what was heretofore considered impossible.

Think for a second of yourself as a migratory bird. Picture too, thousands of years of human migrations; for millennia, much of humanity has been nomadic, or semi-nomadic, moving into unknown territory as they sought out new places to live, new challenges bringing fresh experience. Evolution itself is nomadic, ever moving forward, ever vacating what has been, and where. The pull of the future is the pull of the unknown; it is the magnetic pull of life itself. And it is this magnetism of the future that gives life to the present moment, and activates it internally. Actually, there is no real divide between future and present so long as we allow our future to move fluidly within the present. This is the real meaning of what has sometimes been called "the Now."

If we strongly activate the bio-electrical power within our own brains, we are bound to generate a magnetic field at right angles to the vector of our intention. So, if we hold within us a clear image of what we seek to experience, or to attain, such situations will automatically be drawn towards us. What we seek will seek us out, like an echo seeking the source of its sound; like a reflection seeking the original image. The surrounding matrix will have been stirred up and a corresponding response will be initiated. In this way, we participate in creating our own reality, for better or for worse. For, depending on what we actively seek, or actively deny, so will our returns be.

Why are some people winners and others losers? Why do some people accrue great wealth and others poverty? Why do some generate precious circles of friendship and love, while others, though outwardly successful, never succeed in bridging the terrifying gap between human hearts? Much of this has to do with things sought after strongly within the inner person. What is sought after in this way sends out a resonant image, and this image draws to it magnetically a corresponding response.

It is interesting to observe how single-minded people are often able to realize their objectives. Is this simply because they are very focused and strong-willed? No, it is more than that. It is because of the electromagnetic nature of intention. When we focus on an object of desire to such an extent that we, in a sense, lose ourselves in its pursuit, then we have sent out a laser-like beam that transmits the image of our intention. Since this image has been made by our own consciousness, within our own dreaming faculty, the more strongly we invest it with emotion (with desire and with conviction,) the more powerfully it will be projected on to the screen of the world "out there." And this "out there" is really not distinct or separate from what is "in here." They are co-extensive. They form a continuous part of the all-enveloping matrix, the zero-point field.

In your head, you hold the capacity to form images. When you dream, or daydream, light is generated internally. This light, this electricity within the brain, allows you to see your own reality, even with eyes closed, even when fast asleep in the dead of night. Now, consider your head as though it were a giant movie projector. Imagine the visual contents of your desires, of your deep, heart-felt intentions, to be pro-

NICHOLAS CORRIN, L.Ac.

jected strongly outward on to the screen of the "out there", the screen of space-time. The stronger and brighter the light stream of intention is generated from within the mind, the greater its action potential. The greater the current that is beamed outward, the more powerful the magnetic field that will automatically build at right angles to this current. In this way, intention, when properly and powerfully directed, is always magnetic.

At this point, we should remember that magnetic fields are capable of re-shaping physical structures. Along with vertical, spiraling movements and pyramidal forms, magnetic fields can alter the properties of matter, most particularly by affecting the hydrogen bonds within water molecules. As hydrogen is the primary element of the periodic table, and the most common element in the universe, it is no great stretch to imagine magnetic fields affecting the very structures of what we call physical reality. What if the magnetic force of intention and focused desire were able to affect the "structure" of those intangible fields that subtend the visible, physical fields, drawing up out of them the very images that we carry in our own imaginations? We have already seen, in the dramatic healings described above, how the magnetic force of the imagination can melt tumors "like snowballs on a hot stove."

Put simply, the magnetic field of the earth is essential for all life since it interacts with the bio-electrical currents without which no organism can survive. Because evolution has endowed human beings with powerful brains with inbuilt capacities for shaping consciousness, our very thoughts and intentions can interact with the zero-point field (the all-enveloping plenum) via interaction with the earth's magnetic field. In such a way can we participate in creating our own destinies.

There is, however, a caveat. In order for us to be able to magnetically influence the field so as to draw to us the events that we desire, we must cultivate self-awareness. Otherwise we will only succeed in manifesting the contents of our own unconscious, which may be very damaging for us. We will inevitably draw to us what we unconsciously believe to be real, true, or inevitable. Perhaps, beneath our advocacy of free will, we secretly believe in fate. Or perhaps, beneath our optimistic exterior, we harbor dark needs to punish ourselves, or to see ourselves fail. Or again, perhaps despite our nice words about justice and equality, deep inside, we mostly seek power over others, not intimacy and mutual respect. We may be filled up with complex or contradictory feelings, all of which will "blur" the image we are trying to put out. In the end, our projected image may be so grainy and indistinct that almost no magnetic field effect is generated. Or what we draw to us may be a "mirror-image" of our own confusion and indecisiveness. Only by clarifying our own hearts can we hope to activate the magnetic effect successfully.

TO PRAY OR TO MEDITATE?

But wait—are we talking here about prayer or about meditation? Both—and neither.

Usually, prayer is thought of as an asking for something which is lacking. And usually, meditation is thought of as becoming very still, observing one's thoughts and perhaps receiving some flash of insight or deepened perspective. Prayer is typically thought of in the active voice, and meditation in the passive voice. But what we are talking about here is in between: it is the third voice, neither active nor passive, but in between.

It is, as we have seen, the third voice, somewhere in between active and passive, that allows the red hawk to master the winds, and the trout to remain perfectly still in rushing waters. The third voice, this active-passive way of being, is

NICHOLAS CORRIN, L.Ac.

what enables us to be one with the flow yet at the same time to master it and draw from it what we need. It is the feminine side of power giving birth to the masculine side. It is strength drawn from submission, and invention drawn from attention.

In *The Isaiah Effect*, author Gregg Braden recounts his exploration into what he calls the "lost mode of prayer." He traces this mode back at least as far as the Essene communities of the Holy Land, and notes their profound influence on the Buddhist monasteries of Tibet. [87] What is this lost mode of prayer, that Braden calls the "missing key?" It is when "we focus upon the feeling of our heart's desire, rather than the thought of our knowing world." So it is not an idea in our heads that we must project, asking for its manifestation. It is a feeling of conviction vibrating strongly in our hearts of this desired image already being there—of its already happening.

We must feel that what we deeply desire and hold in our imagination is real and actual. It must not be hypothetical and set in the future. In the imagination, it must already be experienced as a reality. Then, a seed will start to germinate in the zero-point field. Body, heart and mind must be in alignment for this to happen: there can be no cracks if we wish to be successful. Our prayer-meditation must be engaged in by our whole being: physical, emotional and mental. This generates a vibratory signature which must draw to it a response from the field of reality "out there." In this way, the "out there" will be shaped by the "in here."

Braden's real awakening to this possibility occurred when a native American friend of his took him along to a solitary prayer ceremony he was conducting out in the hills of northern New Mexico, in a wild spot covered with juniper, sage and pinon. At that time the land was (as it is again today) in the grip of drought. David, Braden's friend, had gone there to pray for rain. There was a stone circle already laid out in that light filled yet desolate landscape. David removed his shoes and walked in silence about the stone medicine wheel. After a very short time, perhaps a few brief minutes, he returned to tell Braden the work was done. What, already? Later that evening, clouds broke, the weather shifted and by the next day, children were playing in the mud.

What had David done? It is what he had not done that is crucial. He had not prayed for rain. "When I was young, our elders passed on to me the secret of prayer. The secret is that when we ask for something, we acknowledge what we do not have. Continuing to ask only gives power to what has never come to pass." Instead, David expressed gratitude from within his heart to the desert, the wind, the heat and even to the drought, acknowledging their existence. Next he imagined, fully and exuberantly, rain. He felt it, he smelled it, he splashed around in it. And it came to him, as bidden.

"We must first have the feelings of what we wish to experience...creation is already complete. Our prayer becomes a prayer of thanks for the opportunity to choose which creation we experience." In the plenum of the zero-point field, everything is already there. The heart, like a fisherman, can draw out of this ocean the part of reality it imagines.

IMAGINATION + BELIEF + GRATITUDE = ACTIVATION = MANIFESTATION

The imagination is not fantasy, it is the interface between us and the elusive forces that govern reality. Imagination, when used in this way, becomes the third voice between prayer and meditation. But imagination, if it is to have the power to bring something to life, must be fully lived by the one imagining. "Unless you yourself enter the image and think from it, it is incapable of birth".[88] Thus, the imagination is also like a river, and we must be ready to plunge into it, to risk ourselves in it, to become one with it, to lose ourselves utterly in it so that the object of our inner focus can be activated. In the heart, we can desire from a place of wisdom, not mere self-seeking. When we imagine the best for ourselves, we simultaneously imagine the best for the world.

THIS DREAMING WORLD

I am sure that most people have had experiences where an image clearly popped into their heads and later emerged into "reality." A very common example of this is thinking of somebody and, a short time later, the phone rings and guess who it is? If you search inside yourself, you will find puzzling moments when there appears to have been a direct link between a thought or dream image and something actually happening.

This strange "interference factor" between mental image and external reality first occurred to me clearly in my early twenties. Once again, it was an occasion where I had lost something! My girlfriend and I had been for a beer at a city bar in Manchester, my hometown in England. After leaving the pub, we walked across town, enjoying the balmy summer air. Eventually, we decided to wait at a bus stop to catch the number 42 bus home. About an hour had already passed since we had left the pub. I suddenly realized that my wallet was no longer in my jacket pocket, where it was supposed to be. It was a black, leather wallet that my father had brought back from a trip to Sweden and given to me some years earlier. I was very attached to it. On top of this, it had cash inside it.

With a feeling of complete serenity, a precise visual image now formed itself in my mind, rather like a movie still projected on to a screen. I saw the wallet lying on top of the upholstered bench of the pub, lying at a 45 degree angle to the back of the bench. I saw a thronged mass of people seated around it, drinking. And I "saw" with complete inner certitude that the wallet had remained "unseen" by all those people, as though it were protected by a veil of invisibility.

How did I know this? I cannot say. Even to this day I cannot account for such things. All I can say is that I saw this and there was not a shadow of doubt in my mind. And after I had walked across town to the crowded pub, with all sorts of people milling around inside it—the last place on earth you would want to leave a wallet stuffed with cash—there it was, precisely as I had seen it in my mind's eye.

There is another story attached to this same wallet, and it occurred about three months before this one. My friend and I had taken a train across Europe from London, in order to spend Easter in Italy. It was cold and grey when we got off the train in Turin. We checked into a hotel, did a little sight-seeing, and then strolled down to the river bank for some quiet moments of contemplation. The slow waters of the Po drifted lazily by, as though still in a kind of wintry torpor. The broad expanse of surface water was silver-brown, a mix of copper and earth with nickel highlights. I rested my el-bows on the stone balustrade and, like a gargoyle with my chin propped in my cupped hands, gazed out over the slow, somnambulant waters.

I cannot say how long I must have fallen asleep—for seconds, minutes or... years? For someone who never ever, at that time in my life, slept during daylight, strangely, not only had I drifted off, but I had done so standing up out-side, looking at a river. When I came to, I automatically put my hand in my right pocket and pulled out my black wallet from Sweden. It was empty. I looked again, not believing my eyes: completely empty. I was wearing an anorak with deep, button-clip pockets, and, during my mysterious slumber, somebody must have opened the clip, pulled out my wal-let, removed all the cash from inside, replaced the emptied wallet back inside my pocket, clipped the pocket shut, and disappeared. All this in the space of how many seconds?

I had been foolish enough not to convert any of this cash into travelers checks and, this being a time before credit

NICHOLAS CORRIN, L.Ac.

cards were common, all the money for the trip was gone. Yet I felt that something was being communicated to me, something it might take me many years to fully figure out. Dream and waking reality were not anywhere as distinct as we believed them to be. Instead, they fused, or overlapped. The dream entered the waking world and vice versa. Where was consciousness in all this, and where was the currency of "truth", as represented by the banknotes in my wallet? Anybody's guess. Everything was uncertain, everything was open to question.

Yet there were images and there were powers associated with those images: the river, the wintry light, the black wallet. Perhaps, in another mind, another strand of consciousness, my presence overlooking the river Po had been foreseen, had been dreamed up even. Perhaps the whole incident had unraveled with the same dream like calm and inevitability with which, three months later, I was to recover the selfsame wallet, with all its contents intact.

Though we tend to see ourselves as independent actors on a stage, it is only the entire play that carries meaning, not any particular role taken separately. When we accept that we are just a part of the play, we earn the right to improvise. Otherwise, if we take ourselves too seriously, we get condemned to scripts; and our lives become determined. Whatever is pre-determined is hopeless. To have hope, it is necessary to be able to dream. To follow your dreams is the best way of entering the currents of the dreaming world. Follow your dreams and allow the world to dream itself into being through you. Pursue your own experiences, deeply and passionately sought after, but never forget that you are but one member of a great family of dreamers: clouds, mountains, rivers, plants, animals and people, each projecting their innermost desires on to the screen of the swirling, ineffable void.

POWER THROUGH CONNECTION

The matrix is the mother element, or unifying field, which connects us to each other and to the whole of nature, indeed to all that exists. The matrix—what some call the zero point field—provides a continuum linking everything with everything. And this continuum can be influenced by conscious thought.

We have been exploring the power of thought when highly focused, charged with feeling and particularly when projected outward as an image. This has been referred to as the lost mode of prayer, or as magnetized intention, or simply as awakened potential. Larry Dossey, MD, has spoken and written at length about the use of prayer in medicine today, citing examples of studies conducted at university hospitals where patients have objectively improved after being prayed for at a distance—regardless of the religion, belief system or particular way of praying that the praying participant had. It seemed that the healing benefits transcended any cultural or religious differences.

The fact is that thought is a kind of "substance" which we emit. It is a particular vibratory frequency which can affect other bodies, whether human or inanimate, to greater or lesser extents, via the enveloping matrix in which we all co-exist. Thought, when emitted, disturbs or excites the matrix in such a way that it passes this on to the recipient. Most often, the effects may be too minute or subtle to be noticed. However, when a strong charge of loving intention is built up and projected to the recipient, these effects may be of a far greater magnitude.

Nonetheless, we are dealing here with a double-edged sword. Ill effects can be projected outward as much as good

NICHOLAS CORRIN, L.Ac.

effects. If you carry negativity in your heart, you may be projecting that outward and affecting someone so as to cause damage, even though this may be subtle. And that person whom you are damaging may very well be yourself: if you are emitting a broadcast from the mind which has a high content of anger, vindictiveness, despair or resignation, you may well be pulling back towards your life effects in sync with these broadcasts from your unconscious mind. So it is vital to know yourself well, and to clear yourself of such negativity, otherwise you will, like a magnet, draw to you those very types of events you fear and reject, events which nonetheless resonate with the inner currents of your thinking. This book has been designed to help you break free from such negativity, not by reducing life to some simplistic moral play where good is good and bad is bad and never the twain shall meet. Rather by embracing love as the fundamental energy that brings freedom to the individual, and does so through giving and surrendering the need to control.

The Maharishi Effect is one of the best known examples of focused prayer-meditation producing demonstrable effects: it is another illustration of the third voice we have previously spoken about. In 1972, studies conducted by researchers in twenty-four US cities showed conclusively that crime and violence invariably dropped when as little as one percent of the population engaged in some form of meditation.[89] Further studies followed in Israel, the Phillipines, India and again in the U.S., with data showing analogous results: where there was a certain small percentage of the population regularly engaged in meditation, crime, fire outbreaks and accidents all decreased in the cities studied.

Between 1984 and 1987, a study encompassing millions of meditators at 18 peace meditations was coordinated by Buryl Payne, who found that solar activity was directly affected by the meditative energy. On the day following the peace meditation, solar flares would decrease by "about 30 percent." [90] Payne's study was undertaken as a follow up to previous research by Professor Raymond Wheeler of the University of Kansas. Wheeler had proposed that if we map out the time line of our collective history, we find that "wars occur in cycles of 11 years" and that they "have done so for over 2,500 years, matching in nearly perfect step the cycle of sunspot activity." Payne adds that Wheeler's study was confirmed by Edward Dewey, Director of the Foundation for the Study of Cycles, "who considered it the most important discovery of his life." [91] International battles and warfare normally increase about two years before or one year after the peak in solar cycle activity. The last was estimated to be in 2000, one year before the terrible events of September 2001, which catapulted us into the wars in Afghanistan and then Iraq, the doctrine of pre-emptive war, and the escalating violence all over the world. As we approach 2013, we are entering another cyclical peak.

Crimes, domestic violence, psychotic behavior and war can all be correlated with lunar and solar activity, and with fluctuations in the Earth's magnetic field. The earth's field fluctuations strongly affect us both physically and mentally, as they disturb balances delicately held in body chemistry, unleashing virus growth or metabolic and bio-chemical disturbances with their consequent effects on behavior But if this is so, it is surely a two way street: whatever affects us can also be affected by us. If solar turmoil stimulates human turmoil, then human equanimity can calm down the sun. If there is a unity to everything, then we have the capability to affect it directly by the thoughts and feelings we hold in our hearts and minds. Such things as weather patterns are not as independent of us as we modern, "scientific" people believe. And certainly, the human body—whether our own or someone else's—can be the beneficiary of our healing intentions if that is what we hold in our heart.

In *Power versus Force*, Dr. David Hawkins proposes that

NICHOLAS CORRIN, L.Ac.

there exists a counterbalancing system on the level of the field, whereby different levels of human consciousness interact and counterbalance one another. Hawkins believes that the majority (85 percent of the world's population) is operating at a very low level of consciousness, one easily prone to hatred and to violence, but that relatively small numbers of people who resonate at higher levels have the effect of counterbalancing the downward pull of this mass, despite their inferiority in numbers.[92] Hawkins, who maintains that these findings can be validated through kinesiology, asserts that a loving thought is incommensurably more powerful than a fearful one and that, "even a few loving thoughts during the course of the day more than counterbalance all of our negative thoughts."

If this is so, then it only confirms what has always been said by the wise. Living from the heart offers the only sure path that can guide us through reality. Or, as the Dalai Lama has said, "My religion is kindness."

TAPPING INTO SERENITY

Life is never calm for very long because the life-force itself is a kind of storm. If we look at satellite photographs of hurricane systems, we find spiral forms reminiscent of those spirals exhibited by young nebulae in outer galaxies. The spiral is life itself, emerging out of the blackness. Life is a whirlwind, and it is no accident that it is from such a wind that God speaks to Job in what is possibly the oldest book in the Bible.

The eye in the storm, that stillpoint, is also the gaze of Shiva in Vedic and Hindu tradition. With slightly lowered lids, and gentle smile, Shiva's gaze becomes the contemplation of the Buddha, ever compassionate.

Life and death, interminably entangled, promote a spin of appearances and disappearances, ecstasy and devastation.

But not what we would call justice, in human terms, nor security. And certainly not serenity. Where, then, might we look for serenity?

Serenity is ever present and available to us, but at a different level of experience than daily life. We cannot expect ourselves to lead lives of utter calm, nor to be untroubled by the state of the world, nor by our own sometimes desperate lives, rattled by pain and perceived tragedies and beset by fears and inner demons. Yet serenity is there.

Serenity is there just as the blue sky is always there, behind the overcast blanket of cloud. It spreads above us even at night, behind the veil of darkness, awaiting its own return. That blue expanse is always there for our spirits to enter, even when storms rage about us, and when heavy rains turn the roads to mud. One level of life is always giving birth and always dying. Another level, watching over this one perhaps, spreads to blue infinity. It is from this blue eye in the limitless void that the storms spin outward, like Catherine wheels shedding sparks with all the brilliance and transience of individual existence.

NICHOLAS CORRIN, L.Ac.

FINAL THOUGHTS

The stereotypical human of today is a sedentary being, glued to a computer terminal or a cell phone. This person seems to have lost an enormous amount of instinctual wisdom, a loss consistent with becoming fundamentally disconnected from their own body. Is she, is he, happy? It appears not, if happiness is indeed more than mere fun or entertainment. Despite an ever growing dependency on external gadgets and pharmaceutical stimulants, this contemporary being seems beset with feelings of impotence, anxiety and growing impatience. Where is the relaxed sense of purpose and meaningfulness without which human dignity withers like a severed twig dropped on to concrete?

The alter ego of today's well put together urban human is actually a drifter: half crazed on cheap liquor and drugs, he stumbles, red faced and teetering through lines of oncoming traffic, no longer sure who he is or why the sun rises and sets each day. Bearing no sense of genuine independence, most humans have forgotten what it means to be a sovereign being anchored in the vast expanses and freedom of the limitless skies, the guardian mountain ranges, or what was once an all but impenetrable and deeply sonorous tapestry of woodland. Especially over the past two centuries, we have forfeited our ancestral relationship with nature, increasingly sucked into the predatory vortex of a post-industrial machine whose owners, the super-affluent elite, continue to squeeze out every last drop of life's riches for themselves. There is now a gnawing sense of disquiet and foreboding, as though something is deeply wrong, broken, warped.

The rupture with nature and the debasement of human freedom and dignity has been accentuated by political and financial interests which seem to have no other goal than to further their own gross appetites for control and manipulation. An aura of imminent collapse hangs over the quotidian world like a chemical haze. Once stable nations with their busted economies now descend a dark spiral towards geopolitical conflict, increased surveillance of citizens and further erosion of constitutional freedoms.

The times in which we live, some have suggested, represent an Age of Turmoil, a far cry from that edenic shift in consciousness fantasized by sentimental New Age apologists. Yet this turmoil is no doubt an essential chrysalis phase if old, toxic patterns are to be broken down and reconfigured into new ways of living, new ways of doing business, less parasitical forms of body politic, and healthier people abiding on a healthier planet. The status quo, now revealing itself to be inimical to both democracy and human survival itself, is dragging us into an epoch of turbulence. We may indeed be entering a blizzard of perfect storms, financial, environmental, cultural and biological. Surviving these winds of change, let alone becoming stronger, perhaps even happier, requires a fundamental change in our outlook and our behavior. Certainly there have been multiple times in our collective past when humans, like other animals, have been required to adapt to violent changes in their immediate or global environments. Adaptability, flexibility and courage have always been key assets, but in times of turmoil, they become priceless attributes.

What modes of behavior, what types of outlook can best serve us in periods of unraveling and conflict? If the artificially contrived, protective sheaths malfunction, we suddenly must face the world with greater vulnerability but also with greater immediacy. The vulnerability stems from a heightened sense of our animal physicality. Made of flesh,

NICHOLAS CORRIN, L.Ac.

blood and bone, our physical bodies become more vividly present to us when the computer generated world fails to flicker obsessively away on plasma screens and mobile devices. We have taken the dependability of these devices for granted. But solar storms may wipe out satellite functioning for extended periods of time. Gnawing hunger or cold may become more constant companions, like in the Depression of the 1930's. Environmental disasters of many sorts appear to be stacking up at the doorway. No longer can we take anything for granted.

Yet all this fracturing and possible loss also presents itself to us as a great opening. How much of what we have clung on to, how much of what we have been sold, of what we have bought or bought into, really has served us? Is there perhaps a lighter, cleaner, even a more delightful way of living? And what would that entail?

As presented in this book, letting go is not so much an action as a state of being that brings us closer to the environing natural realm and to our half-forgotten essence. How might we regain this state in the most effective way? My answer to this would be that life is a practice. Practice anything, whether a musical instrument, a foreign language or a complex dance form, and you will eventually become proficient. Practicing letting go through the body - not just the mind - is the most assured way of growing more adaptable, stronger and ultimately, free. The exercises and meditations included in this book have been chosen to provide possibilities for the reader to cultivate deeper states of awareness. Practicing such meditations regularly is the secret to advancement. However, these practices can be taken a good deal further when the body itself is fully engaged in the meditative practices. When the human body moves fluidly in space, the art of letting go is fully embodied. The physical body becomes more flexible, stronger, younger; in a word more attuned.

These practices have been the basis of the author's creation of a series of meditative movements, called Infinite Body Qi-Gong. Practicing these movements not only cultivates grace and power in the human body, it allows the mind to let go of what is inessential and instead to open itself fully to what is given in the enveloping richness and exquisite balance of Nature itself; to what is cosmic, primal, and mysterious. A giant step towards cultivating the Power of Letting Go would be to study the flexible and adaptive gyrations of Infinite Body Qi-Gong. Those interested in learning more about Infinite Body Qi-Gong can contact the author or his assistants at info@fridayharborholistichealth.com for more details of classes, training and workshops.

NICHOLAS CORRIN, L.Ac.

EXERCISES
AND MEDITATIONS

The following exercises and meditations have been designed to help you absorb the ideas in this section, and apply them to your own life.

SHARPEN YOUR VISION

Practice developing inner vision. At times of the day when you have some free time, close your eyes and visualize something—a person, a place, anything. Try to view it as clearly as possible, and from different angles. This is not as easy as it sounds. But with practice, it becomes easier. This is an invaluable tool for you if you wish to project your intention successfully.

CONNECT WITH
YOUR INTENTION

Whatever you carry inside as a heartfelt desire is ready to become your intention. But it must not be blocked by doubt or other negative self-talk. Even after doing the other exercises in this book, there may still be traces in you of negative self-talk that have not been washed away. Don't worry! Just stay on it. Notice this self-talk if it is there, and just continue to connect strongly with what you wish to experience and accomplish in your life. Tell yourself positively that this is possible, that this is why you are here, to have these experiences that you seek with all your heart. Always connect with your intention to have the life you want, even if it does not seem to be happening yet. Never focus on this sense of lack, always focus with trust and belief that what you seek is already coming towards you.

RETURNING TO THE PRESENT MOMENT

1) *Stand outside, or sit indoors in a quiet place where you won't be disturbed.*

2) *Become conscious of your surroundings. If you are in a room, visualize what is directly outside that room, what is in the street outside the building, what is beyond that street, and so on, all the way into the far distance.*

3) *Start to breathe slowly and deeply, inhaling all the way down into your lower abdomen.*

4) *Now allow your thoughts to flow into the future as though a big balloon was inflating outward and forward from your abdomen, and in it were all your hopes, fears and expectations about your future. Once the balloon is fully extended, allow your thoughts to flow into your past, and imagine a balloon inflating back of you from your rear. See the balloon expanding and becoming huge, and see it fill up with all your memories, regrets, attachments, successes, failures, loves and recriminations.*

5) *When both balloons are fully extended, start to deflate them: imagine them shrinking with all their contents, as the twin balloons pull back inside your body.*

NICHOLAS CORRIN, L.Ac.

6) Now there is just you with yourself in the present moment.

7) Connect with the quiet intensity of the present moment and the mystery of just being here.

8) Open your eyes and observe the strange, wordless presence of the space around you and all that it contains. Feel how good it is to be present, simply to be here, alive and aware, and present.

STIMULATING THE THIRD EYE

1) Sit in a quiet place where you won't be disturbed.

2) Make sure your spine is erect, and your pelvis is evenly balanced.

3) Imagine a thin thread attached to the top of your head connecting you to the sky.

4) Keep your chin tucked in slightly to ensure that your neck is quite straight. But stay relaxed.

5) Close your eyes. Breathe slowly and deeply.

6) Focus on the point between your eyebrows.

7) As you breathe in, imagine that you are breathing in light through this point. Imagine that you are breathing in light, and take this light all the way down to your navel as you inhale. Then exhale it out through the point between your eyebrows.

8) As you inhale, lightly contract your perineum, then release this contraction as you exhale.

9) Continue this rhythmic breathing and visualizing for as long as you can maintain your attention.

10) Slowly open your eyes and get up.

11) If you practice this exercise often enough, your third eye will grow and eventually open like a flower.

MAGNETIZING YOUR INTENTION

1) Sit in a quiet place where you won't be disturbed.

2) Close your eyes. Relax your body and mind. Breathe slowly and deeply.

3) First activate the energy center in your lower abdomen.

4) Next, activate your Heart center.

5) Now activate your 3rd Eye by breathing in and out through the point between your eyebrows.

6) Feel each of these energy centers tingling as they become activated.

7) Now, as you inhale, draw energy up from the base of your spine to the pineal gland in the center of your brain. As you exhale, let the energy descend back down to the base of your spine. With each loop of energy, feel the pineal at the center of your brain tingle and grow more charged.

NICHOLAS CORRIN, L.Ac.

8) After looping the energy like this a number of times, the center of your brain will feel as though it carries a strong electrical potential: it is now charged up with energy.

9) Next, allow yourself to visualize something you deeply desire to happen, something you deeply desire for yourself or for another, and that you believe is a good thing. Something you both believe in and desire from deep in your heart.

10) Now project this image out through your 3rd Eye as though it were a slide or movie projector.

11) Keep projecting the image of what it is you desire outward from the center of your brain through your 3rd Eye, with as much detail and clarity as you can, like a photograph or a movie clip.

12) When this has been achieved and your image has been clearly projected out there, watch the image gradually recede into the distance. When it has disappeared, slowly open your eyes, trusting that your intention has now been delivered into the field of potentiality, where it will generate a magnetic response of attraction, and cause what you are seeking to actually occur.

13) Repeat as often as you feel necessary so that your image increases in clarity and conviction.

TAPPING INTO SERENITY

1) Sit a stool, bench or rock. Or, if you prefer, sit on the floor in a cross-legged or lotus position. (If this position is at all uncomfortable for you, sit on a meditation cushion or other support).

2) Make sure your spine is erect and your pelvis is balanced and even. Let your energy sink down into the earth. Sense a deep, magnetic pull from the earth.

3) Extend your arms in front of you and rest each hand, palm down on your knees.

4) Close your eyes. Breathe slowly and deeply down into your belly.

5) Become like a mountain, rising out of the plain. Breathe slowly and deeply. Become a mountain, breathing. As you breathe, take in the moisture, smells, and the breezes that are swirling about you.

6) Become aware of the mists and low lying clouds on your flanks. Sense the darker, heavier clouds building around your summit, overshadowing the landscape below. Feel the heavy pressure of these clouds.

7) Now, breathing inward through the point on the top of your head, draw the breath down to your lower abdomen. Use your breath to connect with the blue sky higher up. Breathe in its light and freedom.

8) Keep breathing into your interior this vision of a deep, free, blue space above you.

9) Breathe this blue light all the way into your core until you are completely filled with it, completely calmed.

10) When you feel ready, slowly open your eyes and come out of your meditation.

NICHOLAS CORRIN, L.Ac.

REFERENCES

1) LYNNE MCTAGGART, THE FIELD.
    New York, Harper Perennial, 2002, pp.5-14.
2) FRED ALAN WOLF, MIND INTO MATTER.
    Needham, MA. Moment Point Press, 2001, pp.143-145.
3) LYNNE MCTAGGART, THE FIELD.
    New York, Harper Perennial, 2002, pp.19-36.
4) DAVID FRAWLEY, YOGA AND THE SACRED FIRE.
    Twin Lakes, WI, 2004, pp.46-49.
5) DAVID FRAWLEY, FROM THE RIVER OF HEAVEN.
    Passage Press, Salt Lake City, 1990, p.135.
6) FRED ALAN WOLF, THE EAGLE'S QUEST.
    Touchstone, NY, 1991, pp.51-52.
7) WAYNE DYER, THE POWER OF INTENTION.
    Hay House, CA, 2004, p.11.
8) IBID, p.11.
9) WILLIAM THOMAS, SCORCHED EARTH.
    New Society Publishers, Philadelphia, 1995, p.67.
10) W.G.SEBALD, RINGS OF SATURN.
    New Directions, New York, 1998, p.97.
11) IBID, p.97.
12) ROBERT BLY, SHADOW: SEARCHING FOR THE HIDDEN SELF.
    Penguin Putnam, New York, 2002, p.9.
13) HANNAH ARENDT, MEN IN DARK TIMES.
    Harvest Books, London, 1970.
14) ROBERT LAWLOR, SACRED GEOMETRY.
    Thames and Hudson, London, 1997, p.17.
15) IBID, p.19.
16) DAVID FRAWLEY, TANTRIC YOGA and the WISDOM
    GODDESSES. Passage Press, Salt Lake City, Utah, 1994, p.234.
17) SEUNG SAHN, ED. STEPHEN MITCHELL, DROPPING ASHES ON THE
    BUDDHA. Grove Press, New York, 1976, p.12.

18) IBID, pp.51-52.

19) PETER TOMKINS AND CHRISTOPHER BIRD, THE SECRET LIFE OF
PLANTS. Harper and Row, New York, 1989, p.98.

20) DAVID ABRAM, THE SPELL OF THE SENSUOUS.
Vintage Books, New York, 1997, pp. 163-166.

21) LOREN EISELEY, THE IMMENSE JOURNEY.
Vintage Books, New York, 1959, p.63.

22) IBID, P.63.

23) FRED ALAN WOLF, MIND INTO MATTER.
Moment Point Press, Needham, MA, 2001, pp.73-74.

24) KIIKO MATSUMOTO and STEPHEN BIRCH, HARA DIAGNOSIS:
REFLECTIONS ON THE SEA.
Paradigm Publications, Brookline, MA, 1988, p.70.

25) IBID, p.71.

26) ROBERT LAWLOR, SACRED GEOMETRY.
Thames and Hudson, London, 1997, p.22.

27) DAVID FRAWLEY, YOGA AND THE SACRED FIRE.
Lotus Press, Twin Lakes, WI, 2004, pp.241-242.

28) ROBERT MAY, PHYSICIANS OF THE SOUL.
White Cloud Press, Ashland, OR, 2003, p.13.

29) DAVE BUTRILL, EATING AMONG FRIENDS, NATIONAL
WILDLIFE, Feb./March 2006, vol.44. no.2.

30) www.urbanlegends.about.com/library/bi_tiger_and_pigs.htm

31) Interview with KAREN ARMSTRONG, "To Go Beyond Thought",
PARABOLA, vol.31, Fall 2006, p.21.

32) JACOB LIBERMAN, LIGHT, MEDICINE OF THE FUTURE.
Bear & Co., NM, 1991, p.24.

33) PETER TOMPKINS AND CHRISTOPHER BIRD, THE SECRET LIFE OF
PLANTS. Harper and Row, New York, 1973, p.82.

34) IBID, p.86.

35) TOM SCHRODER, OLD SOULS.
Simon and Schuster, New York, 1999.

36) THEODOR SCHWENK, SENSITIVE CHAOS.
Rudolf Steiner Press, London, 1996, pp.37-51.

37) PAULO COELHO, THE ZAHIR.
HarperCollins, London, 2006, p.90.

38) RICHARD GERBER, VIBRATIONAL MEDICINE.
Bear & Co., VT, 2001,pp.147-151.

NICHOLAS CORRIN, L.Ac.

39) David Frawley, YOGA AND THE SACRED FIRE.
Lotus, WI, 2004, p.29.

40) Jacob Liberman, LIGHT, MEDICINE OF THE FUTURE.
Bear & Co., NM, 1991, P.7.

41) Brian Breiling, LIGHT YEARS AHEAD.
Celestial Arts, Berkely, CA, 1996, p.277.

42) IBID, p.236.

43) Richard Gerber, VIBRATIONAL MEDICINE.
Bear & Co., VT, 2001, pp.119-172.

44) Richard Feynman, QED.
Princeton University Press, NJ, 1988, p.15.

45) Lynne McTaggart, THE FIELD.
Harper Perennial, New York, 2003, p.40.

46) Bruce Lipton, THE BIOLOGY OF BELIEF.
Mountain of Love/Elite Books, Santa Rosa, CA, 2005, pp.75-95.

47) Lynne McTaggart, THE FIELD.
Harper Perennial, New York, 2003, p.40.

48) Lawrence E. Badgley MD, A New Method For Locating
Acupuncture Points and Body Field Distortions. American Journal
of Acupuncture, Vol. 12, July- Sept. 1984.

49) Brian Breiling et al., LIGHT YEARS AHEAD.
Celestial Arts, Berkeley, CA, 1996, p.278.

50) Lynne McTaggart, THE FIELD.
Harper Perennial, New York, 2003, pp.19-36.

51) Benoytosh Bhattacharrya, THE SCIENCE OF COSMIC LIGHT
THERAPY. Firma KLM, Calcutta, 1976, p.45.

52) Lynne McTaggart, THE FIELD.
Harper Perennial, New York, 2003, p.220.

53) Robert Lawlor, SACRED GEOMETRY.
Thames and Hudson, London, 1997, p.23.

54) Lynne McTaggart, THE FIELD.
Harper Perennial, New York, 2003, p.219.

55) Jonathan Goldman, HEALING SOUNDS.
Harper Collins, New York, 1996.

56) Fredddy Silva, SECRETS IN THE FIELDS.
Hampton Roads, Charlottesvilee, VA, 2002, p.217.

57) Daniel Perret, SOUND HEALING WITH THE FIVE
ELEMENTS.
Binkey Kok Publications, Havelte, Holland, 2005, p.133.

58) Ed. Robert Bly, James Hillman, Michael Meade, THE RAG AND BONE SHOP OF THE HEART.
Harper Perennial, New York, 1992, p.160.

59) David Abram, THE SPELL OF THE SENSUOUS.
Vintage, New York, 1996, p.148.

60) Bruce Lipton, THE BIOLOGY OF BELIEF.
Mountain of Love/Elite books, Santa Rosa, CA, 2005, p.46.

61) David Frawley, YOGA AND THE SACRED FIRE.
Lotus, WI, 2004, p.217.

62) Benoytosh Bhattacharrya, THE SCIENCE OF COSMIC LIGHT THERAPY. Firma KLM, Calcutta, 1976, pp.83ff.

63) Thomas Ashley-Farrand, HEALING MANTRAS.
Ballantine-Wellspring, New York, 1999.

64) James Hillman, THE DREAM AND THE UNDERWORLD.
Harper and Row, New York, 1979, p.100.

65) David Abram, THE SPELL OF THE SENSUOUS.
Vintage, New York, 1996, p.140.

66) IBID, p.152.

67) W.G.Sebald, RINGS OF SATURN.
New Directions, New York, 1998, p.57.

68) Ray Dodds, THE POWER OF BELIEF.
Hampton Roads, VA, 2003, p.xi.

69) IBID, p.119.

70) IBID, p.73ff.

71) Ed. Kim Comer, WISDOM OF THE SADHU.
Om Bokks, Andra Pradesh, India, 2001, p.112.

72) IBID, p.181.

73) Guyon Richards, THE CHAIN OF LIFE.
Health Science Press, Surrey, UK, 1954, p.2.

74) David Bohm, WHOLENESS AND THE IMPLICATE ORDER.
Routledge and Kegan Paul, London, 1987, p.132.

75) Callum Coats, LIVING ENERGIES.
Gateway Books, Bath, UK, 1996, p.141.

76) Gregg Braden, THE ISAIAH EFFECT.
Three Rivers Press, New York, 2000, p.90.

77) IBID, P.91.

78) Jeanne Achterbeg, IMAGERY IN HEALING.
New Science Library, Shambhala, Boston & London, 1985, p.80.

79) KENNY ASUBEL, WHEN HEALING BECOMES A CRIME.
Healing Arts Press, Rochester, VT,2000.
80) JEANNE ACHTERBEG, IMAGERY IN HEALING.
NewScience Library, Shambhala, Boston & London, 1985, p.184.
81) BRUCE LIPTON, THE BIOLOGY OF BELIEF.
Mountain of Love/Elite books, Santa Rosa, CA, 2005, p.123.
82) JEANNE ACHTERBEG, IMAGERY IN HEALING.
NewScience Library, Shambhala, Boston & London, 1985, p.172.
83) IBID, p.173.
84) BRIAN BREILING ET AL., LIGHT YEARS AHEAD.
Celestial Arts, Berkeley, CA, 1996, p.277-281.
85) DAVID HAWKINS, POWER VERSUS FORCE.
Hay House, CA, 2002, p.42.
86) CANDACE PERT, MOLECULES OF EMOTION.
Simon and Schuster, New York, 1997.
87) GREGG BRADEN, THE ISAIAH EFFECT.
Three Rivers Press, New York, 2000, pp.123-141.
88) IBID, p.167.
89) IBID, p.236.
90) BURYL PAYNE, MAGNETIC HEALING.
Lotus Press, Twin Lakes, WI, 1997, p.176.
91) IBID, p.177.
92) DAVID HAWKINS, POWER VERSUS FORCE.
Hay House, CA, 2002, p.282.

Selected Bibliography

ABRAMS, DAVID. *The Spell of the Sensuous*. NY: Vintage, 1996.

ASUBEL, KENNY. *When Healing Becomes A Crime*. VT: Healing Arts Press, 2000.

AUROBINDO, SRI. *The Integral Yoga*. Twin Lakes: Lotus Press, 2005.

BECKER, ROBERT. *Cross Currents*. LA: Jeremy Tarcher Inc., 1990.

BHATTACHARRYA, BENOYTOSH. *The Science of Cosmic Ray Therapy*. Calcutta: Firma KLM, 1976.

BLY, ROBERT. *The Shadow*. NY: Penguin Putnam, 2002.

BRADEN, GREGG. *The Isaiah Effect*. NY: Three Rivers Press, 2000.

BRENNAN, BARBARA ANN. *Hands of Light*. NY: Bantam, 1987.

BRENNAN, BARBARA ANN. *Light Emerging*. NY: Bantam, 1993.

BURGER BRUCE. *Esoteric Anatomy*. Berkeley, CA: N. Atlantic Books, 1998.

CALASSO, ROBERT. *Ka*. NY: Vintage, 1999.

CAMPBELL, JOSEPH. *Creative Mythology*. NY: Penguin, 1976

CHIA, MANTAK. *Taoist Cosmic Healing*. Vermont: Destiny Books, 2001.

CLEARY, THOMAS. *Practical Taoism*, Boston: Shambhala, 1996.

COELHO, PAULO. *The Zahir*. London: Harper, 2006.

COATS, CALLUM. *Living Energies*. Bath, UK: Gateway Books, 1996.

COWAN, ELIOT. *Plant Spirit Medicine*. OR: Swan Raven & Co., 1995.

DODD, RAY. *The Power of Belief*, VA: Hampton Books, 2003.

ED. BREILING, BRIAN. *Light Years Ahead*. Berkeley, CA: Celestial Arts, 1996.

ED. COMER, KIM. *Wisdom of the Sadhu*. Andhra Pradesha, India, 2001.

EISELEY, LOREN. *The Immense Journey*. New York: Vintage, 1957.

EVOLA, JULIUS. *The Yoga of Power*. VT: Inner Traditions, 1992.

FEYNMAN, RICHARD. *QED*. Princeton University Press, NJ, 1988.

FRAWLEY, DAVID. *Ayurveda and the Mind*. TL, WI: Lotus, 1996.

FRAWLEY, DAVID. *Tantric Yoga*. Delhi: Banarsidass, 1994.

NICHOLAS CORRIN, L.Ac.

FRAWLEY, DAVID. *Vedantic Meditation*, Berkeley, CA: North Atlantic Books, 2000.

FRAWLEY, DAVID. *Yoga and the Sacred Fire*. TL, WI: Lotus, 2004.

HAWKINS, DAVID. *Power v. Force*. CA: Hay House, 2002

HAWKINS, DAVID. *I, Reality and Subjectivity*. AZ: Veritas, 2003.

HILLMAN, JAMES. *The Dream and the Underworld*. NY: Harper and Row, 1979.

HILLMAN, JAMES, *Revisioning Psychology*. NY: Harper Collins, 1975.

KLOCEK, DENNIS. *Seeking Spirit Vision*. Fair Oaks, CA: R.S. Press, 1998.

LADE, ARNIE. *Energetic Healing*. Twin Lakes, WI: Lotus, 1998.

LAV, D.C. *Yuan Dao*, NY: Ballantine, 1998.

LIBERMAN, JACOB. *Light, Medicine of the Future*. NM: Bear and Co., 1995.

LIPTON, BRUCE. *The Biology of Belief*. Santa Rosa, CA: Mountain of Love/ Elite Books, 2005.

MATSUMOTO, KIIKO AND BIRCH, STEPHEN. *Hara Diagnosis*. MA:Paradigm Publication,1983

RENARD, GARY R. *The Disappearance of the Universe*. CA: Hay House, 2004

MAY, ROBERT. *Physicians of the Soul*. OR: White Cloud Press, 1982.

McTAGGART, LYNN. *The Field*. NY: Harper Perennial, 2002.

PAYNE, BURYL. *Magnetic Healing*, WI. Lotus Press, 1997

RAGNAR, PETER. *The Awesome Science of Luck*. Asheville, NC: Roaring Lion Publishing, 2005.

RAGNAR, PETER. *How Long Do You Choose to Live?* Asheville, NC: Roaring Lion Publishing, 2005.

REES, MARTIN. *Our Final Hour*. NY: Basic Books, 2003.

REES, MARTIN. *Our Cosmic Habitat*. NJ: Princeton U Press, 2001.

RUSSELL, EDWARD. *Report on Radionics*. Essex, UK: C.W. Daniel Co. Ltd., 1973.

SCHWARTZ, BENJAMIN. *The World of Thought in Ancient China*. Cambridge, MA: Harvard University Press, 1985.

SCHWENK, THEODOR. *Sensitive Chaos*. London: Rudolf Steiner Press, 1996.

SEBALD, W.G. *Rings Of Saturn*. NY: New Direction, 1998.

SILVA, FREDDY. *Secrets in the Fields*. VA: Hampton Road Publishing, 2002.

SITCHIN, ZECHARIA. *Journey into the Mythical Past*. VT: Bear and Co., 2007.

SHRODER, TOM. *Old Souls*. NY: Simon and Schuster, 1999.

SUI, CHOA KOK. *Pranic Healing*. Maine: Samuel Weiser Inc., 1990.

SVOBODA, ROBERT AND LADE, ARNIE.

Tao and Dharma.
Twin City, WI: Lotus Press, 1995.

SWIMME, BRIAN AND BERRY, THOMAS.
The Universe Story.
NY: Harper Collins, 1992.

THOMAS, WILLIAM. *Scorched Earth.*
Philadelphia,
PA: New Society Publishing, 1995.

TOMPKINS, PETER AND BIRD,
CHRISTOPHER. *The Secret Life of
Plants.* NY: Harper and Row, 1973.

WILBER, KEN. *A Theory of
Everything.* Boston
MA: Shambhala, 2000.

WOLF, FRED ALAN. *The Eagle's
Quest.* NY: Touchshore, 1991.

WOLF, FRED ALAN. *Mind into Matter.*
Needham, MA: Moment Point
Press, 2001.

WONG, EVA. *Cultivating Stillness.*
Boston, MA: Shambhala, 1992.

NICHOLAS CORRIN, L.Ac.

INDEX

NICHOLAS CORRIN, L.Ac.

NICHOLAS CORRIN, L.Ac.

ABOUT NICHOLAS CORRIN

Born in the UK, Corrin began his undergraduate studies with degrees in French and Italian literature, before pursuing graduate work at the University of London in the Art and Philosophy of the Renaissance. Traveling widely, Corrin taught and continued his research in France, Switzerland and Italy. In 1984, he spent a year in Turkey teaching and researching Aesculepian healing structures. After moving to the US in 1985, Corrin taught Art, History and Writing at various colleges, before undergoing formal training in Oriental and Ayurvedic Medicine at the International Institute of Chinese Medicine, South Baylo  University in California, and later at the American Institute of Vedic Studies in New Mexico.

Corrin also engaged in a decades-long study of Taoist Qi-Gong as well as Vedic meditation. These inner practices eventually led to the discovery of his patented technique, Vibropuncture®. Nicholas Corrin's writings span diverse areas including the dynamics of energy, self-mastery, the science of movement, immunological issues, imaginative writings, and the poetic contemplation of nature. They deliver insights in sometimes startling ways by juxtaposing what might at first seem to be incongruous elements, thus generating new "wholes" and opening up fresh perspectives on life and reality. Corrin currently maintains a private practice in alternative and oriental medicine on San Juan Island in Washington.

NICHOLAS CORRIN, L.Ac.